MUSIC IN
CHILDHOOD EDUCATION

MUSIC IN
CHILDHOOD EDUCATION

Second Edition

Robert L. Garretson

Colorado State University

PRENTICE-HALL, INC., Englewood Cliffs, New Jersey

Library of Congress Cataloging in Publication Data

GARRETSON, ROBERT L
  Music in childhood education.

  Bibliography: p.
  Includes index.
  1. School music—Instruction and study—United
States. I. Title.
MT3.U5G36 1976   372.8′7   75-31905
ISBN 0-13-606988-6
ISBN 0-13-606970-3 pbk.

Printed in the United States of America

10 9 8 7 6 5 4 3 2 1

PRENTICE-HALL INTERNATIONAL, INC., *London*
PRENTICE-HALL OF AUSTRALIA, PTY. LIMITED, *Sydney*
PRENTICE-HALL OF CANADA, LTD., *Toronto*
PRENTICE-HALL OF INDIA PRIVATE LIMITED, *New Delhi*
PRENTICE-HALL OF JAPAN, INC., *Tokyo*
PRENTICE-HALL OF SOUTHEAST ASIA (PTE.) LTD., *Singapore*

TO NANCY AND JOHN

CONTENTS

vii

chapter 7

TIMBRE, 179

chapter 8

FORM, 208

chapter 9

TEMPO, DYNAMICS, AND EXPRESSION, 226

chapter 10

MUSICAL STYLE, 248

chapter 11

CONTEMPORARY INFLUENCES
ON MUSIC EDUCATION IN AMERICA, 258

chapter 12

MUSIC AND OTHER CURRICULAR AREAS, 278

APPENDIX, 285

INDEX, 291

PREFACE

This book is addressed to all those persons interested in the musical education of children—to pre-service teachers, classroom teachers, music specialists, parents, and administrators. It is concerned with the basic premises underlying instructional programs in music, with the developmental aspects of children's growth in music, with the teacher-student relationship as it affects learning, and with the ways and means to teach music effectively to children.

In this second edition, the chapter on music in the modern school curriculum has been completely revised, with a new section added on "modern day approaches to the teaching of music." A new chapter on planning to teach music gives special attention not only to group activities, but also to approaches to individually guided education (IGE). The chapter on the child voice and singing has been carefully edited and updated. Also, in this edition, the author recognizes the current trends in music education and has organized a considerable portion of the content around musical concepts and suggested activities for their comprehension. Included are chapters on pitch and melody; rhythm, meter, and bodily movement; harmony, polyphony, texture, and part-singing; timbre; form and listening; and tempo, dynamics and expression. In addition, new chapters have been included on contemporary influences on music education in America and on music and other curricular areas. The Appendix continues to provide important and valuable source information for music educators.

Today's graded elementary music series reflect a conceptual approach to the teaching of music. Many of the concepts included in this textbook appear in the students' and teachers' books of these series, and teachers will be able to correlate the approaches included here with the graded music books that are used in a particular school. According to theories of conceptual learning, concepts need to be reinforced in each subsequent grade through more in-depth experiences. In the series books, those concepts are restated or elaborated upon at appropriate grade levels, along with concepts newly introduced at those grade levels. Some concepts that are stressed in the books for several grade levels, however, are not restated in an appreciably different way. In this text, such concepts are included only on the grade level at which they are *first* introduced; it is assumed that teachers working with any particular series will continue to stress their fundamental importance. A few subjects, however, involving a general approach appropriate to several grade levels, are included at the ends of the chapters in which they are most relevant.

It is not intended that this text be a comprehensive presentation of every possible concept. Only the most basic are included. Those presented, however, and the suggested activities and skills leading to their comprehension, will provide a structure upon which the music teacher *can* build an organized program of music instruction. The listings of specific activities include questions which may be posed to children to guide their thinking and facilitate their discovery of musical concepts.

For students using this book in methods classes, a list of topics for discussion has been included at the end of each chapter; specific suggestions for further study have also been included for those persons wishing to delve more deeply into particular topics or areas. As a prerequisite to the use of this book in a methods class, it is presumed that a student either will have had a course in music fundamentals, class piano, or both, or will have had previous musical experiences which result in a similar level of comprehension of musical concepts and a similar development of musical skills. In some institutions, however, both music fundamentals and methodology are taught concurrently. This book may be adapted for such concurrent instruction, for the basic musical concepts to be learned are the same—only the approach may need to be somewhat modified. For supplementary information on music fundamentals, see the list of publications in the Appendix.

Music specialists as well as classroom teachers may use this book as a guide in developing a comprehensive music program in the elementary grades. The classroom teacher who is inexperienced in teaching music will find within these pages many activities that can be taught to children and that require only a minimal musical background. Classroom teachers, however, should assess their levels of skill and understanding, determine activities they *can* present, and, based upon the security of these experiences, gradually widen the range of musical activities that they offer to children. It is hoped that this book will assist all teachers in this important process.

For permission to use special photographs, I am indebted to: Robert McSpadden of the Cincinnati (Ohio) Public Schools; Alan Stevens of the Fort Collins (Colorado) Public Schools; Nancy J. Pitz and E'rena Hockenberry of the Jefferson County (Colorado) Public Schools; B.F. Kitching and Company; Peripole, Inc.; Rhythm Band, Inc.; and the University School, Indiana University, and the Daily Herald-Telephone, Bloomington, Indiana.

For permission to use songs, musical excerpts, or poetry from their publications, I express appreciation to: American Book Company, Belwin-Mills Publishing Corp., Boosey & Hawkes, Inc., William C. Brown Publishers, Silver Burdett Company, Grace Eilert, Follett Publishing Company, The Macmillan Company, Nancy Nunnally, Schmidt, Hall & McCreary Company, and Janet E. Tobitt.

For permission to use materials from their publications, appreciation is expressed to: the Contemporary Music Project of the Music Educators National Conference; Educational Media Press; Charles B. Fowler, Author, and Malcolm S. Besson, Editor, *Music Educators Journal;* Institute for Development of Educational Activities, Inc.; and Ronald Thomas, Author, *MMCP Synthesis; A Structure for Music Education.*

R.L.G.

MUSIC IN
CHILDHOOD EDUCATION

chapter 1

MUSIC IN THE MODERN
SCHOOL CURRICULUM

From 1838, when music became a part of the curriculum in the public schools of Boston, music has gained a gradual acceptance as a part of the instructional program in elementary schools. Today it is generally recognized as an integral part of the curriculum. World events of the past two decades, however, have caused educators to reevaluate the purposes, as well as the procedures, of teaching music in the schools.

To be successful, the teacher of music in the modern school must possess a well-defined philosophy of teaching. He or she should have not only a broad understanding of the general purposes of education, but also a thorough understanding of the specific values and purposes to be achieved by the inclusion of music in the curriculum. This understanding is essential if the recipients of the program are to reap its maximum benefits. Understanding the values of music in the education of children provides the teacher with a basis for establishing objectives that are necessary for effective teaching. In general, both classroom teachers and music specialists should strive toward the same goals while remaining cognizant of their own particular roles in the school.

This chapter, then, is directed toward answering two important questions: "What are the values of music instruction in the schools?" and "What are the new directions charted today by music educators and who is responsible for accomplishing these new goals?"

VALUES OF MUSIC IN THE CURRICULUM

Many varied claims have been set forth in the past for the values of music participation, e.g., "music study develops personal discipline," "music participation promotes desirable social attitudes," "singing improves posture," "music study increases one's sensitivity to beauty," and so on. These values are often used to justify the place of music in the school curriculum. While some of these stated claims deserve primary consideration, others have often been of only secondary importance and, in some instances, could perhaps better be fulfilled through other curricular areas. Some educators have been prone to accept too uncritically a myriad of reasons for the teaching of music in the schools. While it is possible for a number of values to be realized through music study, even these are of varying importance. Failure to give thoughtful consideration to the relative importance of these values has caused some teachers to lose sight of the principal objectives which underlie and guide their general approach to teaching.

Aesthetic and Expressive Values

The aesthetic values inherent in music must be considered the primary justification for the inclusion of music education in the schools. Aesthetics may be defined simply as the study of beauty in art and nature.[1] Humans have a distinct need for beauty in their lives, as it serves to refine and humanize their entire being. Aesthetic education, the process of increasing an individual's sensitivity to beauty, is the primary task of the music educator.

It is important that schools help their future citizens to become intelligent *consumers* of music. The uninformed are more likely to become victims of their own inexperience. Therefore, an important function of the music education program is to endeavor to broaden for all students the base of musical experience, which should lead to a greater understanding of the nature of music.

A teacher should never accept standards of taste based simply upon what a particular group initially likes best—often jazz and popular music. This standard of taste is often dependent on limited musical experience. The school should endeavor to provide experiences which the students might not ordinarily have. This means a broad experience with the finest music, which is the cultural heritage of all citizens. The thoughtful music educator, however, will start with music his students readily understand, and will endeavor to explain and clarify relationships and similarities between the familiar and the new or unfamiliar. Such a procedure provides a basis for continual growth and an ever-widening of music preferences.

Closely related to aesthetic education is the need for individual self-expression in as many varied ways as possible. Man expresses many concepts and ideas through language, but language has its limitations.

---

[1] Beauty is a personal thing. What is beautiful to one person may not be to another. Therein lies a reason for broadening a person's understanding of the nature of music.

Certain aspects of human experience are best expressed through other media, such as the dance, the visual arts, or music.

Each individual needs to achieve self-understanding—to create a self-image. Each person is in the process of developing into something, and what one ultimately becomes depends upon the possibilities one envisions and the choices one makes among them. The more opportunities one has for self-expression and exploration of possibilities, the greater his or her potential for self-development. Today's modern society needs creative individuals in all fields of endeavor. Creativity often involves the restructuring of existing components into new and useful patterns as much as the development of completely new elements. The development of creative individuals is, in part, dependent upon ample opportunities for exploring possible solutions to problems in all curricular areas. Music and the other arts can offer varied possibilities for the expression of individual feelings in a creative manner.

Cultural and Personal-Social Values

An important function of the school is the passing on to future generations of our Judeo-Christian heritage, which has developed over hundreds of years. Music, of course, is an integral part of the total culture. It is a part of worship, as well as governmental and military ceremonies, and it is used to enhance the effectiveness of dramatic productions presented through the media of radio, television, and motion pictures. Some music has a soothing and tranquilizing effect and for this reason has been used effectively by industry and in shopping centers and hospitals. It has been used to stir emotions at political conventions, and as a means of developing group cohesiveness and singleness of purpose at various other types of meetings. Music as a force in American life cannot be ignored.

The objective of world peace depends to a very great extent upon an understanding of other cultures in addition to our own. Music is an integral part of all cultures and the hopes, fears, aspirations, and beliefs of various ethnic groups are often expressed through their folk music. Complete understanding of these peoples cannot be achieved unless all aspects of their cultures, including music, are included in the units of study taught in the schools.

Certain personal and social benefits may also result from music study. Although highly important, they cannot be considered as the primary values to be achieved by the study of music, because these benefits may also accrue from other studies in the curriculum.

It is important that all individuals develop a feeling of self-assurance. This comes about through having a variety and number of successful school experiences. It is a fundamental responsibility of all teachers to assist children toward finding their own strengths so that such self-assurance may be attained. Perhaps some individuals will excel in music, while others will find different fields more rewarding. To best meet the needs of all students the schools should provide a variety of experiences—including music—in the curriculum.

Some writers have endeavored to justify the inclusion of music in the curriculum on the basis of its physical benefits. Actually, the overall physical development of students may best be achieved through planned activities in physical education. Nevertheless, habits of correct posture and proper abdominal-diaphragmatic breathing may accrue from experience in vocal and instrumental music.

During a normal school day various tensions are bound to build up within students in the classroom. These tensions result in fatigue and prevent students from accomplishing their desired goals. The cathartic values of music participation have long been known. Music activities, as well as art and physical education, when interspersed between various academic subjects, can result in a lessening of these tensions and may effect the necessary atmosphere conducive to continued academic work.

The development of social beings able to take their places in adult society is another responsibility of the entire school. Participation in music activities may contribute toward this end. While some classrooms and rehearsal rooms have a more autocratic than democratic atmosphere because of the personalities of the teachers, the music class, because of the nature of the subject, does lend itself toward the development of various social values. The effective teacher can develop attitudes of cooperation, attitudes which also are necessary for a competent performance of the music being studied. Acceptance by peers is highly important to the personal-social development of youth. The importance of individual skills and cooperative group effort needed for the success of musical organizations provides a social setting for the development of mutual respect and new friendships.

Therapeutic Values of Music

Music therapy may be defined as the scientific application of the art of music to accomplish therapeutic aims. Such therapeutic treatment is presently being used in institutions throughout the country and the profession of music therapy is undergoing tremendous growth. Music therapists function in a wide variety of places, including psychiatric hospitals, mental retardation centers, physical disability hospitals, community mental health centers, day care centers, nursing homes, special education schools, correctional facilities, and special service agencies.[2]

[2] *What You As a Careers Counselor Need to Know About Music Therapy* (Lawrence, Kansas: National Association for Music Therapy, Inc.).

Music therapy may assist persons in a variety of ways. For example, it may be used to remediate problems in learning, to assist children in learning appropriate social interaction, to help motivate emotionally disturbed children or those with developmental disabilities, to help children remediate their perceptual motor problems through movement to music, as a form of physical therapy for orthopedically handicapped children, to provide sensory stimulation, and to help hostile, aggressive, and non-cooperative children learn more appropriate behaviors.

There is a growing trend toward using music therapists in the public schools as members of special-education units working with exceptional children. In responding to this trend, a number of music schools are beginning to offer a double major—one in music education and the other in music therapy. Because of the interrelationships of these two programs, pre-service teachers enrolled in them can be better trained to meet the demands placed upon them and to fulfill the varying needs of children in the schools.

Avocational and Vocational Values

Avocational interests, those outside a chosen occupation, serve to enrich one's life and renew one's spirits from the tensions and frustrations encountered in everyday life. Avocational choices will, of course, vary widely according to the needs and interests of individuals. Music is a particularly attractive avocation because persons of all ages may participate. A look into the future would probably reveal a greater use of automation in industry and a subsequently increased amount of leisure time. Therefore, the schools should provide ample opportunity for experience with a variety of types of possible avocational choices.

If the music in our culture is to be perpetuated, then children must be provided ample opportunity for exploring this area as a possible life's work. To be successful in the music profession one must develop certain basic skills and understandings. Therefore, children should have the opportunity to begin their musical studies relatively early in life.

Relationship of Values
to Type of Activities

The aesthetic values of music are paramount in an educational program in the schools; but these values may not necessarily be of central importance when music is used in certain social situations, such as, in adult community sings, or at summer youth camps. In these instances the primary function of the music leader is not merely to instruct, but to use music as a force in creating group cohesion, esprit de corps, or perhaps a recreational atmosphere. This does not necessarily mean that the song leader must lower his musical standards. It simply means that he will often be using music of a different type in order to achieve a different type of goal.

MODERN-DAY APPROACHES
TO THE TEACHING OF MUSIC

An examination of the history of music education reveals a vacillating point of view—in that music educators have often gone to extremes and have either stressed procedures, hopefully to teach music-reading to achieve more effective performance, or they have endeavored to make music a completely enjoyable experience with the objective of providing motivation for more serious musical study. Both viewpoints have been in our philosophy for some time, and most teachers have usually given philosophical support to each idea; nevertheless, in practice they have leaned toward one or the other. Of course, neither of these approaches has succeeded in developing any real degree of musical understanding. If children's musicality is to be developed, then intellectual comprehension must be considered on an equal basis with skill development and affective or emotional response. They are not alternatives, but mutually compatible goals that teachers should strive to accomplish.[3]

It was once felt by some educators that all music experiences should be pleasurable on the assumption that learning would not occur if the child's interest were not held. The words *like* and *interest* were interpreted as being somewhat synonymous. On the other hand, according to McMurray, the pragmatic viewpoint holds that *interest* can result from pleasure on the positive side and even fear on the negative side. For learning to occur, it must be accompanied by an emotional force, whether it be pleasant or unpleasant. As most learning requires some kind of effort, it follows that pleasure cannot always be the only or necessarily the best motivating force. A more realistic learning situation may even be a point of conflict, an irritant, or an obstacle to be overcome.[4] The insightful teacher will, of course, endeavor to devise teaching strategies that will not create apprehension, but will intrigue and challenge students toward learning. Real satisfactions in adult life, after all, do not come by withdrawal from unpleasantries, but from facing up to

[3] Cf. A. Theodore Tellstrom, *Music in American Education, Past and Present* (New York: Holt, Rinehart and Winston, Inc., 1971), p. 255.

[4] McMurray, Foster, "Pragmatism in Music Education," *Basic Concepts in Music Education. The Fifty-Seventh Yearbook of the National Society for the Study of Education.* (Chicago: The University of Chicago Press, 1958), pp. 47–50.

and solving the many diverse problems with which we are confronted. Young children naturally enjoy riddles, puzzles, and games (if they aren't too competitive), and successful experiences with these activities can provide the basis for them to meet new challenges—musical and otherwise.

The Structure of Music and Conceptual Learning

As a result of the success of Russia's space achievements, and particularly with "Sputnik" in 1957, the American public and its professional educators were jarred into a considered reappraisal of the American educational system. After various conferences and points of view set forth in professional journals, many music educators concluded that musicality can best be achieved through developing an understanding of the concepts in the structure of music. Structure is delineated by the elements which comprise a particular subject matter. Understanding the structure of music involves studying its various elements—melody, rhythm, harmony, timbre or tone color, form, and expression—as well as comprehending their interrelationships.

In previous years, unit teaching was much in vogue, with the work being organized around such topics as "Music of the Civil War Period," or "Music of the American West." Each unit included activities, such as songs relating to the topic, folk dances and rhythmic activities, listening to recorded music, and creative activities. The overall results of such planning and teaching were not overly beneficial. The scope of the activities was so broad that there was only a somewhat cursory relationship between them, with the effect of the study having very minimal benefits.[5]

Today, effective teaching units can be built on any of the basic musical elements or on a combination of them. Each unit, therefore, has a certain integrity in that its parts are related to a meaningful whole; and children, when studying the parts, can see them in relationship to a whole and thus maintain a sense of direction as to where their study is leading them. This awareness lends a certain security to the situation, and also provides the basis for a more meaningful learning experience.

It is felt today that the basics of any subject can be taught to children of any age providing they are presented in a way that the child can understand. When taught to young children, concepts should be presented at their simplest level. In the study of melody, for example, concepts such as "melody has high and low pitches," and "melody has

[5] Tellstrom, *op. cit.*, p. 256.

long and short tones" should be introduced.[6] While these concepts are appropriate for initial experiences, subsequent lessons will go into more detail. Basic concepts will gradually be dealt with in greater depth or breadth.[7] Each subsequent experience reinforces a child's understanding of a concept and clarifies and enlarges his understanding of it. The preceding approach is referred to as cyclical development, or spiral curriculum, and is accepted procedure in all areas of the school curriculum.

Approaches to Teaching

There are three basically different approaches to teaching that can and are currently being applied in the classroom. Each of these methods may be considered appropriate under a given set of circumstances. The first is the all-too-familiar *lecture method,* in which the teacher usually begins by making a generalization and then illustrates it with various examples. There are instances in which this approach is appropriate, e.g., when certain types of information must be provided to students in a relatively short period of time. The method, however, should be used sparingly, as there is often a tendency for teachers simply to "dispense information" and then later to evaluate the students' assimilation of the stated facts after they have "regurgitated" back the information in an examination. This is the easiest method, for a teacher can simply relate the facts as he or she knows them. (The degree of retention under this method, however, is the lowest of all the approaches.) It can also be the most deadly in the hands of the uninspired teacher and can serve to turn students completely off the subject being undertaken. The axiom "teachers teach as they have been taught" is one of the unfortunate results of the lecture method.

Another commonly used approach is the *socratic method,* in which the teacher endeavors to draw students out through a carefully devised set of questions. As a result, the students are led from the known to the unknown—through a series of experiences which lead ultimately to a conclusion. Students are asked specific questions that gradually lead them toward comprehension of a new fact or concept. If the students respond with the wrong answers, however, or if they are unable to respond, then the teacher often must provide "clues" or supply a given

---

[6] Some authorities hold the view that a concept is the "residue" left in the child's mind after a particular experience. Therefore, they feel that one can't teach concepts, but can only provide experiences and a framework for their comprehension.

[7] The concept that melody has high and low pitches is basic and appropriate for the understanding of melody by young children. The concept that pitch has various frequencies is related to the same concept, but certainly it is much more sophisticated.

answer before proceeding to the next question. In contrast to the lecture method, this approach involves student activity to a much greater extent, and, as a result, it is often an appropriate approach for a given set of learnings.

The third approach is the *discovery method,* which is in direct contrast to the lecture method. In a way, its basic tenets are diametrically opposed. Whereas in the lecture method the teacher "dispenses" information like so many pills or "pearls of wisdom," the teacher in the discovery method sets up a learning situation so that the students are challenged into finding out things for themselves. Rather than being told about a concept, the child discovers it independently. This concept is not necessarily verbalized, however, and the teacher can often determine from specific musical responses whether or not a student comprehends. That is, if the student can show or perform a concept, it may not be necessary to tell about it, even though in some circumstances verbalizing may be a desirable means of seeking further clarification. Of all the approaches utilized, the discovery method is the most time consuming, yet under it the retention of the learnings is the highest.

In teaching concepts about the diatonic scale, for example, the discovery approach might initially involve experience with singing songs in a given key (usually C), the learning of the letter names, and perhaps building and playing a scale on the resonator bells. Later, after having experience with songs in a related key (F or G), the student may endeavor to build a corresponding scale on resonator bells in this particular key. Through experimentation the child will discover that some alteration in the scale is necessary if it is to "sound right," and that changing one of the tone bars for one a half step lower (B♭) or a half step higher (F♯) will solve the problem. Later still, the child may endeavor to build other scales by experimenting and arranging the proper sequence of whole and half steps. Following these discoveries, he can develop a clearer insight into the necessity for key signatures and how they may serve as an aid to the performer. Key signatures may thus become more meaningful symbols rather than remaining abstract representations of something only to be learned—without any real purpose.

To provide further clarification, the three before-mentioned approaches, the lecture method, the socratic method, and the discovery method, are compared and illustrated in the following chart.[8]

---

[8] From Charles B. Fowler, "Discovery: One of the Best Ways to Teach a Musical Concept." Copyright © 1970 by Music Educators National Conference. Reprinted by permission, from *Music Educators Journal* (October, 1970), vol. 57, no. 2, p. 25.

Three Approaches to Teaching a Musical Concept Through Performance

Concept To Be Taught: Dynamic contrasts provide a source of variety and expressive meaning in music.
Material: "Evening Prayer" by Engelbert Humperdinck

1. Lecture   Teacher points out the signs for dynamics in the printed score and demonstrates how these are to be performed. Signs for crescendo, diminuendo, very soft, ritard, and other dynamic indications are shown, and the names attached. Students practice the music until they perform it correctly according to the composer's markings.

2. Socratic   *Teacher:* How many have noticed that some music is louder or softer than other music? Does anyone see a place in this music where it should be sung very softly? *Child:* Right at the beginning. *Teacher:* Is there a sign there that says "sing very softly"? *Child:* The music says "pp." *Teacher:* That's correct. Is there a sign that says "get louder"? *Child:* poco cresc. *Teacher:* Right. What kind of a sign tells us that we should sing loudly? *Child:* "mf." *Teacher:* Can you draw the sign on the board that tells us to grow gradually louder? Child draws ◁ . When the students' attention has been drawn to all the signs, the piece is performed with the proper dynamics and tempo.

3. Discovery   Students learn a piece of music from a score that contains no dynamic markings. The teacher invites the students to experiment with the way they sing the song, in order to make it more beautiful, or to communicate its message more effectively. Students invent their own tempo, dynamics, and phrasing, appropriate to the text. They may invent signs to indicate their preferences. They can compare their version with the composer's original markings or with edited scores, and try to understand why the composer used dynamics in the way he did.

In summary, in determining the approach or method to use for a particular learning situation, the teacher should consider: (a) the amount of time available, (b) the student involvement desired, and (c) the nature of the music concept. The lecture method, of course, takes the least amount of time and the discovery method the most amount of time. The lecture method involves students in a very passive manner, while the discovery approach actively involves them and allows for the maximum creative use of their imaginations. The socratic method falls somewhere between these two extremes. While some concepts are more adaptable than others to the discovery approach, the socratic method can be used in most situations. It is suggested that the lecture method be used sparingly and only when time is of the essence.

Behavioral Objectives

Teaching objectives in the past have focused upon activities and the development of musical skills. As previously stated, objectives today are centered upon developing an understanding of the structure of music; skills are not considered as ends in themselves, but as means through which objectives are realized.

Today, objectives are generally stated in behavioral terms, i.e., they are stated in a way which will help the teacher to determine whether or not, or to what extent, an objective has been achieved or realized. Inherent in a behavioral objective is a criterion or an indication as to what the children can be expected to accomplish. Examples of behavioral objectives in music are: (1) to be able to recognize syncopation in music and to demonstrate an understanding by improvising syncopated patterns with rhythm instruments, and (2) to be able to identify various instruments of the orchestra and demonstrate an understanding by describing the unique tonal characteristics of particular instruments.

Desirable statements of behavioral objectives generally possess the following characteristics:[9]

a. They describe a pattern or type of behavior that we want a learner to demonstrate.

b. They avoid the use of words with too many interpretations and will include words with few interpretations. For example, words such as understand, appreciate, and enjoy should be avoided and words used with more explicit meanings, such as identify, list, compare, recognize, perform, improvise, and compose.

c. They specify what the learner will do or perform to show his comprehension of the objective.

d. They specify any given limitations or conditions under which the learner is to perform or achieve the objective. For example, "given a list of musical terms, the student will (etc.) . . ."

e. They may specify how well or to what extent the learner is to achieve the objective—through a time limit, or a minimum number, or a percentage of correct responses.

9 Robert F. Mager, *Preparing Instructional Objectives* (Palo Alto, Calif.: Fearon Publishers, Inc., 1962).

Evaluation occurs not just at the end of a unit of study, but *is a continuous, on-going process.* The anticipated result of instruction is behavioral change, which may be overt behavior and directly observable, or covert or internal response. Wherever possible, overt expression is sought to determine if a covert response is occurring.

Overt behavior, such as the achievement of specific skills, is identifiable, readily observed, and evaluated. Covert, or internal response, deals with appreciation or understanding, and its evaluation becomes more subjective and difficult to assess. If, for example, in determining a child's understanding of the highness of pitch, an overt response is sought, such as identifying the higher of two pitches; a more objective assessment of the degree of student understanding is then possible. On the other hand, when an overt expression of a covert or internal response is not possible or feasible, lack of overt expression should not exclude achieving an internal response as a long-range objective, with an expected outcome.[10]

WHO IS TO TEACH MUSIC?

After consideration of the values of music and the objectives we wish to attain, we come to the matter of who is to teach music in the elementary school. Who is to implement these objectives? What are the roles of the music specialist and the classroom teacher and what is the nature of their relationships? Schools vary in their answers to these questions. The following arrangements, however, are most common.[11]

1. The classroom teacher. In schools organized around the concept of the "self-contained classroom," the classroom teacher generally has the responsibility of teaching all the subjects, including music. The teacher, knowing the needs, abilities, and interests of his particular class, is thus able to integrate music with the on-going class activity and make it a meaningful learning experience. Unfortunately, these teachers do not all possess the necessary background and skills for teaching music adequately. As a means of meeting this problem some teachers have assisted each other in the teaching of subjects in which they feel insecure. One classroom teacher, for example, may teach all the music to several classes, while another will teach art, and perhaps still another physical education. Thus the strengths of each teacher are used to the best advantage. Although this comprises at least a workable arrangement, it

---

[10] Cf. Donald J. Davis, "Evaluation and Curricular Development in the Arts," *Toward An Aesthetic Education* (Washington, D.C.: Music Educators National Conference, 1971), pp. 119–122.

[11] Cf. Edward J. Hermann, *Supervising Music in the Elementary School* (Englewood Cliffs, N.J.: Prentice-Hall, Inc., 1965), pp. 3–4.

cannot be said to be a widespread practice. Teachers who enjoy music and see its values, and who feel adequate in teaching it, will employ it whenever possible and appropriate. Those who feel inadequate about teaching music will shy away from it and sometimes ignore it totally. Under this arrangement, therefore, programs in music instruction may range from the adequate to the practically nonexistent.

2. The special music teacher. In some elementary schools, where the administration feels a special music teacher is necessary and desirable, a person especially proficient in music—usually with a bachelor's degree in music education—will have the major responsibility for the teaching of music. Of this arrangement, quite a wide variation in practice exists. In some situations, the person may be simply a traveling music teacher, perhaps visiting on a rotational basis a number of schools. The teacher's schedule generally allows a periodic visit to each classroom with lessons ranging from twenty to thirty minutes in length. The frequency of the visits depends, of course, upon the number of schools and classrooms for which the teacher is responsible. In certain instances, the relative infrequency of the teacher's visits, because of a heavy teaching load, makes the visitations barely worthwhile. In school systems with adequate finances, and where an adequate number of teachers are employed for the task, satisfactory results may be expected. To teach music adequately, however, sufficient time must be provided for both planning and teaching. For a teacher to move hurriedly from classroom to classroom, without giving consideration to the on-going class activities and the needs and interests of the students, generally negates the values of the visit.

In other situations, one teacher may be assigned to a single school, with the responsibility for teaching all the music from grades one through six. In some instances the teacher will make regularly scheduled visits to each classroom. In others, the children (generally only those in the intermediate grades) will move to a special music room for instructional periods of varying length, depending upon the local school situation. In still other schools, the music specialist may teach only those students in the intermediate grades, with music instruction in the primary grades being the responsibility of the classroom teachers.

3. The music consultant and the classroom teacher. Growing out of the administrator's recognition of the necessity for good working relationships, as well as the most prudent and economical use of the music specialist's time, is the trend toward the increased use of the position known as the *music consultant*. In this approach, the responsibility for the teaching of music is shared by the music consultant and the classroom teacher. The function of the music consultant is to aid and assist classroom teachers in their growth in professional competence. Underlying this approach are the administrator's beliefs that classroom teachers *can* teach music, that music ought to be a part of the daily experience of children rather than simply a twice-a-week activity, that most teachers will need some special help if the total program is to be effective, and that the music consultant does possess a unique background that makes it possible to give special help to those teachers who need it. The use of music consultants has been successful in many communities, particularly where the administrator has carefully clarified the nature of the responsibilities of both the classroom teachers and the music consultant.

The music consultant may assist classroom teachers in many ways. He may travel to a number of schools on a rotational basis to visit the classrooms of teachers who need and request assistance in their teaching. (Some classroom teachers are highly competent in the teaching of music and need only a minimum amount of help.) The specialist may observe a lesson and offer suggestions. It must be understood that the specialist provides aid because the classroom teacher requests assistance in teaching, and not because of a quasi-administrative responsibility. This is the key to effective working relationships. The specialist does not prod the classroom teacher, but serves as a resource person, ever ready to give needed assistance. Whenever the teacher-consultant relationship is good, the consultant may give a demonstration lesson in the classroom and perhaps launch a particular unit of study. Perhaps the classroom teacher, in planning a new unit of study, needs suggestions on appropriate materials. The consultant with a broader background and reference library of books, music, and recordings, can provide invaluable help and assistance.

Workshops in teaching elementary school music can be most helpful to classroom teachers. Such workshops might be scheduled twice monthly, perhaps for an hour and one-half after school. When teachers are cognizant of their needs and interested in improving skills and understandings, these sessions can be highly beneficial. Teachers should participate wholeheartedly in all the activities which they expect to teach their children. Music skills and understandings are accomplished best by *doing* and not by simply talking about them.

Topics for Discussion

1. Why is it important for teachers to have a well-defined philosophy of education?

2. How might one account for the fact that in past years music educators have been inclined to emphasize procedures that either develop music-reading skills *or* provide "enjoyment" for the purpose of motivating children to pursue more serious music study?

3. What is the relationship of "whole" learning to the teaching of musical concepts based on the structure of music?

4. Describe circumstances in which the lecture method, the socratic method, and the discovery method might best be employed in teaching, to the exclusion of the other approaches.

5. Teaching objectives in music have a different focus today than in the past. Discuss the reasons behind this change.

6. Compare the functions of the classroom teacher, as regards to music teaching, with those of the music specialist. Indicate the specific desired contributions of each to children's musical development.

Suggestions for Further Study

Birge, Edward Bailey, *History of Public School Music in the United States.* Washington, D.C.: Music Educators National Conference (a reprinting of the 1928 edition, available in either cloth or paperback).

Hermann, Edward J., *Supervising Music in the Elementary Schools.* Englewood Cliffs, N.J.: Prentice-Hall, Inc., 1965.

Hoffer, Charles, *Teaching Music in the Secondary Schools* (2nd ed.). Belmont, Calif.: Wadsworth Publishing Company, Inc., chapter 3.

Kaplan, Max, *Foundations and Frontiers of Music Education.* New York: Holt, Rinehart & Winston, Inc., 1966.

Langer, Susanne K., *Feeling and Form.* New York: Charles Scribner's Sons, 1953, chapters 1–3, 7–10.

————, *Philosophy in a New Key.* New York: New American Library, 1948, chapter 8.

Livingston, James A., Michael D. Poland, and Ronald E. Simmons, *Accountability and Objectives for Music Education.* Costa Mesa, Calif.: Educational Media Press, 1972.

Mager, Robert F., *Preparing Instructional Objectives.* Palo Alto, Calif.: Fearon Publishers, Inc., 1962.

MENC, *Toward An Aesthetic Education.* Washington, D.C.: Music Educators National Conference, 1971.

POUNDS, RALPH L., and ROBERT L. GARRETSON. *Principles of Modern Education.* New York: The Macmillan Company, 1962, chapter 8.

REIMER, BENNETT, *A Philosophy of Music Education.* Englewood Cliffs, N.J.: Prentice-Hall, 1970.

SCHWADRON, ABRAHAM, *Aesthetics: Dimensions for Music Education.* Washington, D.C.: Music Educators National Conference, 1967.

TELLSTROM, A. THEODORE, *Music in American Education, Past and Present.* New York: Holt, Rinehart & Winston, 1971.

chapter 2

PLANNING TO TEACH MUSIC

Although it is acknowledged that even the most carefully laid plans can go astray, this can never be considered an acceptable excuse or reason for *not planning,* but only a commentary on the unpredictability of human events. There is little question but that the most successful teachers carefully and deliberately plan their teaching. They give thoughtful and careful consideration to the needs and abilities of their children, determine reasonable objectives, and then devise strategies to accomplish these objectives.

Learning activities, if they are to be effective, must be carefully conceived. The teacher must know what he wants to accomplish during a given period and specific teaching strategies must be devised. So that the procedures will become crystallized in the teacher's mind, it is essential to prepare a written plan in outline form. Writing clarifies one's thinking and serves as a useful teaching guide. All teaching plans, once they are used, should be carefully filed for future reference. They are not only a record of what has been covered, but are also an invaluable reference in assessing one's overall planning efforts and in preparing new plans for the ensuing term or year.

In planning, a number of factors need to be given consideration, including the learning environment, the backgrounds of the children, the type of classroom organization prevalent in particular schools, the inclusion of large group activities, and the utilization of Individually Guided Education (IGE).

THE LEARNING ENVIRONMENT

In planning to teach music in the elementary school, one of the first considerations is the classroom environment in which children are

17

to experience music. Is the atmosphere of the room pleasing and conducive to learning? Is the room organized so as to stimulate learning? The following are a number of ideas for the teacher to consider:

1. Teaching aids can be helpful if posted on the walls of the music room, usually immediately above the chalkboard. Include prints or photos of various composers and musical instruments, and so forth.

2. Displays of student work should also be posted on the room walls. Children's creative efforts, such as songs, poems, and music notation, are meaningful displays and constant reminders of satisfying musical accomplishments that may "set the stage" for even further musical accomplishments. It may prove helpful if the efforts of the music teacher are coordinated with those of the art teacher, who can help the children arrive at aesthetic principles (e.g., on size, shape, color) concerning the most appropriate way to display their creative work.

Jefferson County (Colorado) Public Schools
Photograph by Nancy J. Pitz.

Wall displays may contribute to the learning atmosphere of the music room.

3. A "listening center" may be designated in the classroom and a record player permanently set up, with earphones available, so that children

can listen to recordings of their choice without interrupting the rest of the class. It is indeed desirable to secure a "listening station" with multiple jacks and earphones so that several children can listen together. The "listening center" may be made not only attractive but also more interesting to children if record jackets are displayed on the wall above the record player. Pertinent printed information about the music and composers, as well as listening guides for individual study, should be made accessible to the children and should form a part of the "listening center."

4. A musical instrument corner in the classroom may also be designated and instruments displayed on a table and made available for children to experiment with. Such instruments as Autoharps, melody bells, resonator bells, Orff instruments, guitars, and percussion instruments should be a part of all music classrooms and should be displayed in such a way that they stimulate the children's desire to experiment with them.

Ft. Collins (Colorado) Public Schools

An "instrument corner" where children have easy access to various musical instruments.

The teacher should periodically expand the children's environment beyond the school classroom to include locations in the community-at-large, for example, by visiting churches for organ concerts and demonstrations, and concert halls and music schools for special concerts and demonstrations.

UNDERSTANDING CHILDREN'S BACKGROUNDS

Long-range planning is an essential prerequisite to effective teaching and should be accomplished well in advance of the beginning of the school year. A broad general plan should be developed in which the content to be covered during a particular six-week period or semester is identified and elaborated upon. It is generally accepted that teachers need to consider the background and accomplishments of their students and should begin "where they are." If the children's achievements are known to the teacher, then a basis exists for planning the ensuing years' activities. If the teacher is new to the school, however, appropriate information needs to be sought. The following are some suggested means for securing the necessary information:

1. Determine the children's background by discussions with their previous teachers. Examine course outlines and endeavor to determine what specific areas were covered and what was accomplished.

2. Review examples of all creative work available, including poems, songs, and summaries of creative dramatizations.

3. Listen to any available tape recordings of previous classwork or programs.

4. Examine health records available in the office to determine if any students have hearing or visual deficiences. This information needs to be known at the beginning of the year so that appropriate seating arrangements, as well as other teaching plans, can be made.

5. Some school districts also use standardized qualitative tests to determine aptitude and achievement, the latter including mastering of terminology, comprehension of concepts, and so forth.

During the initial part of the year, however, overall plans may be adjusted, providing that additional information is gained about the children's level of musical development, and after skills have been assessed and the children's knowledge about music has been more carefully determined.

WHAT TYPE OF CLASSROOM ORGANIZATION?

Some teachers advocate a totally open classroom, others a more conventional classroom organization. Regardless of the type of organization, the most important thing is what actually goes on in the classroom! What really happens? Are the large-group activities exciting musical events or are they dull and uneventful? Does the open classroom create an atmosphere of eager anticipation, or does it lend to chaotic confusion?[1] The answer, of course, lies in the teacher, who will probably discover that careful planning is absolutely essential to any type of effective learning, regardless of the type of classroom organization used, and that the appropriate organization of the class is dependent upon the activities engaged in to fulfill specific objectives. In determining the best overall approach, it would be wise for the teacher to utilize an approach that is compatible with the philosophy of the particular school and the individual teachers with which the music teacher is associated. Whatever the position of the local school, however, teachers should refrain from the tendency to avoid any and all experimentation simply because of "what others might think."

PLANNING FOR GROUP ACTIVITIES

At the end of each session in which a music class meets, the children should have a clearer understanding or grasp of some musical concept or idea. Concepts, however, are not simply taught to children. Rather, the teacher plans and sets up activities for children first to *experience* and then to *discover* musical concepts. Children's activities should be guided—and through experimentation, discussion, and finally verbalization of the experiences, they will become more meaningful; in addition, the teacher will have an added measure of the degree of their comprehension.

Prior to the recent emphasis on conceptual learning, a major point of emphasis in teaching elementary-school music was the development of musical skills, e.g., skills such as singing, playing instruments, reading music, and creating music. While these skills are still considered by many to be valid objectives, they are no longer conceived of as ends in themselves, but are seen simply as a means through which children can learn about music. And, of course, singing songs or simply playing records for children for an entire period *is not* teaching music and was never considered as such. Perhaps an occasional "songfest" might be justified as a recreational activity, but not as a substitute for a learning activity.

In planning musical experiences of any kind for children, the teacher should keep in mind that *music is an aural art* and an affective experience, i.e., one involved with the feelings and emotions of persons. In view of the present emphasis on musical concepts and structured learning, the teacher should avoid any tendency to over-intellectualize

[1] For a straightforward discussion of the educational possibilities inherent in the open classroom, see Herbert R. Kohl, *The Open Classroom: a Practical Guide to a New Way of Teaching* (New York: Vintage Books, 1969).

the learning process and should strive toward helping children achieve the joy and excitement that results from discovery.

The following is a suggested outline for planning group activities in music:

I. A. Scope of the lesson, specific concepts to be taught.
   B. Objectives expressed in behavioral terms.
   C. Materials and equipment needed.

II. A. Initiatory activities or ways of beginning the lesson.
    B. Teaching strategies—activities in which children engage to realize or achieve objectives.
    C. Culminating activities—ways of summarizing and highlighting the concepts which the children "discover."

III. A. Evaluation—Did the children learn what was anticipated? What were the strengths and weaknesses of the lesson, and how will this judgment effect planning for subsequent lessons?

In part I of the outline, the teacher's concern should be with what is to be accomplished. Specific daily objectives should be expressed in behavioral terms; that is, what do we want the children to accomplish and how will we know when they do? Consideration also needs to be given at this point to the music materials and equipment needed to accomplish the desired objectives.

Part II involves the lesson proper. The first concern is with initiatory activities, or how to introduce the lesson in a way that will fully motivate the students, i.e., that will create excitement about the subject and a desire on the part of the class to explore the topic further. Curiosity needs to be aroused and student energies set into motion in a single direction. The second consideration involves utilizing specific teaching strategies or activities designed to lead children toward the discovery of a basic musical concept, which is the stated objective of the lesson. Through the discovery approach, the teacher can optimize the opportunities for creative, stimulating, and exciting learning, thus avoiding any tendency to overstress conceptual learning to the point where it becomes dull and routine. The third consideration involves culminating activities, or ways of concluding a lesson so that it will become most meaningful to the students. Children should be encouraged to verbalize their "discoveries" and express them in their own words. After this, the teacher can paraphrase and summarize the student expressions. Through this means their new-found understandings will become clearer and more in focus.

Part III of the plan involves the teacher's evaluative process after the lesson. Questions will be asked concerning the overall effectiveness of the lesson and the strengths and weaknesses of the presentation. "What were the more effective techniques and what procedures should be abandoned, or at least revised, during the next lesson?" "What factors should be kept in mind in planning for the next lesson?"

In summary, the preceding daily lesson plan contains three parts:

1. Objectives: To teach children an understanding of a specific musical concept.

2. Activities: Designed to guide children toward the discovery of a specific musical concept or idea.

3. Outcome: Fulfillment of the behavioral objective, or behavior by children demonstrating that they comprehend the concept.

    Or, yet even more simply stated, "What are you going to do?"; "How did you do it?"; and "What was the result?"

The approximate amount of time for each portion of the plan should be estimated and generally adhered to; however, the teacher should be flexible and make adjustments if necessary. The teacher should be aware of and sensitive to the children's needs and responses and react accordingly. For example, if the group is unusually quiet, then they should be drawn out, perhaps through extra discussion. If the group is overly excitable, then the teacher should endeavor to speak more calmly, and perhaps slow down the pace. If the group is generally unattentive, then the teacher should consider increasing the pace of the lesson and project his excitement about the on-going activity. Enthusiasm can be contagious!

In class discussions, the teacher should analyze children's responses. Are they comprehensive enough? Do they show understanding? If not, then the teacher should consider another approach. Different analogies and other musical examples may be used, and additional time should be allowed for further class exploration and discussion.

PLANNING FOR INDIVIDUALLY GUIDED EDUCATION (IGE)

Planning for Individually Guided Education (IGE), or Personalized Systems of Instruction (PSI), as it is known in some areas, certainly takes a special type of consideration and effort, perhaps much more than the planning for the traditional group activities. The results, however, are generally more than worth the effort, especially when children are observed developing the greater independence and self-reliance that results from pursuing activities of special significance and highly personal meaning.

IGE schools are organized according to a multiunit plan, rather than by grades. A school is divided into units and an arrangement might include four units, each with a staff of 3–6 teachers, 1–2 teacher aides, and 75 to 150 children. A typical organization of a multiunit school of 600 students is as shown on page 25:[2]

As will be noted in the diagram, children, teachers, and aides are divided into units that involve overlapping age-ranges of children. Children are placed in units according to their backgrounds and abilities and are grouped within each unit according to their interests and achievements. The teachers in a specific unit work together as a team, with one of the teachers serving as the unit leader. Teachers in a unit meet together regularly for planning purposes and assessment of pupil progress. In planning activities, a given teacher may schedule projects involving a large class, a small group, or working with a particular child on a one-to-one basis. Such flexibility becomes possible through a "team" effort. Each teacher is given an opportunity to contribute his or her own special subject-matter expertise and is encouraged to develop and draw upon his or her own unique strengths. A music teacher who is assigned to an IGE school should schedule time to meet periodically with the teachers in the different units, so that plans can be coordinated and the most appropriate learning experiences can be designed for the children.[3]

Individualized instruction implies that the students move at their own rates of speed, but not always at a rate that the teacher prescribes. In other words, the same goals do not hold true for every child. An objective is for individual children to set their own goals and thus move at their own paces. The teacher's role is that of a facilitator (or coordinator, or resource person) who helps each child find those media and experiences that will be of most help in achieving the chosen goals or objectives. Because there is so much knowledge available, a child cannot be taught everything; therefore, it is the teacher's responsibility to help the child find the most appropriate resources for learning.

Initially, it is essential that the music teacher explore widely all

[2] *Individually Guided Education* (Dayton, Ohio: Institute for Development of Educational Activities, Inc., 1970), p. 7. Used with permission of the Institute for Development of Educational Activities, Inc., an affiliate of the Charles F. Kettering Foundation.

[3] Some music teachers may be inclined to "go their own way." Effective communication among teachers and "teamwork" is absolutely essential to the achievement of the objectives of an IGE school.

ORGANIZATION OF MULTIUNIT SCHOOL WITH 600 PUPILS

Central Office Staff	State Department of Public Instruction Consultants

Principal

Unit A	Unit B	Unit C	Unit D
1 Unit Leader	1 Unit Leader	1 Unit Leader	1 Unit Leader
4 Teachers	4 Teachers	4 Teachers	4 Teachers
1 Instructional Aide	1 Instructional Aide	1 Instructional Aide	1 Instructional Aide
1 Clerical Aide	1 Clerical Aide	1 Clerical Aide	1 Clerical Aide
150 Pupils Age 5, 6, 7	150 Pupils Age 7, 8, 9	150 Pupils Age 8, 9, 10	150 Pupils Age 9, 10, 11

▨ = Instructional Improvement Committee

possible resources and maintain a system of classifying the materials that are available. In developing resource materials, the teacher should work closely with the school librarian, who can be of inestimable help in locating, securing, and classifying information and materials. In accumulating special files on given topics, the teacher will identify many valuable additions simply by being cognizant of the need and aware of the problem that prompted formation of the file. Children can also be of great help in collecting materials if they are alerted to the need for specific types of items.

Although IGE is certainly easier to accomplish in a multiunit school, it is not impossible in the traditional school, and music teachers should still strive to plan in such a way that individual needs are met. Music is a *personal* art, and if it is to become a meaningful part of children's lives, then teachers need to give every consideration to its varied possibilities.

The music teacher may help meet individual student needs by organizing a given class according to special-interest groups. For example, on a given day, a class may be divided into several small sub-groups, each of which explores an area of special interest.

Ft. Collins (Colorado) Public Schools

The Listening Center enables a small group of children to work independently from the rest of the class and to pursue topics of special interest.

One group may choose to work at the "listening center" (a group of record turntables equipped with individual earphones or headsets) to listen to a specific recorded selection. Another group may wish to work quietly reading children's books on topics of special interest. Still another group may explore a special topic by viewing various filmstrips. Another activity may focus on playing music games involving music notation. Other possible groupings may include children who wish to explore or learn to play musical instruments, such as guitar or piano.

With four or five groups involved in activities of a different nature, children are encouraged to work independently. In the event that one teacher in a unit is working with a large group, one or more teachers or aides may be available to assist with the small-group instruction. In the event that this arrangement is not possible, then the teacher may appoint a particular child within each group to serve as the resource person and to assist the other children whenever and in whatever ways he or she is able. For example, a child who has had several years of piano instruction may help others in a group in learning to play a specific piece. Obviously, these "resource persons" within a group should alternate according to the nature of the project, not only so that the strengths of all the children are capitalized upon, but also so that each may have the opportunity for leadership experience. Careful discussions with all members of a class will help to identify their special interests, and careful observation of their achievements will help to identify their unique strengths. With certain activities, the teacher may find it appropriate and desirable to record a set of instructions on a cassette tape. The children can then first listen to these instructions and then begin their chosen activity.

In utilizing IGE or in organizing students into small groups, some teachers, because of their backgrounds, may express concern about the "confusion" in the classroom. Noise, as such, does not really bother students the way it does adults. What initially may sound or appear like confusion, may later "groove" into more homogeneous and agreeable sounds.

One teacher, in an attempt to provide individualized experiences, set up a plan that allowed for two unstructured or "free" days a week. On these days about fifteen different music classes were offered. Students could select a class of their choosing from a wide variety of offerings, including, for example, music theory, song writing, beginning guitar, music of the black man, and the history of classical music. Class size was approximately twelve to fifteen, and every six weeks the student would rotate to another class. The objective was to expose as many students as possible to the program. On the three structured days of the week, the students would engage in activities more appropriate to a large class, such as singing, playing, and basic musicianship.[4]

Another approach is for the teacher to prepare *individual study guides* on a variety of topics, thus enabling children to pursue their own special interests. Children should be given a choice of topics they wish to pursue. The teacher may wish to maintain special study packets with a variety of source materials and study suggestions included. (Children themselves can contribute to these packets and can be of great assistance in identifying pertinent information.) Each study guide will include the title, a statement of learning objectives (after completing the guide, I will be able to _____), and a detailed procedure of study. The study procedure will give careful instructions on what to read or what to listen for on the recording or cassette, and will provide a series of questions to answer or ways in which to respond. (As an alternative to printed study directions, the teacher may wish to record the directions on a cassette tape recorder.) The guide will also include suggestions for self-evaluation and thoughts for pupils to consider prior to evaluation by the teacher.

In preparing individual study guides, teachers will find the publication *How To Write Learning Activity Packages for Music Education* by Joseph W. Landon most helpful. Two examples from this publication —one for second grade and the other for third grade—are included to illustrate the approach.[5]

LAP No. 1   *Title:*   Sounds in Music   *Time Allotment:*   20 minutes

Class: Second Grade (classroom music)   *Performance Level:*   II

Concept: Single tones of the melody follow one another to form a characteristic and recognizable melodic structure.

Behavioral Objectives:
   Given the opportunity to experiment with 3 resonator bells, C, D, and E,

Materials:
   Resonator bells C-D-E
   1 mallet
   Pencil

The student will:
1. Discover different sounds that these resonator bells produce.
2. Develop critical judgment between high and low sounds.
3. Demonstrate the ability to arrange and play these pitches in order from low to high.
4. Discover a tune familiar to him which can be played by these bells.
5. Create a tune of his own.

---

[4] Leonore M. Nelan, "Reach Children with Music," *Instructor* (October, 1971), pp. 73–74.

[5] Joseph W. Landon, *How To Write Learning Activity Packages for Music Education* (Costa Mesta, Calif.: Educational Media Press, 1973), pp. 40, 42–43. Used by permission.

Instructions to the Student:

1. Hi! There are 3 bells on the table. Play these bells using the striker next to the bells. Play them all again.

    Do they ring? _____

2. Now listen to the bells as you play them. Do all the bells sound alike?

    _____ How are they different? _____

    _____

3. Find the bell that sounds the lowest. What is the letter name on this

    bell? _____

    Find the bell that is the highest. What is the letter name on this

    bell? _____

    What bell is left now? _____

4. Arrange the bells:

Low

Middle

High

    Write the
    letters of   _____   _____   _____
    the bells

5. Are your bells in the order of
           C   D   E   ?
        _____   _____   _____

6. Play these letters on the bells—*hit each bell once each time you see the letter.*

        E D C D E E E   D D D   E E E
        E D C D E E E E D D E D C

    What song did you just play?

7. Make your own song on the bells. Write the letters of your song in

    order _____

LAP No. 3   *Title:* Even-uneven
                     Rhythm Patterns   *Time Allotment:*   10 minutes

Class: Third Grade (classroom music)   *Performance Level:*   III

Concept: Rhythm patterns consist of groups of long and short tones. These
                may be combined into even or uneven patterns.

Behavioral Objectives:
    Presented with a series of familiar sounds of varying duration,

Materials:
    Pencil
    Paper
    Box of rhythm instruments (can be home-made)

The student will:
1. Distinguish differences between even and uneven rhythm patterns.
2. Imitate these different patterns by playing the sounds on rhythm instruments.
3. Relate long-short, even-uneven rhythms to blank notation corresponding to the duration of the rhythm patterns.
4. Create original rhythm patterns in which these sounds are used.

Instructions to the Student:

Hello! Today we will learn about rhythms. You already know that music does have lots of types of rhythms put together, and that a song has a beat. The beat of a song is like your heart beat; it goes on and on, sometimes fast, sometimes slow, but it always is there.

Some other things you do also have rhythm. When you swing on the playground, your swing goes back and forth in a steady rhythm. If you jump rope, your rope makes a steady patter on the sidewalk. Have you ever skipped to school? _____ If so, you make a skipping sound as you hop along. Does a clock ticking away have a rhythm? _____ Does the tic toc continue at the same speed? _____ Have you ever listened to a coffee pot perk? _____ Does it have a steady perking noise? _____ If we were the clock, we would go _____ _____, _____ _____, _____ _____. We could write that this way. . . . .

<u>tic</u>   <u>toc</u>   <u>tic</u>   <u>toc</u>

We would call this an *even* rhythm. Can you think of a way to write the coffee pot sound above the following words to make an *even* rhythm?

<u>perk,</u>   <u>perk,</u>   <u>perk,</u>   <u>perk</u>

1. Have you ever ridden on a horse? _____ Does the horse make a sound of clip clop, clip clop? _____ That is an *uneven* sound, and would look like this:

     <u> </u> .   <u> </u> .   <u> </u> .
    clip clop   clip clop   clip clop

The clip has a longer sound than the clop. Clip(long) Clop(short)

2. If we were writing an even rhythm, it would look like this:

   — — — —   — — — —   — — — —

3. And the uneven rhythm would look like this:

   — - — - — - — - — - — - — -

4. Choose a rhythm instrument out of the box. Play this rhythm on that instrument.

   — - — - — - — - — - — - — - — -

5. Now choose a different instrument. Play this rhythm.

   — — — — — — — —

6. Try one more different instrument playing this rhythm pattern.

   — — — —   — - — - — - — -   — — — —

7. Is this an even or uneven rhythm? _ _ _ _ _ _ _ _ _ _   _____

8. Is this an even or uneven rhythm? __ _ __ - __ - __ - __ -   _____

9. Write an uneven rhythm. _____

10. Write an even rhythm. _____

11. Use both kinds of rhythms as you write another example. _____

    _____

    Play the last example you just wrote. Did you like the sound? _____

    Why? _____

    _____

12. Put away the instruments you have used. Thank you for doing such a nice job today.

Still another approach to IGE is a plan for individualized study in which individual pupils choose their own topics, the way in which they plan to pursue them, and the way in which they are to be evaluated. Such a plan is usually more appropriate for older, more mature pupils who are highly motivated and have had previous experience with IGE. It is suggested that such students give thought to and submit to the teacher answers to the following questions before beginning their study.[6]

[6] Adapted from Robert J. Starr, "A Suggestion for Individualizing Instruction Within a Traditional School Organization," *Audiovisual Instruction* (October, 1971), pp. 68–69.

A Proposed Individual Learning Activity

1. This study is proposed by _____

_____.

2. I want to learn more about _____

_____.

3. My study will take me about (a) one week (b) two weeks (c) three weeks (d) a month.

4. I plan to use the following resources in my study (indicate choices): (a) books (b) films (c) filmstrips (d) recordings (e) interviews of persons

(f) other(s) _____

_____.

5. I will show what I have learned by (indicate choices):

   a. identifying   f. classifying

   b. selecting   g. describing

   c. reporting   h. other _____

   d. demonstrating   _____

   e. comparing   _____.

6. I wish to be evaluated by:

   a. reporting what I have learned

   b. demonstrating what I have learned

   c. my written report

   d. my new and creative ideas

   e. other _____.

IGE is becoming a topic of increasing interest to music teachers, as many realize that through this type of organized structure more effective teaching may be accomplished. In some localities, groups of music teachers periodically share ideas with each other on how best to implement IGE, and a body of literature pertaining to it is gradually developing.

SELECTION OF TEACHING MATERIALS

The range and variety of teaching materials available to the music teacher is greater today than ever before, and for new teachers, the choice of appropriate materials can sometimes be perplexing. Selections are based not simply on an awareness of available items, but more upon a particular person's assessment of their worth, which is directly influenced by that person's philosophy of teaching. To bring this problem more into focus, the broad range of materials may be summarized as follows:

1. Basic music series. Nine different companies publish a basic music series, each of which includes a variety of musical activities appropriate to the musical development of children in various grade levels, i.e., from kindergarten usually through the sixth grade (see the Appendix for a complete listing of available series). Most of the series books are designed by well-known music educators around an approach intended to develop a conceptual understanding of music. All the series are usually promoted as a complete program of musical experiences, including songs, suggested recordings for listening activities, bodily movement, instrumental experiences, and other activities. Some of the series also include experiences in related arts, such as visual art and poetry. Certain states and local communities sometimes "adopt" a particular series in music, as well as in language arts and mathematics, and a set of books is provided for both the children and the teachers in all the schools. In spite of the completeness of each series, however, teachers generally find it necessary and desirable to supplement their adopted series with other materials, usually with song and record collections, but sometimes through the acquisition of an "extra" set of series books from another publisher when funds are available.

2. Song and record collections. Various song collections are available to the teacher who is seeking supplementary materials (see the list at the end of Chapter 3). Songs in most collections are included that have general appeal to children, including folksongs from around the world, action songs, and so forth. As to record collections, several companies, including RCA Victor and Bowmar Educational Records, produce record series with instrumental and vocal music appropriate to the musical development of children of various grade levels (see pp. 286–287 for further information).

3. Songs composed by children. As a part of the total music-learning experience, children are often encouraged and assisted by the teacher to write their own songs. From this experience they not only gain insight into the creative process, but also develop a high degree of motivation that is reflected in the quality of other musical experiences. While children gain from the creative process, they will also gain from performing the creative endeavors of other children, and teachers should file and maintain all these materials for use by other children at an appropriate later date.

4. The Orff and Kodály approaches to music education. The Orff Schulwerk, published by B. Schott's Söhne and available in the United States through Belwin-Mills Publishing Corp., was prepared by Carl Orff as a program of music education for use in German schools. The Kodály method, published by Boosey and Hawkes, was prepared by Zoltán Kodály and adopted as the state system of music instruction in Hungary. Most music educators feel that, although both systems are valid, it is difficult to adopt in total a system prepared for another culture; there are many teachers who disagree with this point of view, however, and use one system or the other almost to the total exclusion of other systems of teaching. Still other teachers will modify and adapt aspects of the Orff and Kodály systems and integrate these ideas with systems prevailing in American education today, including the basic music series (for a discussion of both the Orff and Kodály approaches to music education, see chapter 11). Textbooks also have been written that enable teachers to adapt the ideas in these systems to their own classrooms.[7]

5. Popular youth music. There are a number of teachers who utilize popular music, including Afro-American music, rock, and other popular styles, as a part of the children's overall musical experience. Children are already familiar with some of these styles, and their interest and motivation toward such learning experiences are presumed to be much higher. There are some teachers who use these styles of music almost to the total exclusion of all other music.[8] Some prominent music educators recommend the use of popular music, and one firm provides monthly listening guides in nine-month subscriptions.[9]

Years ago, it was a most common practice for school systems to adopt a basic music series and use it almost exclusively for the musical education of their children. Today, however, there are teachers and school systems who feel it unnecessary to adopt a particular music series, but rather encourage teachers to use a variety of supplementary materials and to devise their own activities. Among this group are persons having had first-hand experience with the Manhattanville Music Curriculum Project—a highly creative and innovative music-instruction program (see p. 268). Some systems hold periodic workshops to encourage and assist teachers in using this approach, the curriculum of which will include a wide variety of activities and experiences.

---

[7] See, for example, Lawrence Wheeler and Lois Raebeck, *Orff and Kodály Adapted for the Elementary School* (Dubuque, Iowa: Wm. C. Brown Company, Publishers, 1972).

[8] Teachers who use current popular materials should be cautioned that duplicating them without the express written permission of the publisher is unlawful and can only lead to embarrassment and a possible lawsuit.

[9] For a sample issue, contact *POP HITS*, 3149 Southern, Memphis, Tenn. 38111.

In summary, teachers are encouraged to maintain an open mind about the validity of all teaching materials and activities appropriate for use with their children. They are also cautioned against going overboard for any single approach or source of materials, and urged to develop a curriculum with a wide variety of musical types and styles, which is the musical heritage of all children.

CREATIVITY IN TEACHING

What is creativity? To some persons the term *creative* means only the development of something new and original. According to this viewpoint, which has long been held, it would not be a completely creative act merely to perform music written by someone else. Around 1925, however, a concept appeared which implies that all learning is creative with reference to the learner. The thought implicit in this belief is that the learner must fully comprehend ideas, concepts, and relationships so that they are something more than merely words or symbols and thus they become a part of the learner's total experience. Since no one else can ever do this for any student, such learning can be said to be "created" by the learner. A key word which aptly describes this process is "discovery"; for a child to discover a new fact or relationship, insight and understanding are necessary and must come from, or be "created" within, the individual. Another related term is *re-creative,* often used in connection with the traditional viewpoint of creativity. Persons using this term would usually take the position that while musical performance is not a new creative act, the performer must at least possess a certain degree of insight and musical understanding if the music is to be interpreted in a musicianly manner.

What are the implications of this new viewpoint of creativity for the teaching of music? In singing a song or playing an instrument, a creative approach requires that the music be meaningful to the performer, who must be able to perform it in a manner that gives personal satisfaction. Musical artistry is dependent upon the degree of musical insight the performer possesses; creativity, however, is not dependent upon an arbitrary or fixed level of musical proficiency and insight. For example, a second-grade student who possesses a reasonable understanding of the text and mood of a song and the relationship between the words and the music, and who is able to relate past experiences to this song, is likely to perform or "re-create" it in a highly satisfactory manner. This can be a truly creative act, commensurate with the degree of insight which the child possesses. Furthermore, an experienced adult who possesses a knowledge of the stylistic aspects of the music, and who is sensitive to all the necessary subtle nuances, will be less likely to perform in an unmusical and mechanical manner. The insight leading to a creative performance must come from within the individual and cannot be simply imposed upon a person or group. This does not mean, however, that teachers cannot facilitate the development of insight, for this is one of their primary functions.

The teacher's point of departure, however, should not be, "Shall I plan for a creative work, a re-creative act, or simply a discovery?" but rather, "What can I do to provide meaningful learning experiences for the class?" The teacher can begin by providing a classroom atmosphere conducive to effective learning and by exploring with the students all information that will contribute to improved performance.

While some educators are critical of the use of the term "creative" to describe these activities, most will admit that this particular philosophy has contributed to the development of more desirable learning situations. Actually, it is less important whether the teacher uses the word "creative," "re-creative," or "discovery" in connection with music activities, and more important what he or she actually does in the classroom to provide meaningful learning experiences. The teacher who is really dynamic and imaginative in the teaching of music will most certainly provide the children with an ideal background for those experiences which result in the "creation" of the completely new and original.

Topics for Discussion

1. Discuss the effects of poor and haphazard planning upon the quality of the educative process.

2. What evidence does psychology present us in regard to the advantages of careful planning?

3. Discuss the learning environment as it relates to the learning process.

4. How does the nature of classroom organization relate to the type of planning that a teacher does?

5. Describe the three main parts of a lesson plan for group activities.

6. Why is it desirable to evaluate the effectiveness of each lesson plan after it has been taught? What procedures would you use in the evaluative process?

7. Describe the organization of a multiunit school.

8. What is the basic purpose of Individually Guided Education (IGE)?

Suggestions for Further Study

BAIRD, PEGGY FLANAGAN, *Music Books for the Elementary School Library*. Washington, D.C.: Music Educators National Conference, 1972.

BONEY, JOAN, and LOIS RHEA, *A Guide to Student Teaching in Music*. Englewood Cliffs, N.J.: Prentice-Hall, 1970.

BRUNER, JEROME, *The Process of Education*. New York: Vintage Books, 1963.

————, *Toward a Theory of Instruction*. Cambridge, Mass.: Harvard University Press, 1966.

DUNN, RITA STAFFORD, and KENNETH DUNN, "Practical Questions Teachers Ask About Individualizing Instruction—and Some of the Answers," *Audiovisual Instruction*, January, 1972, pp. 47–50.

GARY, CHARLES L., ed., *The Study of Music in the Elementary School: A Conceptual Approach*. Washington, D.C.: Music Educators National Conference, 1967.

GINOTT, HAIM G., *Between Parent and Child*. New York: Avon Books, 1969.

HOLT, JOHN, *How Children Learn*. New York: Pittman Publishing Company, 1969.

IGE Implementation Guide. Dayton, Ohio: Institute for Development of Educational Activities, Inc., 1970. (System materials include motion pictures, filmstrips with audio cassettes, and printed materials.)

"I Is In: Individualizing in Music Education," *Music Educators Journal* (November, 1972). Part 1: Children Are Different (3 articles); Part 2: Six Plans in Operation; Part 3: Freedom Within Order: Open Education (3 articles); Part 4, For Further Reading.

Individually Guided Education. Dayton, Ohio: Institute for Development of Educational Activities, Inc., 1970 (a 24-page overview of IGE in words, pictures, and diagrams for the general public and educators).

Individually Guided Education in the Multiunit Elementary School. Madison, Wis.: Wisconsin Research and Development Center for Cognitive Learning.

KAPFER, PHILIP G., and GLEN F. OVARD, *Preparing and Using Individualized Learning Packages for Ungraded, Continuous Progress Education*. Englewood Cliffs, N.J.: Educational Technology Publications.

KLAUSMEIER, HERBERT J., et al., *Individually Guided Education in the Multiunit Elementary School—Guidelines for Implementation*. Madison, Wis.: Wisconsin Research and Development Center for Cognitive Learning, 1970.

LANDON, JOSEPH W., *How to Write Learning Activity Packages for Music Education*. Costa Mesa, Calif.: Educational Media Press, 1973.

LIVINGSTON, JAMES A., MICHAEL D. POLAND, and RONALD E. SIMMONS, *Accountability and Objectives For Music Education*. Costa Mesa, Calif.: Educational Media Press, 1972.

MAGER, ROBERT F., *Preparing Instructional Objectives*. Palo Alto, Calif.: Fearon Publishers, 1962.

MASLOW, ABRAHAM H., *The Farther Reaches of Human Nature*. New York: The Viking Press, Inc., 1971 (Part II, Creativeness, chapters 4–7).

MESKE, EUNICE BOARDMAN, and CARROLL RINEHART, *Individualized Instruction in Music*. Reston, Va.: Music Educators National Conference, 1975.

NELAN, LENORE, "Reach Children With Music," *Instructor* (October, 1971).

chapter 3

THE CHILD VOICE
AND SINGING

Singing is a natural and emotionally satisfying childhood experience. Very young children are often initially exposed to singing through a mother's lullaby or by hearing the informal singing of other members of the family. Presentation of a variety of types of songs commensurate with the child's level of comprehension is an integral and important part of the many morning television programs designed for children of pre-school age. Learning to sing is initially an imitative process and most children learn to do so quite as naturally as they learn to speak. Singing is also as natural a form of personal expression as speech and young children may often be observed singing to themselves—singing simple songs they have learned and which appeal to them, and even expressing various thoughts, however brief, through song. An increasing number of children today attend nursery or pre-schools for one or two years prior to the time they enter kindergarten. A most important objective of these schools is helping the children to learn to work together cooperatively and to develop self-confidence. Music activities, and singing in particular, become important means for achieving these objectives and should be an integral part of the school's activities. Children, therefore, do enter the elementary school with a certain amount of background experience in music, however varied it may be. It is important for the teacher to realize this and to understand that children should not be expected to accomplish beyond the limits determined by their physical maturity.

THE CHILD VOICE

Hearing the myriad of vocal sounds on an elementary school playground has caused some observers to wonder about the voice quality which teachers should strive to develop in children. Actually there should be no doubt. In practice, teachers can develop almost any quality they strive for, because the human voice has an inherent ·flexibility which enables it to "imitate" a variety of types of sounds. The vocal mechanism of a child, however, is smaller than that of an adult and lacks the maturity and development which occur through continued use and training. The question then remains, what quality is most natural

Cincinnati Public Schools

Music for very young children is informal and intimate.

and characteristic of the child voice? In the author's opinion, the proper quality should be light, clear, and flutelike. It may even be described as ethereal in nature. This does *not* mean to imply that children's voices should always sound like angels', because certainly in the interpretation of a song the voice quality or color may and should differ to the extent necessary to reflect the moods of the music. But it does mean that children's voices should be kept reasonably light in quality and the heavy, darker quality characteristic of mature voices should be avoided. Even with adult singers, the development of a dark, heavy voice quality, when not sufficiently supported by the breath, will result in flatting, an excessively wide vibrato, and other intonation difficulties. The problem, of course, is more acute in children's voices because of the lack of bodily strength and the general lack of development of the entire vocal mechanism. Therefore, if satisfactory results are to be obtained in singing, the child voice must necessarily be kept light and flutelike in quality. It is often helpful to think of lining the child voice on the o͞o vowel. Even some vocalization on this vowel will be helpful in developing the concept in the children's minds of the voice quality they should be striving for. Various teachers have also found it helpful to differentiate between two types of voice qualities—the type used on the playground and that used for singing.

The voice range of the young child is somewhat limited. This fact must be understood if the teacher is to select songs that will not prove harmful to children's voices and that may be sung with a reasonable degree of ease. The old axiom that the range of children's songs should lie within the treble staff is applicable for children in the intermediate grades, but not for very young children. While some children in the kindergarten and first grade may have a voice range from G below middle C to fourth-space E, many others who have not yet completely discovered how to use their voices may have, for example, a range of only a fifth, from first-line E to third-line B. Initial songs for kindergarten children should therefore be selected with this latter group in mind. As children grow in their vocal capabilities, songs with more extended ranges may be utilized.

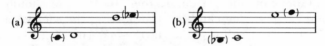

Suggested pitch range for songs in
a. kindergarten-primary grades, and
b. intermediate grades

It should be understood that the voice range increases gradually as a result of both bodily maturation and vocal training. Obviously, no abrupt changes in range can be expected to occur between the third and fourth grades, or between any grades. Vocal development in some children may be considerably ahead of the group and others may lag behind the average. Even some whole classes may be found to be ahead of others on the same grade level.[1] Therefore, as a necessary means of encouraging the optimum development of the children's voices, teachers should be careful to select songs well within the range limits of the majority of the group. Songs with extreme range may have a detrimental effect upon their voices and are not conducive to expressive singing.

Most of the songs found in the basic music texts have been carefully selected in consideration of the musical capabilities of the students, as well as their interests and the units of study generally undertaken at

[1] Factors determining this difference may be the amount of singing experience, the type of training, and the teacher's voice quality and attitudes toward music.

each particular grade level. Teachers using these tested materials may still encounter a few difficulties, but the authors of each series *have* considered the problem of range, as well as difficulty, in preparing the books for each grade level. When songs are obviously too high for a particular group, they may be lowered in pitch a half or a whole tone. It is generally unnecessary and often undesirable, however, to lower the pitch of these songs more than a whole step. Certainly the development of the high range will be facilitated only if children are encouraged and given ample opportunity to sing in a high, light head-voice.

The *tessitura,* or "average range of a song," is actually a more important factor to consider in selecting a song for a group than is the occurrence of an occasional high or low note. If the tessitura of a song is too high, then undue vocal strain may occur, the expressive qualities of the music may be lost, and the development of the children's voices may be hindered.

The voice range of some teachers is limited and some, therefore, make the mistake of lowering the pitch of a song to a key a third or more below the given pitch of the song merely to suit their own convenience. It is really grossly unfair to ask an entire class to adjust to the vocal limitations of one person. Rather, the teacher should adjust to the natural range of the children. Considering the somewhat restricted range of young children in particular, the majority of teachers can make the necessary adjustment with a little effort.

Teachers should endeavor to sing with a light tonal quality, as the heavier chest tones of the adult voice are not easily carried into the upper register. Since children are likely to imitate the voice quality of their teacher, the proper model of a light, flutelike quality (in so far as is possible for the teacher) will facilitate the development of the child voice.[2] As an aid in lightening the voice it is suggested that teachers vocalize periodically on the o͞o vowel, attempting to keep the voice light and the resonance high and forward.[3]

ASSISTING THE UNCERTAIN SINGER

Some children "find" their singing voices sooner than others. In the past this rather natural occurrence has caused no end of concern to classroom teachers, as well as to some special music teachers. In discussing

[2] For models of children's singing voices, refer to the recordings of songs which accompany the basic music series, most of which include some children's voices of quite good quality.

[3] For a discussion of resonance in the adult voice, see Robert L. Garretson, *Conducting Choral Music,* 4th ed. (Boston: Allyn & Bacon, Inc., 1975), pp. 69–78.

and conferring about these children, teachers have used various terms such as "monotones," "non-singers," and "out-of-tune singers," as well as "uncertain singers." The first three of these terms reflect, in general, a somewhat negative attitude toward the problem. The term "uncertain singer" is definitely the most descriptive of the children's problem as well as being a more precise one. Some persons have advanced the idea that certain children are incapable of learning to sing. This may be true only of deaf children and those with serious speech defects. Any child with normal speech and hearing can learn to sing—not always expertly, but at least adequately.[4] Viola Brody states that, "Every child who has a larynx, which functions in speech, can learn not only to perform vocally, but to perform with a pleasing quality."[5]

Causes of Difficulty

If teachers are to assist children in "finding" their voices they must be cognizant of the causes of the problem. An adequate understanding is essential to the development and maintenance of the proper attitude, as well as for providing a basis for the continual exploration and implementation of means to assist each child toward the fulfillment of his own potential. In general, a child's difficulties may stem from one or more of the following causes.

Physical immaturity. It is generally understood that some boys and girls physically develop sooner than others. This fact is quite obvious when one observes the differences in height, weight, and bodily coordination of any group of first-grade children. More careful observation is necessary to note that some children are able to focus their eyes upon the printed page more readily than others. Their inability to use the singing voice properly may, likewise, stem from lack of physical development. This lack is no more unnatural than, and is often related to, the immaturity of the rest of the body.

Lack of experience. Children come to any given first-grade class with a variety of backgrounds of experience with music. Some have attended nursery school for one or more years, others have had the benefit of possessing and listening to their own record collections. While many children have had the opportunity to listen to children's programs on television, not all will have maintained the same degree of interest, nor reaped the same benefit from them.

[4] There are even cases where children with less than normal speech and hearing have been known to develop limited singing ability.

[5] Viola Brody, *An Experimental Study of the Emergence of the Process Involved in the Production of Song* (unpublished Ph.D. Thesis, University of Michigan, 1947), p. 78.

Psychological blocks.   Some children have developed psychological blocks, or "negative sets" against participation in music activities in general, and singing activities in particular. Such negative sets generally occur because of some unpleasant experience with, or associated with, music. Perhaps the attitude on the part of the child was caused by some biting or sarcastic remark made by another child, or by some type of behavior on the part of the teacher. Children's negative sets may be caused by one, or perhaps by a combination of several factors. In any case, the child "retreats" within himself because of fear—fear of being unsuccessful, or of being ridiculed. Rather than attempt to sing, the child convinces himself that he is unable to do so and, therefore, behaves accordingly. Sometimes the child's fears are real and sometimes only imaginary. Whatever the case, his musical development is stunted, and he is unable to make further progress until his attitudes are changed and he achieves some degree of self-confidence.

Often the attitude of the teacher has a direct bearing upon the development of positive attitudes toward music. The teacher who is understanding of children's problems, and who strives patiently to help each child develop his or her maximum potential, will have a minimum amount of such "singing" problems in his class.[6]

Some years ago it was in vogue for teachers to seat their students near the piano in three rows for the singing lesson. The best singers were placed in the last row, in order that the other children might reap the benefit of hearing their "in-tune" voices. An intermediate group of children, who posed some problems but whose singing was generally satisfactory, was placed in the second row. The children having vocal difficulties were placed in the front row near the teacher, where they could receive the maximum amount of assistance. In theory this idea seems feasible and in some instances it has proved practical and helpful. In other situations, however, the procedure has caused quite negative results. Problem situations usually developed when teachers, probably for the convenience of a quick seating arrangement, assigned various names to each group. Ofter the name of a particular bird was assigned to each group. The "superior" group in the last row might have been called "canaries," the intermediate group in the second row might have been called "robins," and the problem group in the first row was given some other bird's name. For all practical purposes, it might as well have been "crows," because this is the self-concept that this group of children developed about their singing abilities. The author has discussed this problem with hundreds of in-service teachers. Many recall that they were

6 For a further discussion of negative sets, see Ralph L. Pounds and Robert L. Garretson, *Principles of Modern Education* (New York: Macmillan, 1962), pp. 59–63.

the "crows" and still remember the stigma that was attached to this system of grouping. Many attribute their present singing difficulties to this early experience with music. Fortunately, the grouping system described above is not particularly prevalent today. It is given as an example, however, of an undesirable learning situation and a classroom atmosphere unconducive to effective learning. While teachers may not group children as previously described, they may likewise contribute to the development of negative attitudes toward music by various unguarded remarks or by facial expressions which express impatience, nonapproval, or even disgust. It is, therefore, absolutely essential that teachers carefully examine their own attitudes toward music, and endeavor always to utilize a positive attitude in dealing with children.

Tone-matching Devices

Tone-matching devices may be used as a means of helping young children to match particular pitches more accurately or to sing various intervals more readily. Tone-matching devices will be found to be most effective when they grow out of the on-going class activity. Thus, a natural means of motivation is provided, with the children highly interested and engrossed in the total learning experience. Tone-matching devices may grow out of a variety of classroom situations, but, perhaps the most natural approach is to relate them to particular songs. The following example illustrates one approach.

Following the class's singing of a song, such as "Three Little Kittens," the teacher might say, "Boys and girls, our kittens in this song seem to get into all sorts of difficulty. I suspect they are the kind who might wander away from home and get lost. If the kittens really were lost, their mother would worry, and perhaps call to them, so they might find their way home. *Let's play a game!* I'll pretend that I am the mother cat and you are the kittens. When I call "meow," you will answer back on the same pitch! So all our kittens won't be answering at the same time, I will point to some of you one at a time. We may not have time today for all our kittens to answer, so some of you will have your chance another day."[7]

The purpose of tone-matching devices is, of course, to assist children to learn to use their singing voices more adequately. The teacher, then, should begin with the group of children who have the most difficulty,

---

[7] A suggested approximate pitch for this tone-matching device is F (first space, treble clef); however, the actual pitch should be varied according to each child's vocal range. Herein lies the value of the teacher's knowing well the capabilities of each child. If the teacher can select a pitch the child can most readily match, then the child's confidence may be developed and his or her singing improved.

and concentrate upon them. All children in the class should periodically have the opportunity to participate in such activities, however. Such participation will not only be beneficial to the child who has "found" his voice, but will also support the teacher's real purpose for using tone-matching devices, which is to assist those children having difficulty. This is important because young children in general do not like to be different, nor to be singled out of a group for any purpose. The children who are having the most difficulty are in many cases likely to be slow developers, sometimes shy and reticent as well. The addition of too much obvious pressure may only add to their adjustment problems and they may withdraw or retreat further into their world of inactivity in which they feel safe from criticism.

The humming sound (as in "meow") is easily produced by the children and is a good beginning point. However, infinite possibilities for tone-matching exist and should be utilized. For example, children might "moo" like a cow, "hoot" like an owl, howl like the wind "ooo . . . ooo . . . oo," "squeak" like a mouse, or "baa" like a lamb. The "tick-tock" of a clock and "toot-toot" of a train are other possibilities. Some kindergarten and first-grade teachers prefer to call the morning role by singing each child's name and requesting an answer on the same pitch. The falling minor third is common to the experience of most children, having been called on this interval by their parents or by other children.

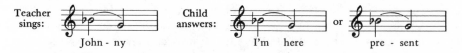

Another approach to tone matching would be simply to select appropriate intervals from particular songs. For example, the following intervals might be utilized after the singing of any song about bells.

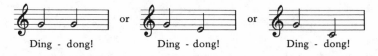

Still another approach is to ask the children to match the pitches of particular instruments as they are played. The added experience of hearing and matching pitches of varying timbre can contribute substantially to the child's musical development. Instruments that may be used are the melody bells, the xylophone, the recorder, the piano and, later, any of the band or orchestral instruments that the teacher may play adequately. Although not a musical instrument as such, considerable benefit may also be derived from the children matching various pitches which the teacher might play on the pitch pipe.

The use of puppets, which children can manipulate on their hands, may be found most helpful for use with tone matching activities. The teacher may sing a musical question (a particular set of pitches or a melodic pattern) through her own puppet, and the child may answer through his or her own puppet. Children can be totally fascinated by this activity. Through this approach, children are less likely to feel that they have been singled out for special attention, as their singing is done through the puppet. Some may even feel the puppet is singing rather than themselves. At the very least, the attention is diverted away from themselves and toward the puppets.

Jefferson County (Colorado) Public Schools.
Photograph by Nancy J. Pitz.

Puppets provide a means of child play which may be utilized for tone-matching devices.

Regardless of the type of motivation, pitch or particular interval, and the timbre or quality of sound which the teacher utilizes for tone-matching, three basic principles apply to their use and each should always be given careful consideration.

1. Establish rapport. The teacher should endeavor to establish rapport with each child. It is helpful to move to a position relatively close to the child and attempt to "personalize" this musical experience. Initial responses are likely to be somewhat subdued, and to hear the child adequately the teacher must be reasonably close.

2. *Adjust to the child's pitch level.* The teacher should select a suitable pitch level for each child (based upon familiarity with the child's background and previous musical experience). Utilizing tone-matching devices in the approximate middle range of the child's singing voice will generally facilitate an accurate response. When, however, a child is unable to match the teacher's pitch and invariably responds on a higher or lower pitch, the teacher should immediately select the child's pitch in singing any subsequent notes or melodic patterns. In other words, it is best to select the pitch of the child's first response. After a reasonably accurate response is achieved on this pitch, the teacher may then sing the next pitch or pattern just a bit higher or lower. In this manner, the exercise proceeds at the child's own level and an experience is provided that can more likely lead to some degree of success. Such a feeling of accomplishment and success provides a desirable attitude and motivation for such future learning experiences.

3. *Be positive in your remarks.* The advice "accentuate the positive" certainly applies in dealing with young children as well as with other individuals. A teacher should always reassure the child concerning his or her progress. Some children, when not meeting success, are likely to become discouraged. Often a series of unsuccessful experiences sets up a barrier in the child's mind against future effort. The child may think, "I just can't do this, so why try!" The teacher plays a vital role in the development of the children's attitudes. Facial expressions, tone of voice, and specific remarks all have a definite effect upon the child's opinion of his own worth. In addition to assuming a sympathetic, understanding attitude, a teacher should utilize such remarks as, "That's better! Now just a little higher!"

SONG-TEACHING PROCEDURES

Since in the initial stages of musical development children learn songs through an imitative process, usually called rote learning, it is essential that teachers utilize good tone quality and proper diction. Appropriate tone quality, as discussed in the preceding section, should be light, with the heavy quality of the chest register being avoided. As regards diction, care should be taken to pronounce correctly all words and to enunciate them in a clear, distinct manner. A generalized American approach to pronunciation should be followed, and when there is doubt about particular words a dictionary should be consulted. Clear enunciation depends in particular upon the precise articulation of the consonants; the teacher should concentrate on the exact movements of the articulating organs, i.e., the tongue, lips, teeth, palate, and the lower jaw. Clear enunciation is usually facilitated when the teacher exaggerates the lip movements in presenting a song to the children. Careful attention to diction is important if children are to hear and understand the words of a song, for the rapidity with which the song is learned depends to a certain extent upon the children's understanding of the words.

The Whole-song and Phrase Methods

The actual performance time of songs selected from basic music texts for the elementary grades will vary from between twelve to sixty seconds. Songs for very young children are generally quite short—sometimes only two phrases in length. Songs for older children, of course, will be longer and some may have a number of verses. In teaching rote songs a teacher may use one of two procedures: a whole-song approach, where the children hear the entire song and repeat it after the teacher; or the phrase method, where after hearing the entire song, the children repeat each phrase after the teacher. Of course, the whole-song approach is utilized primarily for songs which are shorter in length, whereas the phrase approach is utilized for songs which are longer and more difficult in nature. What is difficult for one group, however, may not necessarily be difficult for another. Factors which determine the teacher's choice of method or approach are the length and difficulty of the song, the children's previous musical background and experience, their basic musical aptitude, and the motivation and interest they possess in regard to the song. Specific steps in these two methods are outlined as follows.

Whole-song method.

1. Motivate the children to learn the song through the use of appropriate pictures, stories, or questions.
2. Ask the children to listen for something specific in the song before its actual presentation.
3. Present the song to the class.
4. Ask questions about the students' understanding or enjoyment of the song.
5. Sing the song one or more additional times, depending upon the group's readiness to participate.
6. Have the class join in singing the song.

Phrase method.

Steps 1 through 5 are the same as in the whole-song approach. When children are ready to join in (step 6), the teacher sings one phrase at a time and the children repeat each phrase after him. After each phrase has been sung, the complete song should be sung at least once from beginning to end.

Regardless of the approach used, it is important that the teacher motivate the children to learn the song, whether by showing pictures which evoke interest, telling a story, or simply asking the class questions about their interests which might lead to a discussion of the general subject of the song. The purpose of the motivation is simply to focus the students' attention upon the topic to be studied in order that the most desirable learning situation be created. Motivation need not be lengthy, but should be direct and to the point.

Before the teacher's initial presentation of the song, the class should be asked to listen for something specific in the song as it is sung. The teacher may do this by telling the class to "listen carefully while I sing the song, because afterwards I am going to ask you some questions about it." This request should never be made in the form of a command, but more in the manner of sharing a special secret with the class. After the song has been presented the teacher should ask the class some specific questions about the words in each phrase. Teachers will want to give careful thought to the phrasing of these questions so that the desired response will focus the group's attention upon the central thought in each phrase. This is important because a clear understanding of the ideas involved in the song will facilitate learning it.

In questioning the children about various aspects of the text, the teacher should insist that they raise their hands. This eliminates, to some extent, the mass mumbling effect of group answers. While a group response is justifiable in some instances, it is generally more desirable to allow only one student at a time to answer the teacher's questions. In this way, the students are more likely to listen for and hear each other's responses. It is also desirable for the teacher to strengthen the idea by paraphrasing each student's response. The child's answer, coupled with the teacher's embellishment, allows the children more opportunity to grasp the concepts in the song.

If, after the teacher's initial presentation of the song, the children are unable to answer or discuss particular questions pertaining to it, the teacher should sing the song one or two additional times. In each instance, the teacher should ask the class to listen again for the answer to a particular question. Even when children can answer all questions about a song correctly, it is not too likely that they will be able to sing the melody with any degree of accuracy after only one hearing. Therefore the song should still be repeated one or more times. The actual number of repetitions will depend upon the length and difficulty of the song, the children's previous musical background, and their ability to grasp new concepts. Prior to each repetition, the teacher should provide the class with a reason for the repetition. After the initial presentation, it is desirable in some cases to ask questions about the first two phrases only, with the remaining questions being asked following the repetition. In the event that the children display a reasonable degree of understanding of the words, the teacher may have the class focus their attention upon some technical or appreciative aspect of the music. An appropriate direction for younger children might be, "Listen for the highest note," or "Listen for the points of rest." Older children might be asked, for example, to listen carefully and count the number of phrases in the song. Finally the children are asked to join the teacher in singing the song and, depending upon the factors previously discussed, the teacher will use either the whole-song or the phrase approach. Actually, in practice, a teacher may wish to use a combination of both approaches. That is, the initial presentation might be through the whole-song approach, but then, after the children have sung the song once or twice, a phrase method may be used to attack certain musical problems, such as faulty singing of certain intervals, or inaccurate rhythmic patterns.

Using Recordings

A considerable number of the songs in the basic texts have been recorded; sets of records are available for each grade level and may be obtained from the publishers. These recordings may be effectively utilized in the presentation and study of songs. Of course, the teaching procedure followed must of necessity be the whole-song approach; instead of singing the song, as in steps three and five, the teacher would simply play the recording. The other steps in the whole song approach should be followed as suggested (see p. 49).

Recordings of songs in the basic series have proven extremely helpful to classroom teachers. Many teachers who feel somewhat inadequate about teaching songs have been able to implement a reasonably successful singing program without possessing any outstanding vocal skill. Some teachers have utilized recordings as a means through which they learn the songs, in order that they personally may be able to present them to their classes. Of course, this self-improvement is a most desirable step for teachers to take, for they will be able to make the songs more meaningful and enjoyable to their students than can ever be possible through the use of a recording. This does not mean to minimize the value of recordings. They can serve as an enriching musical experience. Being able to listen to a professional rendition of a song will often assist the children in developing a broader musical perspective.

Recordings are also helpful to music specialists for the same reason, i.e., broadening the student's musical horizons. They may also be of help to classroom teachers and music specialists alike when they are unable to use their voices adequately because of a cold or laryngitis.

Getting Started

Two problems involved in beginning a song are those of establishing the proper pitch and setting the correct tempo. Both are of some concern to the beginning teacher and should be given careful thought.

Establishing the pitch. All teachers should possess a pitch pipe and, of course, learn how to use it properly. The fundamental purpose of the pitch pipe is to provide the correct pitch for not only the teacher, but for the children as well. Occasionally the pitch may be given by the piano or some other readily available instrument; hearing sound in various media can be a helpful and beneficial experience for children. The quality of the pitch pipe, if properly blown, is generally easier for the children to hear however, and the pitch is easier to match. In addition, a pitch pipe may be easily carried in one's pocket and is always conveniently available for immediate use. The same cannot always be said for the availability of other instruments. Initial teacher experiences with the pitch pipe sometimes result in two tones rather than one being sounded. This somewhat embarrassing problem can be avoided if the teacher will place the thumb immediately below the tone-opening to be played and bring the thumb up to the mouth. Before blowing, the lips should be puckered slightly and breath directed into the instrument in a relatively narrow stream. In providing the pitch for children, the teacher should sustain the tone for a reasonable length of time and avoid short puffs. It should be remembered that the pitch is not only for the teacher, but for the children as well.[8] A pitch pipe has one thing in common with other instruments—a certain amount of practice is essential to achieve a desirable tone quality. Therefore, the teacher should possess a definite familiarity with the pitch pipe before attempting to use it in the classroom.

Setting the tempo. When in doubt about the correct tempo of a particular song, the teacher is advised to study the text carefully. A

---

[8] A generally accepted practice is for the teacher to play the tonic pitch or keynote on the pitch pipe, then to sing the tonic chord, followed by the beginning note.

thorough analysis of the words will reveal the basic mood of the song, and this has a direct bearing on tempo. In addition, the teacher should recite the text of the song, for the rhythm of the words coupled with the overall mood will dictate the most desirable tempo. Other factors, such as the maturity and musical backgrounds of the children should also be taken into consideration. However, these should be considered subservient to the dictates of the rhythm of the words and the overall mood of the song.

In teaching a song, the teacher should prepare the class for its beginning and establish the desired tempo by utilizing the phrase, "Ready, sing!" These two words should, if possible, be sung on the beginning pitch of the song and in the desired musical tempo. In songs of 4/4 meter, for example, if the music begins on the first beat of a measure, the words, "Ready, sing!" should be spoken precisely on beats three and four preceding the first note of the song.

In addition to preparing the group with verbal commands, it is also desirable for the teacher, particularly in the intermediate grades, to use a preparatory conducting movement.[9] These movements are illustrated on page 122. It is not suggested that elementary school teachers conduct the entire song they are teaching, but rather only a measure or two, primarily to help the group to get started and to establish the tempo. In the initial stages, the experience of watching for the conductor's movements and listening for the verbal command serve to reinforce each other and tend to make each more meaningful. As the students become more alert to the teacher's conducting movements, however, the verbal directions of "Ready, sing!" may be gradually eliminated. In addition, the teacher may assist the group in starting by a slight nod of the head and through appropriate facial expressions. All of these movements combined provide the best preparatory movements for the children.

Maintaining Rapport

Teacher-student rapport is most readily attained when the teacher establishes eye contact with the students in all parts of the room. This is best achieved through slow, casual movements of the head and body. A few steps taken toward one side of the room, a pause, and a return to another part of the room also improve rapport. Teachers should avoid a rigid, stationary position, as it can quite conceivably give the impression of boredom or simply lack of enthusiasm—certainly not desirable traits for any teacher. Facial expressions reflecting the overall mood of a song may also contribute to improved rapport.

[9] For a detailed presentation of the basic conducting movements, see Robert L. Garretson, *Conducting Choral Music,* 4th ed. (Boston: Allyn & Bacon, 1975), chapter 1.

Other Teaching Considerations

Whether the teacher utilizes the phrase or the whole-song approach to teaching a song, it is generally advisable initially to present the complete song to the class in order that the children may develop a concept of the whole song. With this concept in mind, the class is better able to relate the parts, which they hear and study, to the whole song. In teaching songs with an extensive number of verses, however, this practice generally should not be followed. It is best to consider the "whole" in this case to be one complete verse, rather than the total of all the verses. As the class usually has a strong desire to participate, it is generally advisable to allow them to do so as soon as possible. Once the class has adequately learned the rhythmic and melodic patterns of the song, the learning of additional verses becomes a relatively easy task. In short, be sure the students know the "tune" before introducing additional verses.

In songs involving the repetition of words and phrases from previous verses, such as encountered in the song "MacDonald's Farm," difficulties often stem from confusion over the order of the repeated words. In such songs, learning can be facilitated by printing the entire word series on the chalkboard before the initial presentation. Students can then follow the visual patterns of the word progressions while the teacher sings, and much unnecessary confusion may be eliminated. This procedure may be used from approximately the second grade on, depending, of course, upon the students' ability to read and understand the words which the teacher has written on the chalkboard. If the song is used for some recreational purpose, however, then the amusement which comes from the sometimes natural confusion over words may be justified. In such cases, the teacher may prefer not to use the above-suggested procedure.

In teaching action songs there is sometimes a question as to when the teacher should introduce the actions. Should it be during the initial presentation of the song, concurrently with the melody, or after the students have learned the melody and words? There is no single answer to this question. The proper procedure will vary according to several factors —namely, the length and difficulty of the song, the nature of the actions, and the children's concentration abilities. In some songs, learning simple actions concurrently with the music often facilitates the learning process, as the motions serve to pinpoint and reinforce the retention of the important or key words.[10] In other instances, teaching the actions too soon may distract the students' attention from the music, and certain melodic and rhythmic patterns may be learned incorrectly or, at least, will take a

---

[10] An example of a song in which the actions may facilitate the learning of the music is "The Teapot," *The First Grade Book* (Boston: Ginn and Company, 1949), p. 7.

longer time to be learned correctly.[11] The question, therefore, is whether the actions add to or detract from the music. To determine the answer, the teacher should consider carefully all the previously mentioned factors.

ALTERNATIVE PROCEDURES FOR
TEACHING SONGS

Teachers need not always use the same standardized procedure for teaching songs. One approach may involve a careful analysis of the music for the purpose of developing tonal and rhythmic independency. This process emphasizes helping the child to interpret independently the symbols on the printed page. The teacher's role is to guide the students' analysis—not to provide it for them (once a child has heard a song, there is no longer any reason to analyze the score in the same way). Reading skills may be developed only through lots of experience in actual reading, i.e., experience in relying upon one's own musical memory in attempting to recall the actual sound of the notation. A suggested teaching procedure, then, for developing skills in music reading is as follows:

1. Have the children *scan* the score looking for familiar and unfamiliar tonal and rhythmic patterns. The teacher may guide the class in, for example, finding phrases that are alike, phrases that are different, phrases that are almost alike but slightly different, finding and framing like tonal and rhythmic patterns, and identifying new elements in the score, such as unfamiliar tonal and rhythmic patterns, accidentals, or new words.
2. Examine the meter signature. Does the music swing in twos or threes? (This step may be omitted for very young children until they have reached sufficient maturity to be introduced to the concept.)
3. Chant and/or clap the rhythm of the song. In chanting, the class may respond according to the actual names of the notes. For example: "quarter, quarter, eighth, eighth, half note, etc." In clapping, make sure that the class responds to the pulse by squeezing the hands together on each pulsation except those that are clapped (see p. 119 for example). It is not always necessary to chant or clap the entire song, but usually only the basic patterns. Call attention to identical rhythmic patterns in various phrases.
4. Examine the key signature and locate *do*. Then determine if the tonal center of the song is *do* or *la*. If it seems to be neither, is it in the Pentatonic mode? (This step may also be omitted for very young children until they have reached sufficient maturity to be introduced to the concept—generally in the fourth grade.)

[11] An example of a song in which the suggested actions may hinder the learning of the song is "The Bus," *The Magic of Music* (Boston: Ginn, 1970), p. 153.

5. Sing syllables (or numbers) of certain basic tonal patterns.
6. Sing the song.
7. Repeat any of the above steps whenever further clarification of certain aspects of the song is needed.

The above procedure is based upon the idea that children develop skill in reading through experience in analyzing the score and attempting to recall from their musical memory the way the music should sound. A considerable amount of time, therefore, should be devoted to this procedure. Admittedly, however, teaching all songs in this manner is not necessary or even desirable. The procedure is time-consuming, and a teacher may often teach a song with another objective in mind. For example, the teacher may wish to emphasize only the relationship of a particular folk song to the culture from which it emanated. Therefore, he would want the class to learn the song as readily as possible so that the time may be devoted to other aspects of study about that culture. This procedure will quite naturally involve the teacher's either singing the song or playing a recording of it. In this case, once the children have heard the song, it would be of little value as a reading song. The following procedure is then suggested:

1. Provide the children with an overall concept of the song by singing it entirely through, playing a recording of it, or playing it on the piano while the class follow the song in their books.
2. Have the children identify unfamiliar words and then briefly discuss the meaning and mood of the text.
3. Identify the meter and tonality. Does the song swing in twos, threes, or fours? Is the song in major or minor tonality?
4. The class should then sing the song with the teacher.
5. Identify tonal and rhythmic difficulties and endeavor to overcome them. Difficult tonal patterns may be sung slowly with syllables or numbers, and rhythmic problems may be approached through chanting or clapping. (Most rhythmic problems, however, may be corrected rather quickly by having the class recite the text in the correct musical rhythm. Once the rhythm is corrected, the melody of the song is sung more readily.)
6. Sing the song a second time.
7. Discuss the mood and meaning of the song again, emphasizing what it means to the class and what it may have meant to the folk from whom it emanated.

Topics for Discussion

1. Describe the natural tonal characteristics of the child voice.

2. Since children are likely to imitate the teacher's voice quality, what model should the teacher use?

3. Discuss the problems of the "uncertain singer." What factors are involved in the child's lack of musical development?

4. Describe in detail how the attitudes of a teacher may affect children's development of a positive or negative outlook toward singing.

5. What are some necessary personal attributes of a successful music teacher?

6. What techniques and methods can a teacher use to develop interest and enthusiasm in a child who refuses to sing?

7. What factors influence the teacher's choice of either the whole-song or phrase approach to the rote teaching of a song?

8. Discuss the relationship between the children's understanding of the words of a song and the rapidity with which they will be able to learn the music.

Suggestions for Further Study

GARRETSON, ROBERT L., *Conducting Choral Music* (4th ed.). Boston: Allyn & Bacon, Inc., 1975, chapter 2.

INGRAM, MADELINE, and WM. C. RICE, *Vocal Techniques for Children and Youth*. Nashville, Tenn.: Abingdon Press.

NORDHOLM, HARRIET, *Singing in the Elementary Schools*. Englewood Cliffs, N.J.: Prentice-Hall, 1966.

SWANSON, BESSIE R., *Music in the Education of Children* (3rd ed.). Belmont, Calif.: Wadsworth, 1969, chapter 6.

Films and Filmstrips[12]

The Pitch Pipe (Johnson Hunt Productions), b&w, 13 minutes, college.

What Does Music Mean? Young People's Concert Series, Leonard Bernstein (McGraw-Hill Films), 1 hour, elementary/college.

12 Addresses of producers and distributors of educational films are listed in the Appendix, pp. 287–288.

Suggested Song Materials

BERTAIL, INEZ, *Complete Nursery Song Book*. New York: Lothrop, Lee & Shepard, Inc., 1947.

BAILEY, CHARITY, *Sing a Song with Charity Bailey*. New York: Plymouth Music Company.

COLEMAN, JACK L., IRENE L. SCHOEPPLE, and VIRGINIA TEMPLETON, *Music for Exceptional Children*. Evanston, Ill.: Summy-Birchard Company, 1964.

COLEMAN, SATIS N., and ALICE G. THORN, *Singing Time; Another Singing Time; The Little Singing Time; A New Singing Time*. New York: The John Day Company.

CROWNINSHIELD, ETHEL, *Mother Goose Songs* (1948); *Sing and Play Book* (1938); *Stories that Sing* (1945); *Songs and Stories About Animals* (1947); *Walk the World Together* (1951). Boston: Boston Music Company.

DALLIN, LEON, and LYNN DALLIN, *Heritage Songster*. Dubuque, Iowa: Wm. C. Brown.

DAVISON, ARCHIBALD T., and THOMAS W. SURETTE, *140 Folk-Tunes* [Rote Songs for grades I, II, and III]. Boston: E. C. Schirmer Music Company, 1944. (Also available with piano accompaniment.)

GLAZER, TOM, *A New Treasury of Folk Songs*. New York: Bantam Books, Inc., 1961.

Juilliard Repertory Library, Cincinnati, Ohio: Canyon Press, Inc., 1970.

KAPP, PAUL, *A Cat Came Fiddling and Other Rhymes of Childhood*. New York: General Music Publishing Company, Inc., 1956.

KODÁLY, ZOLTÁN, *Fifty Nursery Songs* [within a range of five notes], London: Boosey & Hawkes, 1962.

LANDECK, BEATRICE, *Songs to Grow On* (1950); *More Songs to Grow On* (1954). New York: Edward B. Marks and William Sloan Associates. (Songs recorded by Folkway Records.)

NYE, ROBERT, VERNICE NYE, NEVA AUBIN, and GEORGE KYME, *Singing With Children*. Belmont, Calif.: Wadsworth, 1962.

RICHARDS, MARY HELEN, *Pentatonic Songs for Young Children*. New York: Harper & Row, Publishers, 1967.

SEEGER, RUTH C., *American Folk Songs for Children* (1948); *Animal Folk Songs for Children* (1950); *American Folk Songs for Christmas* (1953). Garden City, N.Y.: Doubleday & Company, Inc.

Songs Children Like. Washington, D.C.: Association for Childhood Education.

Songs for Every Purpose and Occasion. Minneapolis: Schmitt, Hall & McCreary, 1938.

SNYDER, ALICE M., *Sing and Strum*. New York: Mills Music, Inc., 1957.

TOBITT, JANET E., *The Ditty Bag*. Pleasantville, N.Y.: Janet E. Tobitt, 1946.

VANDRE, CARL, *Easy Songs for Young Singers*. Minneapolis: Handy-Folio Music Company.

WOOD, LUCILLE F., and LOUISE B. SCOTT, *Singing Fun* (1954); *More Singing Fun* (1961). St. Louis: Webster Publishing Company. (Songs recorded by Bowmar Records.)

All Basic Music Series; for listing of books and publishers, see the Appendix, p. 286.

chapter 4

PITCH AND MELODY

This chapter introduces concepts of pitch and melody for kindergarten through grade six and describes activities and skills leading to their comprehension. The grade level at which specific concepts or musical ideas may be introduced is indicated in this and in subsequent chapters. It should never be assumed, however, that a single musical experience is sufficient for the comprehension of a particular concept. Teachers may employ the suggested activities as frequently as seems necessary. To maintain interest, however, the materials and approach should be varied somewhat. (The musical experiences suggested are provided only as examples, and it is hoped that teachers will continually explore the use of other appropriate materials.) Furthermore, the activities suggested are not necessarily meant to be limited to one grade level, but may be utilized in succeeding grades. Only when concepts are set forth repeatedly—each time in a somewhat different context—will they ever become thoroughly comprehended and totally meaningful. And only through careful evaluation of each day's activities can the teacher assess the extent of the children's comprehension and determine appropriate follow-up experiences.

CONCEPTS OF PITCH AND MELODY FOR K–6
AND ACTIVITIES AND SKILLS
FOR THEIR COMPREHENSION

Concepts   Activities and Skills

[The long-range goal of all activities is
the development of children's musicality,
i.e., *increased sensitivity and responsiveness to music.* Following each activity,

the effectiveness of instruction should be evaluated. Concepts need to be reinforced through varied, but similar activities; therefore, the teacher must determine what students really have learned, as this is the critical factor in determining the specific nature of subsequent experiences.]

K–1

Sounds (melody) can be high and sounds can be low (pitches, instruments).

Have the children explore high and low sounds of voices and instruments (triangle, drum); use bodily movements to indicate high pitches (stretching hands upward on tip-toes) and low tones (squatting); identify and play high and low pitches on melody bells, piano, or other instruments. Locate on the score the highest and lowest notes in a song.

Almost any pitched musical instrument, such as the piano, guitar, and tone bells may be used with very young children to help develop a feeling for tonal direction. The teacher may play various tones, beginning with the extreme ranges on the piano, and then ask the children if they were either high, low, or medium pitches. This activity is approached as a guessing game. The teacher may then ask certain children to come to the piano and play either a high, a low, or a medium pitch. This allows the teacher to "check" the child's understanding of the concept; however, the remainder of the class may also be asked to respond as to the correctness of the child's playing. After the children have had some experience with this initial activity, the teacher may periodically play a song familiar to the children in various extremities of the keyboard and ask the class to identify the pitch level.

Another approach would be to sing or imitate contrasting sounds which children hear in everyday life. For example, ask the children to sing up *high* like a little train whistle ("too—too—"), and then down *low* like a big streamliner train ("whoo—whoo"). Still another approach might be to draw on the chalkboard a scene depicting the ground, a fence, and the sky. Discuss these height differences with the class, as low, medium, and high. Next, ask the class to sing phrases on the syllable pitches *do, sol,* and *do:* "down on the ground" (*do*), "up on the fence" (*sol*), and "high in the sky" (*do*). The concept may be made even more meaningful by subsequently asking the class to use appropriate bodily movement while singing. On the first phrase, the class should squat down touching the floor, on the second phrase they should stand almost erect, and on the last phrase they should stand on tip-toe and reach "high in the sky."

Melodies can go up and melodies can go down (rise and fall; ascend and descend).

Children should have a variety of experiences singing songs with rising and falling pitches. After they have reviewed a particular song, ask the children to use their hands and show how the melody of the song "goes up and down."[1]

The teacher may also "diagram" a song by writing diagonal lines and

---

[1] In addition to the songs found in the basic music series, teachers will find it helpful periodically to intersperse other songs, particularly those with a limited tonal range, such as those found in *Fifty Nursery Songs* (within the range of five notes) by Zoltán Kodály (London: Boosey & Hawkes, 1962).

arrows on the chalkboard to indicate the ascending and descending
phrases in the song.

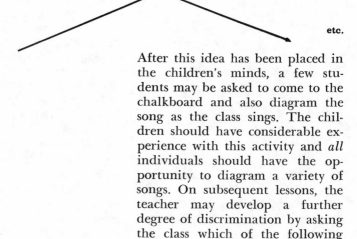

After this idea has been placed in
the children's minds, a few students may be asked to come to the
chalkboard and also diagram the
song as the class sings. The children should have considerable experience with this activity and *all*
individuals should have the opportunity to diagram a variety of
songs. On subsequent lessons, the
teacher may develop a further
degree of discrimination by asking
the class which of the following
lines and arrows best represents
the contour of the musical phrase.

*Melody has long sounds and short
sounds.*

Chanting the words of familiar
songs and poems and then clapping the rhythms is a helpful way
to create awareness of differences
in melodic duration. Ask children
to identify the words on which the
long and short sounds occur. Then,
ask a small group to show the class
their understanding by taking
large steps for the longer notes
and small steps for shorter notes.

Have children describe the durational qualities of different percussion instruments; e.g., the triangle
might be described as a "long
sound" because it rings, whereas
the rhythm sticks may be described
as a "clicking or short sound." On
another day, ask several children

to select instruments that have either long or short sounds.

Grade 2

"Notes" are placed on a staff to tell us how high or low, or long or short each pitch is to be sung.

In the second grade, when children are usually first provided with individual songbooks, the basic learning procedure might be best described as a *hearing, doing,* and *seeing* process. Children should hear lots of music; they should learn to sing or play it by imitation; and they should then be led into observing on the printed page what they have sung or played. This procedure is sometimes called the "rote-note process." Through this approach children are gradually led to a clearer and more complete understanding of notation and what it represents—organized rhythm and melody.

The teacher may begin by asking the class to turn to a specific page of their books and examine a song that they have sung but not seen in notation. The question might follow, "Do you know this song?" or "Do you recognize this song?" If the answer is "Yes," the next question should be "Why?" Most of the group will undoubtedly say that they recognize the title or some of the words. The next question might be, "If this song did not have a title or words, would you still recognize it?" The answer is likely to be "No."

The children may be told that the notation is simply a "picture" of what they have already heard and sung, and that "notes" are placed on a "staff" to tell us how high or low, and how long, each pitch is to be sung. Both the staff and some simple notation should be illustrated on the chalkboard at this point. Then the teacher may say, "As I sing the song, follow the words, and the notes above them, and see if you can tell me what happens." It is hoped the children will notice that when the teacher sings an ascending passage the notes also ascend on the printed page. And as the teacher sings lower, the notes descend on the printed page. This can be an important musical discovery for the class.

Following this experience, children should become further oriented to staff notation by drawing whole notes on designated lines or spaces. To introduce the activity, the teacher should first call attention to the difference between the lines and spaces on a staff placed on the chalkboard. A note may then be written and the class asked if it was drawn on a line or a space ("Which line or space, 1st, 2nd, . . . ?"). Selected children can then come to the chalkboard, draw a note, and the class can then decide on which line or space it was drawn. As an alternative, children may be asked to draw notes on staff paper provided them.[2]

On still another day, children may draw several notes on lines, spaces, or lines and spaces, either at the chalkboard or at their desk. To

[2] It is not to be implied in any way that the drawing of notes on lines and spaces will teach children to read music. This activity is suggested simply as an introduction and orientation to music notation. To develop music-reading skills, many other activities must follow, as indicated in this and other chapters. Educational films and filmstrips with recordings may also be used to help achieve this goal. See the following titles listed at the end of this chapter (p. 91): *Discovering Melody* (United World Films, Inc.), *Exploring Music Reading* (Classroom Materials Co.), *Introduction to Music Reading* (Classroom Materials Co.).

evoke curiosity and to motivate the children further, the teacher may ask the class if they would like to hear how some of the various combinations of tones they have written would sound if played on the piano (or some other instrument).

Tones can stay on one pitch or move up and down. (Melody moves up or down or stays the same.)

Ask children to examine the notation of various songs and to find where the tones (notes) remain the same and where they move up and down. Help them also to discover similarities of notation in different phrases of a song.

Ample opportunity should be provided for children to experiment in playing different scales on the xylophone, the resonator bells, the step bells, and the melody bells. Initially, the teacher may set up specific tone combinations on the xylophone or the resonator bells, and then children should be encouraged to devise their own. Scales may also be devised using tuned water glasses, bottles (see the concept below), and different sizes of flower pots.

When a bottle scale is prepared, the pitch of the bottle lowers as more water is poured in.

Pour water into a bottle and frequently tap the side with a metal spoon or hard mallet. Ask the children to note how the pitch changes as more water is poured into the bottle. Tune several bottles to make a partial scale (*do, re, mi,* etc.).

Tones can move in steps (scalewise) or by skips or leaps.

Help children to discover in songs scale tones that appear alternately on lines or spaces, and skips that appear on lines or spaces (or farther apart). Does the melody move in steps or in skips? To reinforce the visual impression, provide several children with eight resonator bells and let them arrange a short tune either by steps or by skips (and later by combinations of steps and skips). In playing, encourage them to vary the rhythmic duration of each pitch so as to create a more interesting tune.

Keyboard orientation: groups of two and three black keys alternate on the piano keyboard; the black keys on the piano help one to find one's place.

Ask children to find three black keys together, then two black keys together. Find the two black keys nearest the center of the keyboard. Then locate the white key just to the left of these two black keys. This is middle C.

An octave is an interval of eight scale steps.

How many C's can you find on the piano? Each C just above another is an octave! Play an octave. Can you find an octave in song notation?

Grade 3

A scale is a "ladder" or arrangement of ascending and descending pitches.

Although children will experience a variety of scales and tonal systems, the major scale may be introduced first by distributing individual resonator bells of the C-major scale to eight children at random. Each may be asked to play his tone bell and the class decides which is lowest. The pitch should be identified by letter name and number and the notation placed on the chalkboard or a flannel board. Each subsequent ascending tone should be identified in a like manner. Finally, after the scale is complete, ask the group to play it ascending and descending (see "Little Dove," *The Magic of Music,* Book 3, for a good scale song). Provide a similar experience with the tones of the d-minor scale.

The scale may also be displayed on the chalkboard as shown below, showing visually the relationship between one scale step and another.

re
_____

do

ti
- - - - - -

la

sol

fa

mi

re

do
_____

ti

la
- - - - -

Another device to portray the diatonic scale is to illustrate it in the form of a ladder.[3] The rungs of the ladder between the third and fourth degrees and between the seventh degree and the octave should be placed rather closely together to show this half-step relationship. These tonal relationships should be pointed out to the children and they should be asked to listen carefully as they sing the scale with either syllables or numbers.

do	8
ti	7
la	6
sol	5
fa	4
mi	3
re	2
do	1

[3] For further information on the construction of the diatonic scale, see pp. 74–77.

In addition to listening for the half steps between *mi* and *fa* (3 and 4), and *ti* and *do* (7 and 8), the class should experience the strong upward pull which both the third and seventh scale degrees have toward their upper neighbors. One way to illustrate this is to ask the class to sing an ascending scale beginning on *do,* then stopping and holding *mi.* They will sense the pull toward *fa.* Also sing the ascending scale and stop on *ti.* They will also sense the upward pull toward *do.* To illustrate the pull toward the tonal center or *do,* have the class sing the ascending scale beginning on *do* upward for an octave, and then sing downward stopping on any particular tone. The feeling of incompleteness will be felt by the group and most will desire to continue the descending scale downward to its natural resting place of *do.*

In addition to using the visual device of a ladder to illustrate the diatonic scale, it is desirable to utilize the piano keyboard, the stepbells (calling attention to the smaller steps between 3 and 4, and 7 and 8), the melody bells (turned on end), and the fingers of the hand to show the up and down movement of the scale. In using the hand for such an illustration, the teacher may point with the index finger of the other hand to the fingers and the spaces between, simulating the lines and spaces of the musical staff.

Hand signals may also be used to indicate the different steps in the diatonic scale.

Various positions of the hand, each representing a different scale step, are used in the Kodály method, as well as by other European music educators.[4] *Do,* is a closed fist; *re,* an open hand with the palm facing diagonally upward; *mi,* an open hand with the palm facing downward; *fa,* a clenched hand

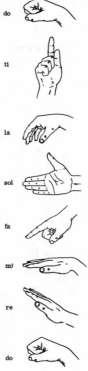

do

ti

la

sol

fa

mi

re

do

with the thumb and forefinger pointing diagonally downward; *sol,* an open hand with the thumb pointing upward and the palm facing the body; *la,* a relaxed hand with the fingers and thumb pointing downward; and *ti,* a closed hand with the thumb and forefinger pointing upward. Through these hand signals children are helped to *hear* through their ears what they *see* through their eyes.

[4] Some sources credit the development of hand signals to the English clergyman and publisher John Curwin (1816–1880); other sources indicate their much earlier use.

After the children have had some experience using these signals, the teacher may utilize them for ear-training exercises, involving various intervals and melodic patterns. They may also be used to assist children whenever difficulties occur in singing songs.[5]

Tones of a melody are represented by notes on a staff (five lines and four spaces).

Comprehension of the meaning of the staff and notation may come about through meaningful and real experiences. A good beginning may occur when the children have the opportunity to manipulate various materials. It is suggested that each student in the class make a staff on a sheet of white construction paper with the lines drawn about an inch apart. Notes may be made out of black paper using a quarter as a model. Small wooden blocks, however, are easier to handle and are generally preferable to paper notes (see photograph, p. 72). A felt board may also be used, but initially it is best to have the class create their own staff and notation. After completing their materials, the class may be asked to place their notes on lines, then on spaces, and then alternately on lines and spaces.

Notes move up or down by steps or skips on the lines and spaces.

Ask the class to place their notes on the staff by steps (lines and spaces alternately) and then by skips (on lines or spaces). They should then be encouraged to experiment freely in placing notes— by either steps or skips, or by combinations of steps and skips. Ask selected children to sing or play the patterns they devised. When a

---

[5] For further information about the Kodály method, see chapter 11, pp. 263–267.

child needs assistance, the teacher may sing the tune with him so that the whole class may hear.

Some melodies move mostly by steps and some by skips.

Children need lots of experience in scanning music notation. The teacher should frequently select a specific song and ask the class to identify the phrases that move mostly by steps and those that move by skips. The teacher may then sing a short phrase and ask the class to identify it by line.

Melody is made up of patterns.

After the students have an understanding of the purposes of the staff, the teacher may select a few pitches, i.e., those of a tonal pattern from a familiar song, write them on the chalkboard, and then, after giving the class the title of the song and the page number, ask them to locate the written phrase in the song by framing the pattern with their index fingers.[6] This procedure of comparing a pattern on the chalkboard with those in the books is helpful in training the eye to identify the more minute differences in music notation. While this device facilitates visual development, aural development may occur when the teacher sings a phrase of a song, using a neutral syllable, rather than writing it on the chalkboard. The students are asked to identify the phrase in the song by relating to the teacher the words beneath the music, or by framing the appropriate phrase. Initially, the students may be able to identify such phrases by observing the general configuration of the notation or

[6] An example of an appropriate song to use for this purpose is "Out on the Ocean" (*The Magic of Music*, Book 3). After the class has identified the initial pattern (first measure), see how many identical patterns they can find in the song (four).

the "ups and downs" of the music. As they grow in their capacity to identify phrases, or perhaps motives, they will become increasingly aware of the precise differences in the musical notation.

"Music-building" games are another device that will help to cement eye-ear relationships. To prepare for these "games," the students should each draw a staff with about an inch between the lines, and make approximately five note heads about the size of a quarter from black construction paper. An alternative to notes made from paper is to use small wooden blocks (or unit cubes), which have the advantage of being easier for children to manipulate. Once the staff and notes have been

Jefferson County (Colorado) Public Schools.
Photograph by Nancy J. Pitz.

Placing note heads (or blocks) on a staff is not only a means to orient children to music notation, but through music-building games, this activity can help to develop tonal awareness and "cement" eye-ear relationships.

assembled, the group is ready to play a game. The teacher says: "*Do* is on the first space, so place one of your notes there. I will sing *do,* followed by two other notes. See if you can place them on the proper lines or spaces on the staff." Suggested patterns to use in the beginning are *do, re, mi,* and *do, mi, sol.* As the children progress in developing this skill, the teacher may use a variety of patterns, preferably selected from the song repertoire of the children.

A sequence is a tonal pattern repeated a step higher or lower.

Singing the syllable patterns given below can provide children with an aural familiarity with sequential patterns, as well as develop greater familiarity and flexibility in the use of syllables.[7] Following this preparatory experience, have the class examine selected songs and help them discover a sequence in a song as a means of understanding the structure of melody. Does the sequential pattern repeat on higher or lower pitches? How is it alike and different from sequences in other songs?

Ascending:	*do-mi-sol, re-fa-la, mi-sol-ti, fa-la-do, sol-ti-re, do.*
Descending:	*do-la-fa, ti-sol-mi, la-fa-re, sol-mi-do, fa-re-ti, do.*
Ascending:	*do-re-mi, re-mi-fa, mi-fa-sol, fa-sol-la, sol-la-ti, la-ti-do, ti-do-re-do.*
Descending:	*do-ti-la, ti-la-sol, la-sol-fa, sol-fa-mi, fa-mi-re, mi-re-do, re-do-ti-do.*

---

[7] Although many teachers make minimal use of syllables, one of the contemporary methods, the Kodály method, makes considerable use of syllables—it is the very backbone of the method. The values of using syllables as a means of clarifying tonal relationships should not be overlooked.

For suggested songs for study and analysis, see "Blow the Winds Southerly" (*Discovering Music Together,* Book 3).

"Valentine, Valentine" (*Exploring Music,* Book 3)

"Chebogah" (*Exploring Music,* Book 3)

"Joyous Chanukah" (*Silver Burdett Music,* Book 3)

Children should also have the opportunity to listen to sequence in recorded instrumental music. They may endeavor to identify sequence aurally, or the notation may be written on the chalkboard. The following works are suggested for listening and study: "Fairies and Giants" from *Wand of Youth* Suite No. 1 (theme 2*) by Edward Elgar (*Adventures in Music,* Grade 3, Volume 1, RCA Victor); "Waltz" (Dance of the Nubians) from *Faust* (theme 1*) by Charles Gounod (*Adventures in Music,* Grade 3, Volume 1, RCA Victor).

Keyboard orientation: The black keys on the piano can help one to identify pitches.

Identify the pitch D between two black keys and ask the children to locate as many D's on the piano as they can. Likewise, identify E (just to the right of two black keys) and other diatonic pitches in the scale.

Grade 4

Major scales are built on the intervals of whole step, whole step, half step, and whole step, whole step, half step.

Children should understand how major scales are constructed. Before an explanation is attempted, however, they should have had experience in singing scales and have developed an awareness of the half steps between the third and fourth and the seventh and eighth degrees

* For notation, see the Teacher's Guide which accompanies the album.

of the scale. The experience, while singing, of observing the scale as a ladder with the third and fourth, and seventh and eighth rungs close together is also helpful.

With these experiences as a basis, the teacher may show how the diatonic scale is built upon two tetrachords, one superimposed upon the other (the tetrachord is a part of the ancient Greek scale, consisting of four tones in the order of "whole step, whole step, half step.") Children may more readily understand the combination of tones by observing these steps on the piano keyboard. The whole steps are easily noticed because of the placement of the black keys; each black key represents a pitch a half-step higher or lower than the adjacent white key.

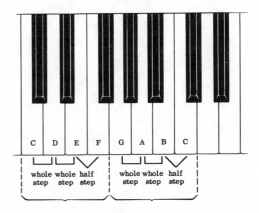

Have children play the C-major scale on the melody bells or the piano (white bars or keys only). Help the class to discover the "whole step, whole step, half step patterns" in the scale and to recognize that a whole step occurs between two white keys when there is a black key in between.

Children should understand that composers cannot always be restricted to the key of C and that they generally begin their "scales" on other pitches. The teacher may then play a scale beginning on G, playing only the white keys. Let as many children as possible observe the piano keyboard while others follow a dummy keyboard or a facsimile of some type. Before the teacher plays the scale the class should be asked to listen carefully to it. (Some children may wince a bit as the F natural is played.) The teacher should then ask them how the scale sounded. Perhaps some children will immediately comprehend why the scale sounded strange. If not, play it again slowly, asking the class to watch for the "whole, whole, half step combination." It will eventually become evident that the teacher is playing whole, whole, half step, and whole, half, whole step. The teacher should then ask the class how the latter tetrachord might be corrected. The answer is simply to raise the next-to-last tone by one half step. This results in the combination of whole, whole, half step. It may then be explained that in notating this scale a sharp sign is placed in front of the next-to-last note to indicate that the pitch is raised one-half step. (In using the same procedure for a scale beginning on F, it will become evident that to achieve the right combination of whole and half steps it is necessary to lower, by using a flat sign, the fourth scale degree.)

Although this procedure may seem somewhat detailed, it is a good way to develop an understanding of the reason for key signatures. To strengthen this concept further, the teacher should illustrate the procedure with several other scales, at least those beginning on D, F, and B♭. It is also desirable to devote some time to showing children how key signatures are placed on the staff. The following rules are helpful.

For sharp keys:
  a. The first sharp is on F.
  b. To place the other sharps, count down four lines and spaces. (The third and sixth sharps should be placed up an octave.)

For flat keys:
  a. The first flat is on B.
  b. To place the other flats, count up four lines and spaces. (The third, fifth, and seventh flats are placed down an octave.)

In counting either up or down, make sure the students count the beginning pitch as one and the last pitch as four.

A sharp (♯) raises a pitch one-half step and a flat (♭) lowers a pitch one-half step. A natural sign (♮) cancels any sharp or flat which precedes it within a measure.

Introduce songs with accidentals (♯, ♭, or ♮). Ask the class to scan the song to see if they observe anything unusual about the notation. Identify melodic patterns with accidentals and write them on the chalkboard. After an explanation is provided on the function of the accidental, let children play the pattern on the melody bells or resonator bells. Distribute separate resonator bells representing a pattern to several children in the class, and have them play a pattern. Ask the class to name the child who played the accidental and identify the pitch.

The home tone (or key-note) in a major scale (do) can be determined by examining the key signature.

Before reading a song, children should first identify the key and meter and then scan the page looking for familiar and unfamiliar tonal and rhythmic patterns. Knowing the key and where the home tone is will assist in this process. "In sharp keys, the last sharp is on the seventh scale step, or *ti,* and in flat keys the last flat is on the fourth scale step, or *fa.* Count up or down to find *do.*" Does the song begin or end on *do* (major key)? Does it end on *la* (minor key)? (Determining keys should never be merely an exercise, but should be based on an understanding of the need and function of sharps or flats in a key signature.)

A melody is a succession of tones that move upward or downward in a single line.

Ask children to describe a melody. What does it do? What do different melodies have in common; i.e., how are they alike? Encourage the class to offer a number of definitions, discuss what they like about each, and then agree upon the best definition.

The interval eight scale steps apart is called an octave; the interval five steps apart is called a fifth.

In exploring the keyboard, ask children to count the scale steps from one pitch to another and help them to discover that an "octave" encompasses eight scale steps. Using a plastic keyboard held so all can see, the teacher may help the children to count the scale steps between other intervals and thus determine their names. Place intervals on a staff on the chalkboard and help the children to discover their sounds and their names.

"Melodic contour" means the shape of the melody.

As the class listens to various songs (either through recordings or played by the teacher on the piano) have them draw the "shape" of each melody in the air and then on the chalkboard. Ask the class to compare the different contours. Does the melody move smoothly (by steps) or is it angular (by leaps)? On subsequent days have the children examine carefully many songs in their texts and describe the melodic contour.

A pentatonic scale usually does not have the fourth and seventh scale tones of the major scale. When these "active" tones are missing, there is less pull toward a tonal center.

Children will have had experience in prior grades of improvising in the pentatonic scale. They should, at this level, be given the experience of selecting their own pitches for the pentatonic scale from the resonator bells or a xylophone prior to playing. Through improvising, they will discover that when the "active" fourth and seventh scale steps are not used, there is less pull toward a tonal center.

The tonal center of major scales is do, *and the tonal center of minor scales is* la; *the same key signature is used for relative major and minor scales.*

If a system of syllables or numbers is to be of any benefit to children, they must know how to find the key-note (*do* or *la*) without depending upon the teacher. Initially, the simplest explanation is to tell the class that, for the sharp keys, the last sharp to the right is *ti*, and to find *do* one simply counts up one scale step; for flat keys, the last flat to the right is *fa* and to find *do*, simply count down (*fa, mi, re, do*) four scale steps on alternate lines and spaces.

After locating *do*, the students will want to determine if the song is in major or minor tonality. This may be done by scanning the melodic line. Specifically, they should first look to see if the melody begins or ends on *do*. Songs beginning on incomplete measures may start on any one of several pitches, but those in major tonality will generally end on *do*. If the song does not end on *do,* the student should determine if it ends on *la*. If it does, the song is probably in minor tonality. If the song ends on neither *do* nor *la,* then perhaps it is written in the pentatonic scale, which usually includes the first, second, third, fifth, and sixth degrees—but not the fourth or seventh —of the diatonic scale. Songs based upon the pentatonic scale may end on any scale tone. Popular music today is well known by fourth graders through radio, television, and recordings, and the sounds of various *modes,* including the natural minor mode (*la* to *la*), are very familiar to their ears!

By placing a major scale on the chalkboard, with its relative minor key written a third below, children may see a visual relationship between the two. They may then sing both scales, the major scale beginning and ending on *do,* and the minor scale on *la.*

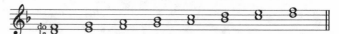

Help children to discover that minor songs borrow their key signature from major keys, and that their tonal center is a third below (*la* to *la*). It may be helpful to have the class sing the C-major scale with syllables ascending and then descending down to A (*la*). Then, sing the relative minor scale from *la* to *la.* Notate both scales on the chalkboard so that comparisons can be made.

Accidentals are sharps, flats, or natural signs indicating an alteration of notes not shown in the key signature.

In scanning a song before singing, children should first examine the key (and meter) signature and then look for any accidentals or pitches not normally occurring in the particular key. Ask them to explain, if they can, why a specific accidental does not belong to a particular key.

The chromatic *scale is made up entirely of half-steps.*

Have the children play a scale, on the melody bells or the piano, beginning on C and using all the white and black keys in order. How many different scale steps are in one octave of the chromatic scale? White and black keys alternate except between what pitches (E to F, and B to C)? Play chromatic scales beginning on other pitches. On how many different pitches can one begin a chromatic scale? Encourage children to devise tunes using selected tones of the chromatic scale and then endeavor to notate them.

Grade 5

An interval is the distance between two tones, and is determined by the number of scale steps encompassed from the bottom to the top pitch.

In a variety of listening sessions, children's attention should be called to the unique sound of various intervals, and in studying songs, they should be asked to identify different intervals, first by counting the scale steps encompassed (make certain that they count the bottom pitch as "one"). Discuss the sound of different intervals. Which ones sound the most pleasing? Which ones sound most dissonant? To reinforce in the child's mind the unique sound of particular intervals, relate them to familiar sounds in particular songs (see pp. 83–84 for examples).

A basic understanding of intervals is helpful in comprehending the musical score. Knowledge of intervals facilitates the placement of sharps and flats in the key signature and contributes to a person's ability to read music—knowing, for example, what a third or sixth sounds like and readily identifying them on the printed page.[8]

second   third   fourth   fifth   sixth   seventh   octave

The student must be able to recognize intervals both visually and aurally. To determine an interval on the printed page, children should be advised to begin with the bottom note, consider it as the first, and count each line and space up to and including the last, or top note. The total number of lines and spaces counted determine the interval. Children should have some experience in determining intervals based on various pitch levels; they should examine lots of music and determine the intervals between notes at points designated by the teacher.

But if visual recognition of intervals is to be of help at all, children must also know how these intervals sound. The best procedure is to relate the intervals to a mean-

---

8 The intervals in the example below are all major intervals, except the fourth, fifth, and octave, which are perfect intervals. Major intervals, when made one-half step smaller, either by lowering the top pitch or by raising the bottom pitch, become minor intervals. Perfect intervals, when made smaller by one-half step, become diminished intervals. If minor intervals are made smaller by one-half step, they also become diminished intervals. Major and perfect intervals, if made larger by one-half step, either by raising the top pitch or by lowering the bottom, become augmented intervals.

For further information on intervals, see any of the books on music fundamentals listed in the Appendix, pp. 285–286.

ingful sound that is a part of the children's musical experience. That is, when discussing an interval of a major third, use the reference point of *do-mi, fa-la,* or *sol-ti,* whichever is applicable.

Another approach is to identify the intervals (both ascending and descending) in certain songs that are easily remembered, and which serve as a familiar point of reference. Following are some suggested examples. Children might add to this list familiar songs that they particularly enjoy.

Half steps (semitones)
Ascending—"Stardust"
Descending—"Habanera"
(from *Carmen*), "Ciribiribin"
Major seconds (whole tones)
Ascending—"America,"
"Happy Birthday," "Polly Wolly Doodle"
Descending—"I Dream of Jeannie," "Turkey in the Straw"
Minor thirds
Ascending—"Go Tell It on the Mountain" (verse), "Drill, Ye Tarriers" (*Making Music Your Own,* Book 5), "Vesper Hymn" (*This Is Music,* Book 6)
Descending—"This Old Man," "Caisson Song," "Everytime I Feel the Spirit"
Major thirds
Ascending—"On Top of Old Smokey," "I Heard the Bells on Christmas Day," "For He's a Jolly Good Fellow"
Descending—"Swing Low, Sweet Chariot"
Perfect fourths
Ascending—"The Farmer in the Dell," "Auld Lang Syne,"

"Flow Gently Sweet Afton,"
"Taps"
Descending—"March of the
Three Kings" (Bizet), "Praise
to God" (*This Is Music,* Book
4)
Perfect fifths
Ascending—"Twinkle, Twin-
kle Little Star," "My Favorite
Things" (from *The Sound of
Music*)
Descending—"My Home's In
Montana"
Minor sixths
Ascending—"Go Down,
Moses," "Fiddlers Two" (*This
Is Music,* Book 4)
Major sixths
Ascending—"My Bonnie Lies
Over the Ocean," "My Wild
Irish Rose," "It Came Upon
the Midnight Clear"
Descending—"Nobody Knows
the Trouble I've Seen," "Sing
Your Way Home" (*Growing
With Music,* Book 4)
Minor sevenths
Ascending—"Calliope" (*Sing-
ing In Harmony,* Book 6)
Major sevenths
Ascending—"El Vito" (*This Is
Music,* Book 6), "Bali Hai"[9]
(from *South Pacific*)
Perfect octaves
Ascending—"Somewhere Over
the Rainbow," "The Christ-
mas Song" (by Mel Tormé),
"Annie Laurie"

*Major scales have half steps be-
tween scale tones 3 and 4 and between 7 and 8; minor scales (natural) have half steps between tones
2 and 3 and tones 5 and 6.*

In addition to singing and playing
music based on major and minor
scales, children will benefit by
writing out various major and
minor scales and by improvising

---

[9] While the first two pitches in this song are the interval of an octave, the
second pitch, because of its relatively short duration, gives way to the third, thus
creating the feeling for the major seventh.

Major scale:

1 2 3 4 5 6 7 8

Natural minor scale:

1 2 3 4 5 6 7 8

simple tunes on the xylophone or resonator bells. Let the children select the home tone and then write the scale on the chalkboard (or on manuscript paper), making certain they use the correct combination of whole and half steps. This will necessitate the use of sharps or flats, depending on the intervals desired. Such an activity helps to clarify the reason for the key signature, which the children should also determine.

In the harmonic form of the minor scale, the seventh scale degree is raised; in the melodic form of the minor scale, both the sixth and seventh scale degrees are raised when ascending and made natural (or lowered) when descending.

harmonic minor scale

melodic minor scale

The theoretical differences between the natural, harmonic, and melodic minor scales may be explained and notated on the chalkboard and illustrated through the study and performance of songs in minor modes. The uniqueness of each mode, however, may best be clarified and appreciated by selecting a familiar song, one in a natural minor mode, for example, and then altering it by singing it in the harmonic or melodic minor modes. These questions are appropriate: "How did we change the minor mode?" "Did this change the effect of the song?" "Which mode do you prefer (for a particular song) and why?"

A minor key borrows its key signature from the major key that is an interval of a minor third above.

From the experience of notating minor scales and making certain that the half steps occur between steps 2 and 3, and steps 5 and 6, children will need to use sharps or flats to indicate the appropriate scale steps. From this experience, they may discover that the minor keys use the same key signature as the major keys a minor third above.

The direction of the note stems— up or down—indicates the correct part for the upper and lower voices to sing or play.

When two-part music is introduced to children, they will discover that the note stems for the higher parts are turned upward and the note stems for the lower parts are turned downward. Occasionally, the lower part may even move higher than the upper part, and the directions of the note stems help to minimize any confusion. Discussion of this fact may prove helpful. Children will also discover that sometimes both parts are to sing in unison rather than in parts, and this is indicated by two stems on one note, going both up and down.

The pentatonic scale is usually built on a whole step, whole step, step and a half, and a whole step.

Although children will have had experience with the pentatonic scale through singing songs and improvising on a given set of tones on the xylophone, resonator bells, or the black keys of the piano, it is important that they clarify their understanding of the intervallic relationships of the tones in this scale by constructing it on a number of different pitches and then improvising on each.

Melodies move by scale and chord patterns.

Children's ability to understand and interpret a musical score can be enhanced by their study of notation to determine the manner in which melodies move. In clarifying the purpose of the staff, the teacher should make sure the children understand the line-space concept for scales and chords. That is:

line line line or *space space space* for chords;
line space line or *space line space* for scale passages.

This concept illustrates one of a number of understandings which teachers sometimes take for granted without realizing that children might not comprehend them.

Which measures move by scale patterns? Can you identify the scale patterns by syllables or numbers? Which measures move by chord patterns? Can you identify the chords?

The whole-tone *scale is comprised of six equally spaced whole steps.*

Without any half steps, which create a feeling for a tonal center, the whole-tone scale achieves a degree of vagueness which was suitable to the efforts of composers such as Debussy, Ives, and others. The whole-tone scale should be notated on the chalkboard and children given the opportunity to experiment with it on the resonator bells and piano.

After specific listening experiences, children may wish to create their own compositions using the whole-tone scale. Suggested orchestral compositions by Debussy for listening are: *La Mer* ("The Sea"), *The Afternoon of a Faun, Nocturnes;* piano compositions are: "Clair de Lune," "Reflections in the Water," and "The Children's Corner."

Charles Ives wrote a song entitled

"The Cage," which includes five sets of the whole-tone scale (*This is Music,* Book 5). Children will benefit by playing the various sets on the melody bells or the piano before singing the song.

A tone row *is a series of 12 tones of the chromatic scale used by composers as a new means to express musical ideas.*

To introduce the tone row to children, select only the 12 tones of the chromatic scale (C to C) from the resonator bells. First, play the tones of the chromatic scale, simply to illustrate the pitches being used. Then blindfold a particular child and ask him to rearrange the 12 tones in any order he wishes (in a random order). Then remove the blindfold and relate to the class that a tone row has been created! Have the child play his row from left to right (the lowest pitches may no longer be to the child's left). Next ask him to play them in the same order, but to create a melody by altering the length of the tones (some short and some longer). Further tonal possibilities may be achieved by playing the row backwards with the same or different rhythms.

For a song written using a twelve-tone row, see "The Quest" by Francis J. Pyle (*The Magic of Music,* Book 5); for a piano work, see Suite for Piano, Opus 25, by Arnold Schoenberg (*Making Music Your Own,* Book 6).

Grade 6

A "blues" scale may be devised by adding two extra tones—the lowered third and seventh scale degrees.

blue notes

Ask children to first play a regular C-major scale on the piano or melody bells and then to play the "blues" scale, adding the flattened or lowered third and seventh scale degrees. Ask the class to describe or verbalize the difference in sound. After singing "Roll, Jordan, Roll" (*This is Music*, Book 6), ask the class to locate the "blue" note in the song. Children should be encouraged to improvise on the piano or bells using this scale. See also the street cry "Sweet Orange" (*This is Music*, Book 6).

Modal scales, each with a uniquely different sound, may be heard by playing octave·scales on the white keys of the piano from the pitches indicated:

To understand the "theory" of each of the modes, have children first play a particular scale on the white keys and then analyze the sequence of whole and half steps. To facilitate their understanding, have them play each mode beginning on other pitches and endeavoring to maintain the correct tonal sequence. The following are examples of music in various modes which children should listen to and/or sing.

Dorian mode, D to D,

"The Mary Gulden Tree"—old English song (*This is Music*, Book 6)
"Nine Hundred Miles" (*The Magic of Music*, Book 6)

Phrygian mode, E to E,

"Summer Is Over" by Ivan Olson, second half (*This is Music*, Book 5)

Lydian mode, F to F,

"Ground Hog"—Kentucky mountain song (*Making Music Your Own*, Book 6)

Mixolydian mode, G to G,

"Norwegian Wood" by The Beetles

*Aeolian mode, A to A,

(See note below)

Locrian mode, B to B.

* The Ionian mode (C to C) is the same as the C-major scale, and the Aeolian mode (A to A) is the same as the A natural minor scale.

"Summer Is Over" by Ivan Olson, first half (*This is Music*, Book 5)

Music of the Middle East often uses a scale with unusual intervals.

Write the Middle-Eastern scale on the chalkboard and let the children play, sing, and analyze it before singing a song on which it is based:

"Ach ya Chabibi" (Israeli love song—*The Magic of Music,* Book 6). After singing the song, ask the class to compare the melodic patterns in the song to the scale on the chalkboard.

(half step, step and a half, and a half step—repeated.)

Topics for Discussion

1. Formulate a sequence of concepts about *melody* that moves from the general to the specific or from the simple to the complex.

2. Describe the conditions under which music notation is introduced to children.

3. How many different instruments may be used to reinforce the concept of long and short sounds?

4. After the concept of a scale has been introduced, how many ways can it be reinforced aurally and visually?

5. What is the best procedure for making key signatures meaningful?

6. Identify various intervals (ascending and descending) in a number of songs that are easily remembered and will serve as helpful points of reference.

7. Innumerable musical scales have been devised in the past. Investigate these in theoretical treatises and determine those that might be appropriate to introduce to intermediate-grade students.

Suggestions for Further Study

COPLAND, AARON, *What To Listen For In Music.* New York: New American Library, 1957, chapter 5.

GARY, CHARLES, ed., *The Study of Music in the Elementary School—A Conceptual Approach.* Washington, D.C.: Music Educators National Conference, 1967.

MACHLIS, JOSEPH, *The Enjoyment of Music* (3rd ed.). New York: W. W. Norton & Company, Inc., 1970, chapter 3.

TIPTON, GLADYS, and ELEANOR TIPTON, *Teacher's Guide: Adventures in Music.* Camden, N.J.: RCA Victor, 1961. (See guides for all albums, grades 1–6.)

Films and Filmstrips[10]

Discovering Melody (United World Films, Inc.), 11 minutes, elementary (ages 5–7).

Exploring Music Reading (Classroom Materials Co.). Filmstrip and recording (grades 1–3).

Introduction to Music Reading (Classroom Materials Co.). Filmstrip and recording, elementary (grades 1–3).

Listen to My Line (EMC Corp., Education Materials Division). Filmstrip, elementary.

Melody in Music (Coronet Instructional Films), b&w or color, 13 minutes, elementary/college.

Musical Atoms—A Study of Intervals, Young People's Concert Series (Bell Telephone Company—inquire about free loan), 1 hour, elementary/college.

What Is Melody? Young People's Concert Series (McGraw-Hill Films), 1 hour, elementary/college.

---

[10] For addresses of producers and distributors of educational films and filmstrips, see the Appendix, pp. 287–288.

chapter 5

RHYTHM, METER, AND
BODILY MOVEMENT

Rhythm is a basic phenomenon of nature and exists all about us —in the sounds of nature's forests, the rhythm of mountain streams and ocean waves, and the man-made sounds of the cities. In the study and performance of music, it is important that rhythm be internalized, i.e., felt inwardly, if a performer is to interpret music in an artistic, musical manner. Lack of rhythmic response is likely to result in a mechanical, unmusical performance. Activities involving bodily response to music provide children with a basis for the comprehension of pulse, duration, pitch, tempo, and dynamics, as well as serving as a stimulus to the creative imagination.

The activities, skills, and comprehensions discussed in this chapter cover all facets of rhythm, from the simple to the complex, and are designed to develop rhythmic responsiveness—a necessary characteristic to musicianly performance.

Bodily movement of various types is also an integral part of the elementary-school physical education program. The overall objectives are similar, with mental and physical coordination being perhaps of greater concern. But the music teacher who utilizes any type of bodily movement as a class activity usually does so with a definite musical objective in mind, and the amount of time devoted to the activity is minimal in contrast to that in the physical education class. Furthermore, the space for movement is often limited in the music room, and the teacher may necessarily opt to have only a small group of children actively involved at one time. The remainder of the class does not sit idly by, but may sing, play instruments, or respond in some other appropriate way. For example, if the select group of children is walking to music, the rest of the class may also "walk" quietly by alternately raising their heels while seated at their desks.

CONCEPTS OF RHYTHM FOR K–6
AND ACTIVITIES AND SKILLS
FOR THEIR COMPREHENSION

Concepts	Activities and Skills
	[The long-range goal of all activities is the development of children's musicality, i.e., *increased sensitivity and responsiveness to music.* Following each activity, the effectiveness of instruction should be evaluated. Concepts need to be reinforced through varied, but similar activities; therefore, the teacher must determine what students really have learned, as this is the critical factor in determining the specific nature of subsequent experiences.]

K–1

There are many ways to move to rhythm (march, walk, run, skip).

Young children are highly receptive to the music they hear and are most responsive to *rhythm.* The teacher should encourage children to explore different ways of moving to music and help them to determine the most appropriate bodily movements for particular songs and instrumental selections (e.g., marching, walking, running, skipping).[1]

It may be found that some children in a given class are somewhat uncoordinated and unable to walk, run, or skip to the tempo of a particular recorded selection. For their initial experiences, therefore,

---

[1] As another means of introducing rhythm to children, use various educational films, such as *Rhythm Is Everywhere* (Carl F. Mahnke Productions). For other titles, see p. 132.

these children should not be forced into responding at a prescribed tempo. At first, for example, they may be asked to walk to the beat of a tom-tom drum or another rhythm instrument, to clapping, or to rhythmic speech patterns. Or, the teacher may improvise appropriate music on the piano. During these activities the teacher should carefully observe the children's bodily responses and adapt the tempo of the music to one that they are physically capable of responding to. This is essential before various recorded selections with a definite prescribed tempo are utilized.

The University School, Indiana University, and
The Daily Herald-Telephone, Bloomington, Ind.

Marching in kindergarten stimulates response to the pulse of the music.

Before the children move to recorded music, the selection should
be played for the class, and they
should be asked to listen carefully
and decide, for example, whether
walking, marching, or running
steps would be the best way to
move to the music. After agreeing
upon the most appropriate bodily
movement, a small group may be
selected to respond, or the entire
class may simulate the movements
while seated at their desks. When
walking or marching, children
should be asked to listen to the
"beat" of the music and try to
"step in time" to it.

The teacher should repeat the preceding activity with music of a
contrasting tempo and rhythmic
movement so that children may
develop a greater awareness of the
actual differences. The following
are some suggested recordings for
this purpose:

Walking:

"Walking Song" from *Acadian
Songs and Dances* by Virgil
Thompson (*Adventures in
Music,* Grade 1, RCA Victor),
"medium steps."

"Pantomime" from the *Come-
dians* by Dmitri Kabalevsky
(*Adventures in Music,* Grade
1, RCA Victor), "slow steps."

"Departure" from *Winter Holiday* by Sergei Prokofiev (*Adventures in Music,* Grade 2,
RCA Victor), "fast steps."

Marching:

"March of the Toys" from *Babes
in Toyland* by Victor Herbert
(*Adventures in Music,* Grade
2, RCA Victor).

"March" from *Soirées Musicales*

by Rossini-Britten (*Adventures in Music,* Grade 1, RCA Victor).

"March" from *Summer Day Suite* by Sergei Prokofiev (*Adventures in Music,* Grade 1, RCA Victor).

"March" from *Love for Three Oranges* by Sergei Prokofiev (*Bowmar Orchestral Library,* Vol. #54).

Running:

"Air Gai" from *Iphigenie in Aulis* by Christoph Willibald Gluck (*Adventures in Music,* Grade 1, RCA Victor).

"The Ball" from *Children's Games* by Georges Bizet (*Adventures in Music,* Grade 1, RCA Victor).

"Run, Run" from *Memories of Childhood* by Pinto (*Bowmar Orchestral Library,* Vol. #68).

Skipping is a bodily movement that children especially enjoy doing in response to music. Preceding this activity, music suitable for the purpose should be played and the children asked to guess the type of bodily movement they feel might be appropriate. With most children, the desired movement is rather easily identified. The class may be further led into a discussion of why they often skip during play and how they feel when they skip. Several children may then be selected for the skipping, or, when adequate space is available, more members of the class may be allowed to participate. Following are recordings appropriate for this activity.

Skipping:

"Gigue" from *Céphale et Procris* by André Modeste Grétry (*Ad-*

ventures in Music, Grade 1, RCA Victor).

"Gigue" from Suite No. 3 in D by J. S. Bach (*Adventures in Music,* Grade 1, RCA Victor).

Classroom teachers may learn to improvise on the piano their own music for walking, running, and skipping. First, they should understand and practice the basic I, IV, V^7, I chord progression.

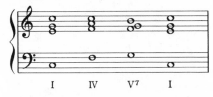

These chords may be played in a tempo and in combinations appropriate for walking, running, or skipping. For walking, the teacher might play:

For running, the teacher may use the same pattern in the right hand, but simply play eighth notes in the left hand:

For skipping, the same basic chord progression may also be used, but the meter should be changed to 6/8 and the rhythmic pattern altered:

After learning these basic patterns, the teacher will undoubtedly wish to improvise others that allow for greater rhythmic and tonal variety. In addition, the classroom teacher will want to either explore and study composed music written expressly for this purpose[2] or to adapt music in various piano books as needed.

The words of a song may suggest ways to dramatize the music.

A creative form of bodily movement may be achieved through dramatizing songs with which the children are familiar. Prior to this activity, the children should have had ample experience with the song, including discussion of the meaning of the words. After a reasonable degree of skill and understanding has been achieved, the teacher may ask for suggestions from the class as to how the various thoughts in the song might be expressed through pantomime (or "acted out"). Songs with several verses, including slightly different but related thoughts, are the most adaptable for dramatization.

The French folksong "I Had a Little Sail-boat" (La Bergère) (*140 Folk-tunes,* Boston: E. C. Schirmer, p. 30) is, for example, particularly suitable for use with children in the kindergarten or first grade. Approximately half a dozen children may be selected to dramatize the song while the remainder of the class provides the descriptive accompaniment by singing the song. In some classes almost all the children will be anxious to participate. In such cases, the teacher should reassure the class and tell

[2] See Robert Pace, *Piano for Classroom Music,* 2nd ed. (Englewood Cliffs, N.J.: Prentice-Hall, 1971).

them that they will all have an opportunity to participate at another time. The first verse in the song describes a "little sailboat." Appropriate actions might be for a small group of children to form a circle, squat on the floor, stretch their arms upward to simulate the sails on a boat, and then rock slowly from side to side in time to the music. The second verse describes an "ugly frog" that "leaped upon her deck." In this verse the children may imagine that they are frogs, assuming appropriate bodily positions and facial expressions. In the third verse, "the ship went topsy-turvy," presumably due to the frog. To depict this, the children may emulate a sinking sailboat, gradually lower their outstretched arms, and "sink" to the floor.

The basic song texts available in each classroom will contain many suitable songs; however, teachers should not limit the many possibilities for such activities to the songs included in any one book. Rather, they should be continually seeking new and suitable materials which may be effectively used for this purpose.

Rhythm has pulse, or beat.

Ask children to listen for the steady, recurring pulsation of the "tick-tock" of a clock, a metronome, or their own heartbeat (with the thumb of the left hand pressed firmly against the inside of the right wrist). Encourage the class to respond to the pulse of the music (either songs or instrumental selections) by clapping, swaying, or walking. Select several children to play a steady pulse on the tom-tom drum, or other appropriate percussion instruments, while other children walk or "march" to the pulse of the music.

After a class has had experience in responding physically to pulse in a variety of ways, the Dalcroze idea of "silent counting" may be introduced, i.e., "pupils march to the music and at a signal stop and count silently the two, three, four, or more beats agreed upon and then take up their march exactly on time."[3]

Rhythm can be even or uneven.

Ask children to select appropriate percussion instruments and to play rhythms that sound like walking, running, and skipping. Which rhythms sound even or uneven? Which instruments sound best on the even sounds? Which sound best on uneven sounds? Have children walk with an even sound (quarter notes played on a tom-tom drum or the piano). Ask them to listen to the music and to step with the beat. When the teacher plays an uneven sound (of any duration) they should stop and stand still. When the even sounds resume they should start walking again. Children enjoy this activity, which makes them listen more acutely to the rhythm of the music.

Rhythm has strong and weak beats.

Children should be asked to listen to selected music for strong and weak beats and should then be encouraged to respond by clapping the loud and softer beats so as to correspond to the stresses in the music. Following this, they should

[3] Beth Landis and Polly Carder, *The Eclectic Curriculum in American Music Education: Contributions of Dalcroze, Kodály, and Orff* (Washington, D.C.: Music Educators National Conference, 1972), p. 20.

portray the differences between strong and weak beats by marking on the chalkboard and in time to the music as follows:

 ; children may then be asked to walk on the strong beats of a song and to pause on the weaker beats.

| 𝅗𝅥 𝅘𝅥 | 𝅗𝅥 𝅘𝅥 | 𝅗𝅥 𝅘𝅥 | etc.

Music has groups of beats.

Slapping the knees on strong beats and clapping on weaker beats helps to emphasize the grouping of beats into twos or threes. Children may also play selected percussion instruments on strong and weak beats. Which instruments sound best on strong beats and which sound better on the weaker beats?

Grade 2

The rhythm of the music may suggest ways of moving one's body.

Bodily movement to music of varying rhythms can provide children with a basis for comprehending different durational patterns. The following are a few examples of instrumental music and suggested activities in which children may participate.

1. "Galloping horses." Music: "The Wild Horsemen" by Robert Schumann (*Bowmar Orchestral Library*, Bol #64). The class should be asked to listen to the music and see if they can tell the way in which the horses are moving. Children should be encouraged to verbalize their ideas (for this as well as subsequent activities), as verbalizing can lead to a clearer understanding of the reasons for their choice. After it has been determined that the music sounds like the horses are "galloping," then four to six children may be selected to "gallop" like horses, preferably in a circle. (A suggested movement is to gallop with one foot always remaining ahead of the other.)

2. "High-stepping horses." Music: "The Happy Farmer" from *Album for the Young,* by Robert Schumann; New York: G. Schirmer, p. 16[4] (*Bowmar Orchestral Library,* Bol #64). The same general procedures may be utilized as suggested for "galloping horses." If adequate space for bodily movement is unavailable, the children may quite easily "step" in place, or pretend to be "rocking horses."

3. "Toy soldiers." Music: "March of the Little Lead Soldiers" by Pierné (*Bowmar Orchestral Library,* Bol #54). The teacher may introduce the music by asking the class to listen and decide how they think small toy (or lead) soldiers would march. After a class discussion of this topic, a small group of children may be asked to demonstrate their own particular conceptions of how these soldiers would march.

4. "Indian dances." Children, both boys and girls, enjoy doing Indian dances, which may be an integral part of their work in a unit of study on Indians, generally undertaken in either the second or third grade. As has been previously suggested, a limited number of children should be chosen to dance at one time. It is also suggested that they dance in a circle, simulating the style of most Indian dances. A variety of recorded selections

---

[4] The music may also be found in various intermediate-grade piano books. See, for example, *Willis' Roadway to Classics for Piano* (Florence, Ky.: Willis Music Co.).

appropriate for use as an accompaniment may be found in the album *Sounds of Indian America* (Indian House, Box 472, Taos, New Mexico 87571).[5]

Teachers may also improvise appropriate music on the piano by playing the eighth note pattern indicated below in the left hand on C♯ and G♯, and any group of the black keys in the right hand.

The above music is simple enough for any teacher to play—even those with very limited musical experience. Children in the second or third grade who have studied piano may also be provided the opportunity to learn this simple accompaniment for dancing. Utilizing one or more drums or tom-toms on the rhythmic pattern

will add to the total effectiveness of the accompaniment.

5. "Ballet dancing." Music: "Ballet for the Sylphs" from *The Damnation of Faust,* by Hector Berlioz (*Adventures in Music,* Grade 1, RCA Victor).[6] Girls espe-

---

[5] Other recordings suitable for this purpose include: *Songs and Dances of Great Lakes Indians,* Folkways 4003; *Music of the Plains Apache,* Folkways 4252; *War Whoops and Medicine Songs,* Folkways 4381; *Music of the Sioux and the Navajo,* Folkways 4401; and *Music of the American Indians of the Southwest,* Folkways 4420.

[6] Other music suitable for this purpose is: "Petite Ballerina," from Ballet Suite No. 1, by Dmitri Shostakovich (*Adventures in Music,* Grade 2, RCA Victor); "Waltz—Dance of the Nubians," from *Faust,* by Charles Gounod (*Adventures in Music,* Grade 3, vol. 1, RCA Victor).

cially enjoy imitating the graceful movements of ballet dancers. They may step, turn slowly, whirl, leap, run, or make other appropriate movements. In some classes there may be children who have had lessons in ballet. These students may be asked to demonstrate some simple movements so that the class may develop a general concept of what to do. Whenever possible, those children may give a brief talk about ballet—including the fundamental movements and how they are adapted in an expressive manner to particular types of music. When children with some experience in ballet are unavailable in a particular school, the teacher should precede this type of rhythmic activity by showing an educational film on this topic.[7]

The RCA *Adventures in Music* record library and the *Bowmar Orchestral Library* both contain many recordings suitable for a wide variety of other rhythmic activities (for specific suggestions see the teacher's guides provided with each album).

Swaying is another way to respond to the pulse of the music.

After singing a song about a tree (or the wind), the teacher may ask the class to pretend they are trees that sway from side to side as they are blown back and forth by the wind. The children may stand, stretch their arms upward to simulate the branches of a tree, and then sway from side to side as they imagine they are being blown about in the wind. The teacher should also participate and demonstrate the importance of responding to the pulsation of the music.

[7] See, for example, *Ballet Girl* (Brandon Films, Inc., 200 W. 57th Street, New York 19, N.Y., 1956), b&w, sound, 23 minutes.

Songs suitable for this purpose are "Wind Through the Olive Trees," *Exploring Music,* Book 2 (New York: Holt, Rinehart & Winston, 1975); "The Wind," *The Magic of Music,* Book 2 (Boston: Ginn and Company, 1970); and "The Autumn Wind," *This is Music for Today,* Book 2 (Boston: Allyn & Bacon, 1971).

Some beats or pulses are stronger than others.

Skipping rope in time to music is an activity that is especially enjoyed by children in the second grade. Most are able to execute this activity quite well; however, all should be advised to listen carefully to the music and to skip on the stronger of the beats or pulses. An alternative activity to skipping rope is the bouncing of a large rubber ball (about the size of a soccer ball) in time to the music. Before undertaking this activity, children should be instructed to use *both* hands and to bounce the ball on the strong beats and hold it on the weaker beats. It is often helpful to practice bouncing the ball for a while before adapting the activity to music.

Rhythm can move in twos or threes.

In selected music, ask the class to listen for the recurring strong beats and the weaker beats in between. Help them to identify the strong beats and the *number* of weaker beats. Have selected children portray the groupings of stressed and unstressed beats on the chalkboard as | ı | ı | ı | ı or | ı ı | ı ı | ı ı | ı ı | ı ı | ı ı . An alternative means of portraying accented and unaccented beats is

or

Melody has tones of different lengths—some are longer than the beat, and some are shorter.

. Have the class listen to many songs and instrumental selections and identify the meter aurally. Does the music swing in twos or threes?

Listen to familiar songs and identify tones that are longer than others; call to the children's attention that some tones move with the beat, some move faster than the beat, and some move slower than the beat.

For the initial experience, use a familiar song such as "Mary Had a Little Lamb." While singing the song, have the class clap the pulse. Then ask the children, "Which words (notes) move faster than the beat?" (ma-ry had a lit-tle); "Which words (notes) move with the beat?" (lamb); and "Which word (note) is longer than the beat?" (snow).

Devise some notational systems to indicate duration:

——— — — ——— — — (line notation); | ⊓ | ⊓ (stem notation); then ♩ ♫♩ ♫ ; introduce and use the names—quarter note, eighth note, and half note.

When children examine a musical score, the teacher may help them to identify the notes that move with the beat (♩), the notes that move faster than the beat (♫), and the notes that move slower than the beat (♩). These notes may be referred to by their actual names and the class may clap, chant, or clap and chant the rhythm of the song. As children gain experience, these relationships will be broadened and clarified. The concept may be reinforced by clapping or playing on selected rhythm instruments the patterns of these three note values as an accompaniment to a song. For example:

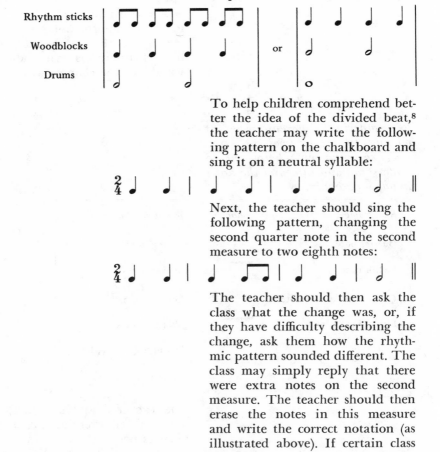

To help children comprehend better the idea of the divided beat,[8] the teacher may write the following pattern on the chalkboard and sing it on a neutral syllable:

Next, the teacher should sing the following pattern, changing the second quarter note in the second measure to two eighth notes:

The teacher should then ask the class what the change was, or, if they have difficulty describing the change, ask them how the rhythmic pattern sounded different. The class may simply reply that there were extra notes on the second measure. The teacher should then erase the notes in this measure and write the correct notation (as illustrated above). If certain class members comprehend the precise notation needed, then let one of them come to the chalkboard and write it.

---

8 The divided beat means that the basic pulse is divided equally into two shorter notes. For example, if the meter is 2/4, the pulse or beat occurs on a quarter note (♩); to divide the beat, two eighth notes (♫) may take its place.

To further clarify differences in duration in children's minds, the teacher may wish to use, at least periodically, the Kodály system of chanting rhythmic notation using different syllables for different notes; for example, ♩ = ta; ♫ = ti, ti; and ♩ = ta - a (for additional information on the Kodály approach, see pp. 263–267). The rhythmic pattern indicated would then be chanted as follows:

ta   ta   ta   ti   ti   ta   ta   ta — a.

Remembering different ways of moving to music (walking, running, skipping, etc.) helps one to understand and interpret the notes in our song books.

Real Name	Symbol	Descriptive Names
Quarter note	♩	walking note
Eighth note	♫	running notes
Quarter and eighth notes	♩ ♪	skipping notes
Eighth-note triplets	♫♪	galloping notes
Half note	♪	slow note (or step, bend)
Whole note	o	a note to hold

The teacher should, of course, call the students' attention to the differences between the various notes on the printed page. Notes may be referred to by their real names, but to young children this name will not hold much meaning, nor will it be likely to be remembered until after they gain considerable experience with printed notation. In the initial stages, it is desirable to refer to notes by names descriptive of their durations. That is, quarter notes may be referred to as "walking notes," eighth notes as "running notes," and so on. Some teachers prefer to use a double reference, i.e., "This is a quarter note and its play name is 'the *walking* note,' because that is the speed at which it moves."

A practice formerly followed by some teachers in teaching a song was to have the children first scan the page, looking for walking, running, and skipping notes, and then, before singing, to have them chant the entire song through, using the appropriate "play names." Some basic music textbooks were even designed to include songs appropriate for this procedure. Today's modern music series, however, make such a procedure somewhat more difficult, because the songs included are selected on the basis of their musical merits (and rightly so) rather than as a combination of notes that are easy for a group to chant. Nevertheless, chanting still has some merit, and when songs include a combination of notes adaptable to this procedure, it may prove beneficial. It is not necessary always to chant the entire song. This may prove tedious, delay the actual singing, and hinder the development of positive attitudes toward music. The teacher should select certain basic rhythm patterns in the music and have the class chant them. For example, the children may chant, while clapping their hands, this pattern:

| quarter | quarter | eighth | eighth | half note |

It is also helpful for the teacher to call the children's attention to the difference in color between the

black notes (♩) and the white

notes (♩). By dramatizing this point somewhat, a more vivid impression is made on the child of the specific differences between quarter and half notes.

In approaching the study of rhythm, the teacher should use a variety of procedures, some which emphasize an aural approach and others which stress visual patterns.

Rhythm patterns may answer one another, as in a conversation.

To open children's ears to a variety of rhythm patterns, and to develop more careful listening habits, a teacher may utilize a "rhythm conversation" (also known as "rhythm talk" and "echo clapping"), i.e., the teacher raps, taps, or claps a rhythmic pattern, or sings it on a neutral syllable, and the children then imitate it. For example:

Initially, simple patterns should be used, and it is suggested that they be selected from songs appropriate to the grade level being taught.

As children develop in their responsiveness to rhythm, the patterns may be extended in length from one to two, and then to four measures.

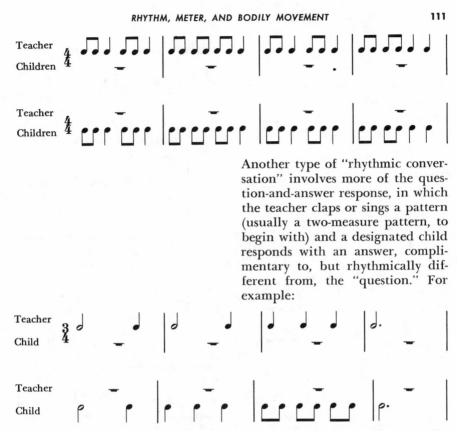

Another type of "rhythmic conversation" involves more of the question-and-answer response, in which the teacher claps or sings a pattern (usually a two-measure pattern, to begin with) and a designated child responds with an answer, complimentary to, but rhythmically different from, the "question." For example:

(Older children will benefit by responding in canon form, i.e., imitating the teacher's pattern one measure later; while clapping one pattern, they will simultaneously be listening to the teacher's next pattern.)

Interesting rhythm patterns can be devised from children's names and names of other things and places.

Ask each child to chant his or her name over and over, and then to clap the rhythm while chanting. Next, write the names in line notation (_____ __ _____). Finally, have the children write their names in regular notation, using eighth notes (♪♪ ♪♪) for the shortest sounds, quarter notes (♩ ♩) for

longer sounds and half notes (𝅗𝅥 𝅗𝅥) for the longest sounds.
The notation should be written on the chalkboard for the entire class to see. The children may also want to write this notation above their names in their notebooks. Activities such as this have unique value in that they give children a more personal experience with rhythm.

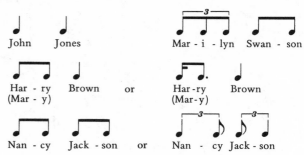

It will be noted that the names of Harry (or Mary) Brown and Nancy Jackson are illustrated in two ways. Depending upon the musical development of the children and their ability to perceive these more subtle differences, it would generally be better to illustrate the names in the latter way, which is certainly more accurate. For younger children, with less experience in notation, the simpler of the two ways should be used. This judgment can be made only by the teacher who knows and understands a particular group's capabilities.

From the experience of notating one's own name may grow the desire to learn how other words would look in notation. The following are some words, combinations of which have been used in the past to clarify various rhythmic patterns in students' minds.

U - tah   Mex - i - co   Lick - i - ty   split   Grass - hop -per

Mis - sis - sip - pi
Cin - cin - na - ti

Hump - ty Dump - ty

From these and similar experiences children may develop a clearer understanding of the fact that the words of a song determine, to a certain extent, the duration of the notes. Following these activities, children may wish to notate the rhythm of short sentences or poems. This may lead somewhat naturally into creating a song as a

Cincinnati Public Schools

Clapping the rhythmic patterns of children's names is one way of teaching note values.

class or group endeavor. (See chapter 9, pp. 242–246 for suggested procedures.)

Grade 3

Rhythm has pulse and accent and may move in twos or threes.

Place a series of quarter notes on the chalkboard, and ask a child to place accents (>) under every second or third note; ask the class to clap the pulse, respond to the accents, and decide if the rhythm moves in twos or threes.[9]

Developing a concept of meter depends upon experience which first leads to a feeling for pulsation in music and an awareness of stress, or accent. In listening to the pulsation of music, children will discover that all the beats do not sound the same. When asked how they differ, a child will usually answer that some beats sound heavier than others. The teacher may at this point provide the children with words that more accurately describe this sound—stress or accent. The teacher may tell the class that most music swings in twos or threes. Ample listening experiences should be provided to clarify this concept. After the class has identified the way in which a particular musical selection swings, a few children may be asked to "mark out" the pulsation and the accents on the chalkboard, for example:

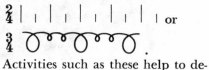

Activities such as these help to de-

---

[9] After children have had ample experience with duple and triple meter, the teacher may wish to introduce quadruple meter and to provide activities that will allow them to differentiate between music that swings twos, threes, and fours.

Bar lines group beats together in "measures."

In the meter signature, the upper number tells us how the notes are grouped, and the lower number tells us the type of note that moves with the beat.

velop the concept of accent through muscular response, as well as through a visual portrayal of strong and weak beats. Children are, therefore, better able to understand the function of the measure bars that set off these groups of strong and weak beats. (The strong beat in the measure immediately follows the bar line.)

On another day place a series of quarter notes on the chalkboard, and ask a child to place a bar line in front of every second, third, or fourth note. Ask the class to accent each note following a bar line and to decide (both aurally and visually) if the beats are grouped in measures of twos, threes, or fours.

Have the children identify the meter of a song (upper number) and the note that moves with the beat (lower number). Then clap, chant, or clap and chant the rhythm with the appropriate terminology, i.e., quarter, quarter, eighth, eighth, half note

(♩ ♩ ♫ ♩). Repeat this approach with a number of songs.

Tell the class that the meter is 4/4 and that a quarter note receives one beat, a half note two beats, and a whole note four beats. Then ask the class to tap the basic pulse (indicated by the teacher). Then play a series of chords, each of the same duration, on the piano and ask the class to count the number of beats in the chords played. Then ask them what kind of note they felt it was. On subsequent lessons the teacher may simply identify the meter, determine or set the pulse, and play the chord progression. About the time that students become accustomed to the quarter note as the beat note, they may then encounter a new meter signature. The teacher may simply announce that 4/2 or 6/8 is the meter signature, describe the number of beats each note receives, and play the durational pattern on the piano.

Following these activities, place notation on the chalkboard without bar lines. Then ask the class to determine the meter and place bar lines in the appropriate locations. Initially, select notation from songs familiar to the class so that the device will be as meaningful as possible. For example, the following notation may be placed on the chalkboard:

Bar lines properly placed will result in the following, more easily identifiable rhythm:

As children mature in their ability to determine the proper location of bar lines, the teacher may select durational patterns from songs less familiar to the group.

Some tones are the same as, some are longer than, and some are shorter than the beat note.

Place the preceding rhythmic figure on the chalkboard, and establish the quarter note as the beat note. Then have the class clap or tap each rhythm (beginning with the quarter notes) and identify the notation that moves with the beat, faster than the beat, and slower than the beat.

Ask several children to select percussion instruments that would be most appropriate for each of these rhythmic figures. Have the children play the rhythms singly and then combine them all together.

Rhythm occurs in patterns.

Identify a specific recurring pattern in a song, and have the students familiarize themselves with it by singing and clapping the rhythm. Then, ask them how many times they can find this pattern in the song.

Examples of songs, and specific rhythmic patterns, suitable for this purpose are:

"We're All Together Again," (*Discovering Music Together,* Book 3).

"Halleloo," (*Discovering Music Together,* Book 3).

"Sleep, My Little One," (*The Magic of Music,* Book 3).

"Sandy Land," (*Exploring Music,* Book 3).

A dotted quarter note (♩.*) can take the place of three eighth notes.*

In songs with 6/8 or 9/8 meter ("When Johnny Comes Marching Home" and "Down in the Valley"), help children to see that the "beat" note is ♩. and that three eighth notes equal one pulse. Help them

A quarter note (♩) and an eighth note (♪) can also take the place of 3 eighth notes. ♪♪♪
♩ ♪

also to discover that the tempo moves too quickly on "Johnny comes marching home" to feel the pulse on each eighth note, and that the beat note is, therefore,

a dotted quarter (♩.).

In the song "When Johnny Comes Marching Home," call the children's attention to the alternate use

of the figures ♪♪♪ and ♩ ♪ and the fact that the rhythm fits the words of the song. If the words of the song were changed, how would you change the rhythm and notation? Select a particular measure, change the words, and help the children to alter the rhythm and notation.

Grade 4

Rhythm patterns are made up of notes of different lengths, and the value of each note is relative to the values of the other notes.

Place the following chart showing relative durational values of notes on the chalkboard as a reference point, and after a brief discussion, have the class examine selected phrases of certain songs.[10] Let the class offer suggestions as to how the rhythm notation of a particular phrase might be altered while still maintaining the correct number of relative note values in a given measure.

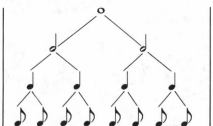

---

[10] In teaching by analogy, the whole note may be compared to a dollar, the half note to the half dollar, and the quarter note to a quarter, and so on. The duration of half notes or quarter notes is a relative matter, depending upon the designation of the beat note.

To help children develop skill in reading different rhythmic patterns, the teacher may place on the chalkboard a number of rhythmic problems encountered in the song books utilized on a particular grade level or, as an alternative, the chart of rhythmic patterns given below. The teacher should first establish the tempo, and the class should maintain it by tapping their feet, clapping, conducting, or beating the pulse of the music on their knees. Then, as the teacher points to specific measures, the children are to sing the patterns on a neutral syllable.

In the study of particular rhythmic patterns, clapping can be most helpful if the teacher helps the children to strive for accuracy. It is most important that children sense the pulse whenever they respond to rhythmic patterns of any type. This response may be facilitated if they are asked to squeeze the hands together on every pulse except those that are clapped. The following example illustrates this approach.

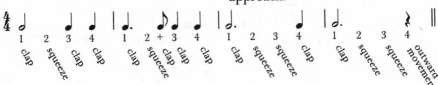

When the hands squeeze together, it is natural for them to move downward slightly in response to the pulse. This movement should be encouraged. It is also important that children respond to the rests in the music. This may be done appropriately by separating the hands in a slight outward movement.

The teacher may later wish to place rhythmic patterns on the chalkboard, asking the children if they can guess the title of the song before clapping the notated rhythm. This approach places the emphasis upon the visual aspects of notation. At other times the teacher may want to use an aural approach to guessing song titles, by rapping, tapping, or clapping rhythmic patterns.

Music is not only organized sounds, but organized silences. There are symbols for rests equivalent to note values.

Children should learn the appropriate symbols for rests equivalent to note values and identify them in various songs. In all music activities they should be encouraged to respond to the rests as accurately as they would to the sounded duration patterns; that is, they should feel and respond to the underlying pulse as indicated in the previous exercise on page 119.

Notes of different lengths can be the beat note.

Children will discover, as they respond to the pulse of music by clapping or conducting, that the beat note (the one representing the pulse) is not always the quarter note, but may be an eighth note, a dotted quarter, or a half note. What is the meter signature that goes with these beat notes? Identify various songs that use these different meters.

Have the children learn and sing the song "The Falling Star" by Howard Hanson (*The Magic of Music,* Book 5), in which the song is in 4/4 meter and the accompaniment is in 12/8. Discuss the effect of using these two meters together.

A conductor beats the pulse of the music.[11]

Conducting experiences will help children respond better to the pulse of the music and will also reinforce their understanding of different meters.

Students in intermediate grades may benefit from learning the basic conducting patterns and utilizing them in response to the pulse of the music. In some instances, the entire class may conduct a particular song. At other times, the teacher may ask one particular student to come to the front of the room and conduct the class in singing a song. The objective of such a procedure is, of course, not necessarily to make "conductors" of the entire class, but simply to provide another means through which they may respond to pulse and accent in music. This does not mean to imply that the basic conducting movements should be taken lightly; rather, each student should learn to conduct as well as possible, within the range or limits of his or her capabilities. The more adept the students are, the more the teacher may expect of them. The following are the basic conducting patterns for duple, triple, quadruple, and sextuple meters.

[11] Considering the maturation and musical development of children, grade 4 seems a logical time to introduce this concept. Some teachers, however, may wish to do so at an earlier time. If so, it is suggested that only duple and triple meter be introduced earlier, and that quadruple and sextuple patterns be delayed until at least the fourth grade and, in some cases, even later.

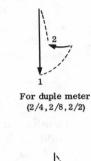

For duple meter
(2/4, 2/8, 2/2)

For triple meter
(3/4, 3/8, 3/2)

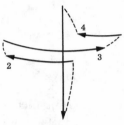

For quadruple meter
(4/4, 4/2, 12/8)

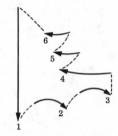

For sextuple meter
(6/8, 6/4)

A tune can be recognized by listening to the rhythm of the music.

In addition to responding to the pulse of the music, students may rap, tap, or clap the rhythm of a song. This helps them to feel the precise rhythmic durations in the various patterns. Another device to develop further awareness of rhythmic patterns is for the teacher to clap or tap out the rhythms of various songs and ask the class to identify the title of each. An alternative would be for the teacher to write on the chalkboard the rhythmic patterns of various songs (usually the first phrase is sufficient) and see if the class can identify them. For example: "Can you identify the tune that is set in this rhythm?"[12]

12 The answer is "Dixie."

3/4 meter in fast waltz tempo has only one strong pulse in each measure.

After "The Skaters' Waltz" has been introduced to the children, have the class respond bodily by swinging their arms in response to the pulse and then by conducting. How many beats does it seem natural to conduct? Why? (There isn't time for three distinct movements.) How many pulses do you feel in each measure? If you sang the song quite slowly, might you feel additional pulses or beats?

6/8 meter in a moderately fast tempo has only two pulses in each measure. Each beat note is ♩..

Again, have the children respond to the pulse, and they will discover only two beats per measure seem natural in moderately fast 6/8 tempo, and that the beat note

is a ♩. rather than an ♪.

Syncopation results when the unaccented portion of a beat (usually the second half) is stressed or accented.

Have children clap the pattern

♪♩ ♪♩ as notated on the chalkboard. Introduce a song with syncopation, such as "Casey Jones" (*This Is Music,* Book 4). Have children identify the number of syncopated patterns in the song. Where does the second note come in relation to the pulse? How do some of the patterns vary slightly? Later,

explore the pattern ♫♩. ♩♪♩ in the song "Cururu Frog," (*This Is Music,* Book 4). How does it differ from other syncopated patterns?

A dotted note receives half again its normal value.

Have the class chant and clap the

rhythmic pattern ♩ ♫♩ ♩. Next, have them respond to the rhythm with the first eighth note tied to

the quarter note ♩♩♩♩ with a slight "push" on the first eighth

note. Then have them respond to

the pattern ♩. ♪♩ and help the class to discover that the two patterns sound identical and that the dot is but a substitution for the eighth note tied to a quarter.

A triplet (♪♪♪) has three notes, but a rhythmic value of only

two (♪♪♪ = ♪♪).

Help the class to discover three notes that seem to fit in a "space" for only two. Explore words that give a feeling for the triplet, such as "Mexico" and "wonderful."

Write the notation ♪♪♪ on the chalkboard and identify it in various songs—aurally and visually. Does the triplet fit the words rhythmically?

Grade 5

In an irregular meter, such as 5/4, the beats can be grouped in combinations of 2 + 3 or 3 + 2.

In studying songs written in irregular meters, i.e., 5/4 or 7/4, children should be asked to examine the musical score carefully to discover if the beats in various measures are grouped in combinations of 2 + 3, or 3 + 2. Are the combinations the same in each measure? Do they alternate in any way? Why do they differ?

Simple meters are those where the beats are grouped in twos, threes, or fours; compound meters are combinations of simple meters and may have 6, 9, or 12 beats in a measure.

Before singing a song, children will examine the meter signature and scan the notation on the page. Their attention should be called to the grouping of the beats within the measure, and after some experience they should readily differentiate between the simple and compound meters. It is always helpful if the teacher will periodically write on the chalkboard the rhythmic notation (without meter signature) of a number of musical phrases and see if after analysis the class can determine the proper meter signatures.

There are different ways of notating syncopation.

In the same song children may find ways of notating syncopation that are different, but which sound the same, for example,

$\frac{4}{4}$ ♩ ♫ ♫ ♩ | and

$\frac{4}{4}$ ♩ ♪♩ ♪♩ |.   These two patterns sound the same. Can you notate other syncopated rhythms that sound different? What tunes were they in?

The meter signature ¢ , *or* alla

breve, *means that a half note* (♩), *rather than the quarter note, is the metric unit, and that two half notes make up a measure.*

To provide children with a better understanding of *alla breve* or ¢ , first have them sing a song written in alla breve in common time of C 4/4 . As a result they will discover that the tempo is too slow. Then ask them to double the tempo so that a half note (♩) is the beat note rather than the quarter note (♩); then relate to them that the meter signature ¢ , or *alla breve,* indicates for the performers to do just what they did!

A half note can take the place of two quarter notes or four eighth notes.

As a review of relative durational values, the teacher may wish to pose such questions as "What can take the place of two quarter notes?" etc.

Grade 6

Shifting from three notes to a beat to two notes to a beat is a typical Latin-American rhythmic device.

The meter of modern music may change frequently within a composition.

Let the class sing a number of Mexican folk melodies, including "Carmen, Carmela" (*The Magic of Music,* Book 6), and help them to discover recurring rhythmic figures that are typical of Latin-American music. Among the patterns they discover will be the shifting from three notes to a beat to two notes to a beat, for example,

Introduce the song "The Side Show" by Charles Ives (*This Is Music,* Book 6), in which the meter changes alternately from 3/4 to 2/4. Chant and clap the following rhythms before singing the song:

1 2 3 **1** 2 **1** 2 3 **1** 2 etc.

with stress upon the first beat.

Also teach the song "Three Laughing Girls" (*The Magic of Music,* Book 6), which changes back and forth from 2/4 to 3/4 meter.

Introduce the concept of additive rhythm, in which an additional beat is added in each subsequent measure, for example:

Listen to several works by Stravinsky and analyze the patterns of additive rhythm.

Accented notes on the second half of the beat are called "after-beats."

Before attempting to analyze the after-beat pattern, it is desirable for a class to have had some experience singing songs or listening to recorded music in which this pattern occurs. Students must have a concept of how after-beats sound before they can be expected to respond with any degree of accuracy. Prior to using the following procedure, the teacher should first establish fully the feeling for the pulse of the music by clapping the hands, tapping the foot, beating the pulse on the knee, or by conducting.

1. The teacher and the class should sing through the following pattern on a neutral syllable:

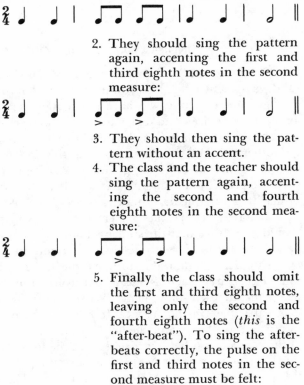

2. They should sing the pattern again, accenting the first and third eighth notes in the second measure:

3. They should then sing the pattern without an accent.
4. The class and the teacher should sing the pattern again, accenting the second and fourth eighth notes in the second measure:

5. Finally the class should omit the first and third eighth notes, leaving only the second and fourth eighth notes (*this* is the "after-beat"). To sing the after-beats correctly, the pulse on the first and third notes in the second measure must be felt:

Polyrhythm is the simultaneous use of several different rhythm patterns.

The simultaneous use of a number of different rhythms can be found in the ethnic music of both Africa and India. Present day "rock" performers, as well as contemporary composers, also utilize this device. Have children listen to the following recorded works and identify as many of the distinct rhythmic patterns as possible. Have them clap, tap, or sing the patterns.

> *Symphony No. 4* by Charles Ives (Columbia, MS-6775)
>
> *L'Histoire du Soldat* by Igor Stravinsky (Columbia, MS-7093)

SINGING GAMES AND FOLK DANCES

Singing games and folk dances may contribute to children's musical development in that they dramatize and lend meaning to the text of a song. Some children who have not found their singing voices, for example, may be drawn to music through this type of activity. In addition, this activity contributes to the development of bodily coordination and is another desirable means of releasing the classroom tensions that build up during the day. Singing games are appropriate to the objectives of both the primary and intermediate grades, while folk dances are utilized primarily in intermediate grades.

Before teaching the movements to a singing game, the teacher should make sure that the students know the song well, so that they will be able better to concentrate their attention on the movements. Whenever feasible, it is desirable to move the students from the classroom to some larger area, such as the school gymnasium, so that they won't be hampered in their movements. When this is possible, the entire class may participate in the activity. In schools where such an alternate location is not available, and the activities must be held within the confines of the classroom, other approaches must be used. For some singing games involving simpler movements, the class may participate in the aisles between the seats. If this procedure is unfeasible, then only part of the class will be able to participate in the rhythmic activity, while the remainder of the group sing the song. This approach is sometimes justified anyway, because it is not easy to concentrate on certain rhythmic movements while singing. In classrooms where only limited space is available, many difficulties can arise when too many students participate at one time. A good procedure is for the class to "take turns" in doing the various activities.

It is generally best for the teacher to demonstrate the games or dances and lead the class through the routine. This approach is preferable to only a verbal explanation, which is often relatively meaningless. In this case, a demonstration is worth far more than any well-chosen words.

A variety of singing games may be found in the basic music series. Directions for these songs are usually given at the bottom of the page or in the teacher's manual. Other sources include record albums of selected singing games and folk dances.[13]

Cincinnati Public Schools

Folk games necessitate that children listen carefully to the rhythm of the music.

Folk dances may also make a valuable contribution to teaching rhythm to intermediate-grade children. The dances, however, are generally more complicated and involved than singing games. Classroom teachers and music specialists, therefore, should not attempt to introduce such activities without adequate knowledge and experience with the dances and an understanding of the best ways of presenting them. In this phase of school activities teachers would do well to consult and cooperate with the physical education specialist, who generally has had specialized training in this area.

13 See, for example, *Singing Games and Folk Dances* (Bowmar Records), Albums 1–6.

Classroom teachers may wish to include folk dances as a part of the study of a particular social-studies unit or topic. They frequently are utilized as a part of the culminating portion of a unit, and perhaps are presented as an assembly program for the school. In such cases, the physical education instructor may teach the dances, with the classroom teacher assuming the responsibility of arranging for appropriate costumes and relating the cultural aspects of the dance to the unit being studied.[14]

Topics for Discussion

1. What does internalization of rhythm mean, and why is it important?

2. Formulate a sequence of concepts about *rhythm* that moves from the general to the specific or from the simple to the complex.

3. Discuss the various types of musical accompaniment that can be used for rhythmic activities. For what type of activity would each be most appropriate?

4. How can the classroom teacher encourage the awkward or uncoordinated child to enjoy and participate in rhythmic activities?

5. In what ways does participation in singing games and folk dances contribute to children's musical development?

Suggestions for Further Study

ARNOFF, FRANCES WEBBER, *Music and Young Children.* New York: Holt, Rinehart & Winston, 1969.

BROWN, MARGARET, and BETTY K. SOMMER, *Movement Education: Its Evolution and a Modern Approach.* Reading, Massachusetts: Addison-Wesley Publishing Co., Inc., 1969.

CLEMENS, JAMES R., *Invitation to Rhythm.* Dubuque, Iowa: Wm. C. Brown, 1962.

COPLAND, AARON, *What To Listen For In Music.* New York: New American Library, 1957, chapter 4.

[14] See Ruth L. Murray, *Dance in Elementary Education* (New York: Harper & Row, 1953), chapters 9–12.

DOLL, EDNA, and MARY JARMAN NELSON, *Rhythms Today*. Morristown, N.J.: Silver Burdett Company, 1965.

DRIVER, ANN, *Music and Movement*. London: Oxford University Press, 1947.

FINDLAY, ELSA, *Rhythm and Movement, Applications of Dalcroze Eurhythmics*. Evanston, Ill.: Summy-Birchard Company, 1971.

FLEMING, GLADYS ANDREWS, *Creative Rhythmic Movement: Boys and Girls Dancing*. Englewood Cliffs, N.J.: Prentice-Hall, 1976.

GARY, CHARLES, ed., *The Study of Music in the Elementary School—A Conceptual Approach*. Washington, D.C.: Music Educators National Conference, 1967.

GERI, FRANK H., *Illustrated Games and Rhythms for Children: Primary Grades*. Englewood Cliffs, N.J.: Prentice-Hall, 1955.

HOOD, MARGUERITE, *Teaching Rhythm and Using Classroom Instruments*. Englewood Cliffs, N.J.: Prentice-Hall, 1970.

HOOD, MARGUERITE V., and E. J. SCHULTZ, *Learning Music Through Rhythm*. Boston: Ginn, 1949.

HUGHES, DOROTHY, *Rhythmic Games and Dances*. New York: American Book Company, 1942.

HUMPHREYS, LOUISE, and JERROLD ROSS, *Interpreting Music Through Movement*. Englewood Cliffs, N.J.: Prentice-Hall, 1964.

KRAUSE, RICHARD, *Play Activities for Boys and Girls*. New York: McGraw-Hill, 1957, chapters 7 and 8.

———, *A Pocket Guide of Folk and Square Dances and Singing Games for the Elementary School*. Englewood Cliffs, N.J.: Prentice-Hall, 1966.

LANDIS, BETH, and POLLY CARDER, *The Eclectic Curriculum In American Music Education: Contributions of Dalcroze, Kodály, and Orff*. Washington, D.C.: Music Educators National Conference, 1972.

LA SALLE, DOROTHY, *Rhythms and Dances for Elementary Schools* (rev. ed.). New York: A. S. Barnes & Company, 1951.

LATCHAW, MARJORIE, and JEAN PYATT, *A Pocket Guide of Dance Activities*. Englewood Cliffs, N.J.: Prentice-Hall, 1958.

MACHLIS, JOSEPH, *The Enjoyment of Music* (3rd ed.). New York: Norton, 1970, chapter 5.

MONSOUR, SALLY, M. C. COHEN, and P. E. LINDRELL, *Rhythm in Music and Dance for Children*. Belmont, Calif.: Wadsworth, 1968.

MURRAY, RUTH L., *Dance in Elementary Education*. New York: Harper & Row, 1953.

MYNATT, CONSTANCE, and BERNARD KAIMAN, *Folk Dancing: For Students and Teachers*. Dubuque, Iowa: Wm. C. Brown Company, Publishers, 1969.

NASH, GRACE C., *Rhythmic Speech Ensembles* (Music with Children Series). Scottsdale, Ariz.: Swartwout Enterprizes, 1966.

———, *Teacher's Manual* (Music with Children Series). Scottsdale: Swartwout Enterprises, 1967.

———, *Verses and Movement* (Music with Children Series). Scottsdale: Swartwout Enterprises, 1967.

RICHARDS, MARY HELEN, *Threshold to Music*. San Francisco: Fearon Publishers, Inc., 1964.

SAFFRAN, ROSANNA B., *First Book of Creative Rhythms.* New York: Holt, Rinehart & Winston, 1963.

SHEEHY, EMMA D., *Children Discover Music and Dance.* New York: Holt, Rinehart & Winston, 1959, chapters 7 and 12.

Skip to My Lou, 17 Singing Games. New York: Girl Scouts of the United States of America.

TIPTON, GLADYS, and ELEANOR TIPTON, *Teacher's Guide: Adventures in Music.* Camden, N.J.: RCA Victor, 1961. (See guides for all albums, grades 1–6.)

TOBITT, JANET E., *Promenade All: A Compilation of Song-Dances.* Pleasantville, N.Y.: Janet E. Tobitt, 1947.

WEILAND, ADELL MARIE, *Music, Rhythms, and Games.* Chicago: Follet Publishing Company, 1953.

WILSON, HARRY R., and BEATRICE A. HUNT, *Sing and Dance.* Minneapolis, Minn.: Schmitt, Hall & McCreary Company, 1945.

Films and Filmstrips[15]

Building Children's Personalities With Creative Dancing (University of California), film no. 5844, college.

Discovering Rhythm (United World Films, Inc.), elementary (pre-school to grade 2).

Let's Begin With the Best (EMC Corporation). Filmstrip, sound, elementary.

Rhythm Is Everywhere (Carl F. Mahnke Productions), b&w, 11 minutes, elementary.

Rhythm Instruments and Movements (Encyclopaedia Britannica Films), b&w, 11 minutes, elementary/college.

Rhythm and Percussion (Encyclopaedia Britannica Films), b&w, 12 minutes, elementary/college.

[15] For addresses of producers and distributors of educational films and filmstrips, see the Appendix, pp. 287–288.

chapter 6

HARMONY, POLYPHONY, TEXTURE, AND PART-SINGING

Harmony results from the simultaneous sounding of two or more pitches, and its study helps one to understand the chordal or vertical organization of music. Harmony, in another sense, is the relationship between chords and their progression from one to another. Harmony adds depth and perspective to the music and enhances the melodic line. Polyphony refers to the horizontal organization of sounds or pitches, where the composer gives first consideration to the interweaving or interrelationship of several musical lines. Rounds and canons are simple examples of music conceived horizontally rather than vertically. In the study of music, the term texture is frequently encountered, and, like a piece of fabric, it refers to the "weave" of the musical structure, which may be harmonically or polyphonically conceived; it may be described, for example, as light and thin, or heavy and weighty; it may be full and sonorous, or graceful and embellished with decorative figures.

This chapter, then, identifies concepts of harmony and polyphony and suggests experiences designed to develop children's understanding of these elements of music. Children should be helped to utilize this knowledge so that it not only enriches their listening experiences, but also develops their ability to interpret musical scores and to sing and play in parts. Through their actual participation in singing and playing harmony, children can more fully understand its structure.

CONCEPTS OF HARMONY, POLYPHONY, AND TEXTURE
FOR K–6 AND ACTIVITIES
AND SKILLS FOR THEIR
COMPREHENSION

Concepts

Activities and Skills

[The long-range goal of all activities is the development of children's musicality, i.e., *increased sensitivity and responsiveness to music.* Following each activity, the effectiveness of instruction should be evaluated. Concepts need to be reinforced through varied, but similar activities; therefore, the teacher must determine what students really have learned, as this is the critical factor in determining the specific nature of subsequent experiences.]

K–1

Harmony creates interest (in contrast to a single melodic line).

To develop their awareness of multiple sounds children should have varied listening experiences, ranging from piano and Autoharp accompaniments to choral singing. In addition, teachers should help young children to create their own harmony by providing them with selected resonator bells, which they may use as an accompaniment to specific songs. For example, the round "Row, Row, Row Your Boat" may be accompanied with a single resonator bell—C or D, depending on the pitch desired (see p. 136). Later experiences may involve the use of two or more pitches, with two or more children each playing a particular pitch, as directed by the teacher.

Grade 2

Harmony results when two or more tones are sounded at the same time.

Continue to create harmony by playing two or more selected tones on the resonator bells as a song accompaniment. Initially the teacher will more than likely find it necessary to "direct" each child as to when to play his or her respective pitch so as to "fit" the harmony. The opportunity should not be unnecessarily delayed, however, for individual children to select the pitches that, according to their own ears, sound the most appropriate for particular chords or measures in a song.

Children should be encouraged to play accompaniments on the Autoharp, beginning with songs which need only two chords (I, V⁷). Provide three children with separate resonator bells (C, E, and G, or

B. F. Kitching & Co., Inc.

Melody Bells, and other mallet-played instruments, provide a desirable individual experience with tonal relationships.

those of any other chord). Ask them to play their tones separately, then together, and to express their feeling about the effect.

The orchestra bells (sometimes called melody bells) and resonator bells resemble a xylophone in the arrangement of their tone bars. All are played by striking the tone bars with a small mallet. Some manufacturers of orchestra bells have painted the bars black and white to simulate the arrangement of the whole and half steps of the piano keyboard. The resonator bells are unique in that each tone bar may be removed from its position in the carrying case and played by individual children. Perhaps the easiest type of instrument to play is one involving a simple muscular movement. Instruments of this type, therefore, and resonator bells in particular, are highly suitable for young children to use. The range of musical experiences with such instruments, however, may vary from the simple to moderately complex.

Beginning experiences with these instruments generally involve playing only one pitch, usually on the first beat of each measure as an accompaniment to a song. Rounds, sung in unison, are particularly adaptable for this purpose. For example:

Row, Row, Row Your Boat

In the example, "Row, Row, Row Your Boat," the symbol X indicates when the bar should be struck. In initial experiences, only one bar or bell should be struck, in this case, C. Later, as children become more adept, they may play the actual pitches of the melody on the appropriate bells, indicated at the beginning of each measure. To provide a variety of materials, the teacher may wish to "arrange" certain songs by marking such tones in the children's books, or, in some cases, by writing the song on the chalkboard so that all may see.[1]

The imaginative teacher will find many uses for these instruments. As children become more adept they may play entire melodies, usually as an accompaniment to class singing. For variety, the bells may be played on one phrase and the children may sing the next. For ear-training, one child may play a short motive while another listens and then attempts to imitate what was sounded.

An ostinato is a musical figure which is repeated to provide a song accompaniment, and children's experience with harmony may be enhanced through the use of ostinati. The Orff instruments are particularly adaptable for this purpose. For example, with the song "Hot Cross Buns"

the following ostinato may be played on the alto xylophone.

[1] It is suggested that music written on the chalkboard for this purpose be in the public domain and not covered by copyright.

Initially, it is helpful if the bars surrounding C and G are removed, leaving only the two pitches for a child to play, and thus minimizing any confusion about the use of the two mallets.

The following ostinati will also be found to be effective accompaniments when played on the instruments indicated.[2]

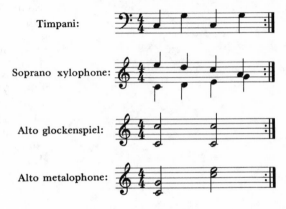

Over a period of time all the children in a given class should have the opportunity to play the different ostinati. A single ostinato may be used as an accompaniment, or ostinati may be combined using as many instruments as are available, with those children singing who are not playing instruments.

For other ostinati, see pages 261–262 in the section on the Carl Orff approach. All these ostinati are only examples, and as children gain familiarity and experience, they should be encouraged to devise their own patterns.

Different chords are played to accompany the singing of songs.

When the piano is used for accompanying singing, children are

2 From Lawrence Wheeler and Lois Raebeck, *Orff and Kodály Adapted for the Elementary School* (Dubuque, Iowa: Wm. C. Brown, Publishers, 1972), pp. 19–20. Used by permission.

generally aware of its harmonic support. Their awareness can be heightened, however, if instead of singing they will hum the melody and direct their attention to the chord changes underlying the melody.

The teacher may wish to play the chord progression I, IV, V⁷, I (or any other progression) with the duration of each chord being a half or whole note at a moderate tempo. Children should be asked to listen carefully for the chord changes and then to verbalize their impressions.

Following this activity, children should have the opportunity to listen for "chord changes" in orchestral music. A suggested recording appropriate for this purpose is: "Bydlo" from *Pictures at an Exhibition* by Modest Moussorgsky (*Adventures in Music,* Grade 2, RCA Victor).

Grade 3

When several pitches are sounded together, we hear a chord.

Let children experiment with a number of different resonator bells, beginning with C, E, and G. See if they can discover other bells that make a similar chord sound (i.e., a major triad). Help the class identify the chords they discover, and suggest that they notate them on the chalkboard. Then ask the children to verbalize the similarities and differences.

Chords change to fit the melody.

Write on the chalkboard the melodic line of a song that moves chordwise, and play all the tones in a measure separately, then together, so that children can begin to see (and hear) the relationship between a given melody and its implied harmony.

Examples of songs suitable for this purpose are:

"Love Somebody"—American folksong (*Exploring Music,* Book 3).

"The Speckled Bird," Finnish folksong (*Discovering Music Together,* Book 3).

"Sweet Betsy From Pike," American folksong (*Discovering Music Together,* Book 3).

"Sandy Land," American singing game (*Exploring Music,* Book 3).

Harmony can be made with instruments or voices.

Children should have the opportunity to listen to many types of orchestral and choral literature to develop an understanding of the different combinations of voices and instruments that can make harmony.

Singing chants is one way to make harmony.

The use of chants based upon simple tonal patterns may enhance the singing of particular songs and serves as an excellent preparation for later experiences in part-singing. Easy chants may be utilized with children beginning in the latter part of the third grade, depending, of course, upon their aptitude and previous musical experience. Very easy chants, involving only a few pitches, are particularly adaptable for use with children with a limited vocal range. In singing chants, the class should be divided into two equal groups, with each group alternately having the opportunity to sing the chant or second part.

While a variety of chants may be located in various books, the teacher may wish to devise his or her own. Songs with a minimum of harmonic changes are the most adaptable for such purposes. Rounds that need only one chord are most appropriate for the initial experiences. An extremely simple, but effective, chant may be devised by having half the class sing a pattern on the first degree of the scale (*do*), while the other half sings the melody of the song. It is often desirable to use this pattern as a brief "introduction," so that the pitch may be more firmly established in the children's minds. For example, the following tonal and rhythmic pattern may be used as a chant with the familiar round "Row, Row, Row Your Boat."

Row, Row, Row Your Boat

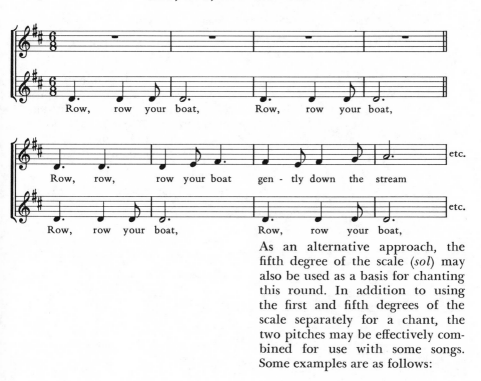

As an alternative approach, the fifth degree of the scale (*sol*) may also be used as a basis for chanting this round. In addition to using the first and fifth degrees of the scale separately for a chant, the two pitches may be effectively combined for use with some songs. Some examples are as follows:

Three Blind Mice

Are You Sleeping?

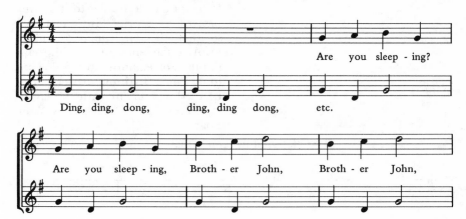

A descending eighth-note pattern on the pitches *do, ti, la, sol* provides a simple, but interesting, chant for such songs as "Mac-Donald's Farm" and "Lightly Row," as well as many others.

In devising a chant for a particular song, the teacher will want to

MacDonald's Farm

consider the selection of appropriate words for the melodic and rhythmic pattern. Generally, the use of some key word in the text may be adapted for this purpose. As indicated in the round "Are You Sleeping," the words "ding, ding, dong" are appropriate to the melodic pattern of *do, sol, do,* and may be said to simulate ringing bells. Likewise, in the song "MacDonald's Farm," the syllables "Ee-i-o—," also taken from the text, are easily adaptable to the descending eighth-note pattern.

The above suggestions are made for the teacher who wishes to devise simple chants for children's initial experiences with harmony. Certainly many other tonal combinations—some much more intricate—are possible and should be utilized. Teachers will find it highly profitable to devise some chants for favorite songs that are appropriate to each group's background and maturity.

The Autoharp is still another way to make harmony.

Children should be provided with the experience of observing the chord symbols indicated above the notation of particular songs and playing an appropriate harmonic accompaniment on the Autoharp.

The Autoharp is played by pressing a button on a bar, to produce the desired chord, and then stroking the strings with a pick or the fingers. Various types of picks may be used, each resulting in a different type of sound—a felt pick for soft, subdued tones, and a plastic pick for louder, more brilliant sounds. There are slots cut in the damper felt on each bar, allowing only the desired strings in the chord to vibrate when the bar is depressed. For example, in the C-major chord, the slots are positioned above most of the C, E, and G strings; when the bar is depressed and the strings stroked, these strings will vibrate while all the others are damped. Autoharps are available in three basic models: the five-bar, the twelve-bar, and the fifteen-bar. The five-bar model is suitable for use with younger children and with simpler music in which only a few chords are needed. With the twelve- and fifteen-bar Autoharps, more chords are available and the player is less restricted in choice of chord and key. The twelve- and fifteen-bar models are recommended for use with intermediate-grade children.

Autoharps provide an effective accompaniment to the singing of

Cincinnati Public Schools

Using the Autoharp in accompanying songs provides a desirable aural experience with harmony.

many songs; often, certain songs in the basic series include the letter names of the appropriate chords with the melodic line of the song. Generally, the player strokes the Autoharp on each beat of the music, sometimes on every other beat, and occasionally on only the first beat of each measure, depending, of course, upon the tempo and mood of the song. Usually, chords are not changed more often than once a measure. Simpler songs, recommended for use with young children, may require no more than two chords, and thus the instrument is easily played by the beginning student.[3]

Grade 4

In dialogue songs the voices answer each other as in a conversation.

In singing a dialogue song, the children are generaly divided into two groups, one group answering the questions or reiterating the statements made by the other. Thus a conversation or dialogue takes place. In dialogue songs, harmony does not occur except where one part briefly overlaps the other. The value of such songs is that they help to develop tonal awareness and vocal independence. Students must listen carefully to the singers in their own group, as well as to those in the other, if entrances and releases are to be precise. The "teamwork" involved in the effective singing of dialogue songs is one of the basic factors that contribute to their enjoyment.

The spiritual "Who Did?", shown here, is a particularly good example of a dialogue song. Teachers will find many other songs of this type in the basic song books for the intermediate grades.

[3] For a helpful educational film, see *The Autoharp* (Johnson Hunt Productions).

Who Did ?[4]

2. *Whale did,* Whale did, *Whale did,* Whale did,
   Whale did swallow Jo-Jo-Jo-Jo.
   Whale did, Whale did, *Whale did,* Whale did,
   Whale did swallow Jo-Jo-Jo-Jo.
   Whale did, Whale did, *Whale did,* Whale did,
   Whale did swallow Jo-Jo-Jo-Jo.
   Whale did swallow Jonah,
   Whale did swallow Jonah,
   Whale did swallow Jonah up.

Harmony is created when you sing a descant to a familiar song.

A descant is a countermelody, a "second" melody, that sounds above the regular melody to create harmony and enhance the tune. Descants may be sung by a selected group of voices or played

4 Used by permission of Silver Burdett Company.

on melody instruments. Recorders and other simple wind instruments are particularly appropriate for learning descants, with half the class playing, and the other half singing (and then alternating). Descants may enhance the effectiveness of many songs commonly used in the intermediate grades. They are particularly helpful as a preparation for part-singing. Simple descants may be introduced in the fourth grade and in some instances the latter part of the third grade, depending, of course, upon the children's aptitude and previous musical experience.

The Mockingbird Song[5]

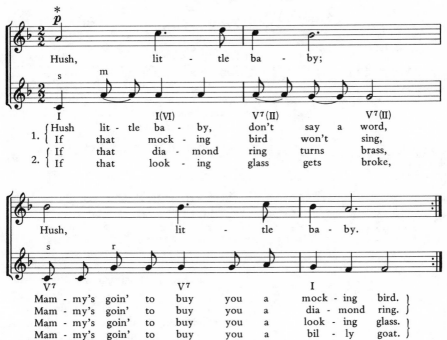

3. If that billy goat won't pull,
   Mammy's goin' to buy you a cart and bull.
   If that cart and bull turn over,
   Mammy's goin' to buy you a dog named Rover.

* Upper part may be sung, or played by a melody instrument.

5 Used by permission of Follett Publishing Company.

All Through the Night[6]

Loo_____ Loo loo loo loo

1. Sleep, my child, and peace at-tend thee   all   thro' the night,
2. While the moon her watch is keep-ing   all   thro' the night,

Loo_____ Loo loo loo loo

Guard - ian an - gels   God will send thee   all   thro' the night;
While   the wea - ry   world is sleep-ing   all   thro' the night,

Loo_____ Loo_____

Soft the drow-sy   hours are creep-ing, Hill and vale in   slum - ber steep-ing;
O'er thy spir - it   gen - tly steal-ing, Vi-sions of de - light re - veal-ing,

Loo_____ Loo loo loo loo.

Moth - er, here, her   watch is keep-ing   all   thro' the night.
Breathes a   pure and   ho - ly feel-ing   all   thro' the night.

Simple descants are included in most of the basic music series and may also be found in various other books.[7] A teacher who understands the harmonic structure of a particular song will find it relatively easy to devise a descant to meet the interests and needs of a particular class.

[6] Used by permission of American Book Company.
[7] For suggested descant books, see the listing on p. 177.

Singing rounds and canons is another way to make harmony.

Rounds and canons are a form of melodic imitation in which two or more parts enter in successive order. A round repeats from the beginning, and the point of imitation is always at the unison (rounds are sometimes called "circle canons"). A canon does not repeat and the point of imitation may be at the unison or at any other interval. Both are valuable in that they can provide relatively easy and satisfying musical experiences in which singers have the opportunity to hear the "interplay" of one part against another. A feeling for harmony may thus be developed and may result in a degree of independence in singing a different vocal line.

Children's success in singing rounds and canons depends, to a large extent, upon their familiarity with the "tune" and their ability to "hold" their respective parts. After children have had considerable experience, they will enjoy singing rounds in three or more parts; initially, however, it is suggested that they be limited to two parts. The following are some approaches to teaching rounds and canons in two parts.

1. The children may sing one part while the teacher sings the other.
2. One group may sing its part, while the other plays its part on one of the simple wind instruments.
3. Both groups may play their parts on simple wind instruments or on a combination of instruments, including melody bells, piano, and simple wind instruments.
4. Two groups of rhythm or per-

cussion instruments, each with a contrasting tonal quality, may be used. This approach, with each group playing the rhythm of the melody, brings out the rhythmic interplay of the parts.

5. Both groups may sing their respective parts.

At all times the teacher should make certain that the children know the melody sufficiently well before dividing them into singing groups, and that students in each group listen not only to themselves, but to the other voices as well. Children will benefit from singing rounds and canons only to the extent that they listen to the relationship between their part and the others.

"Lovely Evening" and "Old Texas" are examples of a round and a canon, respectively, that when sung in a smooth, flowing manner enable a child to sense more readily the relationship of one part to the others. It is suggested, for this reason, that a number of songs of this type be used, particularly in the children's early experiences with rounds and canons.

Lovely Evening

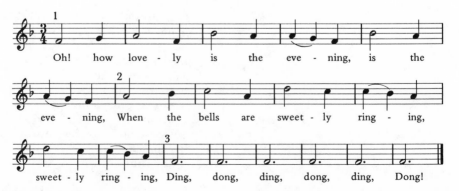

Oh! how love - ly is the eve - ning, is the eve - ning, When the bells are sweet - ly ring - ing, sweet - ly ring - ing, Ding, dong, ding, dong, ding, Dong!

Old Texas[8]

The Australian round "Kooka-burra" and the canon "The Alpha-bet" are sung in a more detached style and are particularly enjoy-able to children because of their humorous character. Many rounds and canons of this type should also be included in the children's reper-toire.

Kookaburra[9]

Koo - ka - bur - ra sits on an old gum tree,

Mer - ry, mer - ry king of the bush is he.

Laugh, Koo - ka - bur - ra, laugh, Koo - ka - bur - ra, Gay your life must be.

8 From *Silver Burdett Music,* Book 4 (Morristown, N.J.: Silver Burdett Company, 1974), p. 89. Used by permission.

9 From Janet E. Tobitt, *The Ditty Bag* (Pleasantville, N.Y., 1946). Used by permission.

The Alphabet[10]

While rounds and canons may be introduced to children as early as the third grade, they should be particularly emphasized at the fourth-grade level, with continuing experience in the fifth and sixth grades. A number of rounds and canons may be found in the basic music series for grades 4–6, and some other sources are listed at the end of this chapter.

[10] From Harry R. Wilson, *Rounds and Canons*. Used by permission of the publishers, Schmitt, Hall & McCreary Company.

The chord structure of certain songs is the same, therefore, they can be sung together to create harmony.

The value of singing two different songs simultaneously, i.e., combined songs, is primarily recreational; the activity does contribute in some degree to the development of a feeling for harmony, however, when it is a cooperative rather than a competitive affair. Before a class sings combined songs, the teacher should make sure that the students know each song reasonably well and that they understand the importance of listening carefully to the other group as well as to their own. The following are a number of pairs of songs that may be combined effectively, either with voices, instruments, or both.[11]

"Are You Sleeping"	"Three Blind Mice"
"The Farmer in the Dell"	"Three Blind Mice"
"Keep the Home Fires Burning"	"The Long, Long Trail"
"Old Folks at Home"	"Humoresque"
"Row, Row, Row Your Boat"	"Three Blind Mice"
"Solomon Levi"	"The Spanish Cavalier"
"Ten Little Indians"	"Skip to My Lou"
"Tipperary"	"Pack Up Your Troubles"

By writing out the notation of two songs on the chalkboard, children can "see" the "compatibility" of the two vocal lines.

Chords are built on line, line, line, or space, space, space.

Write the harmonization of a round on the chalkboard so that children can "see" the intervals that sound so "harmonious." Then, write a series of chords on lines or spaces and have children play them on the piano or the resonator bells.

Chords can be built on any step of the scale.

Write a C-major scale on the chalkboard and let children build chords on each scale step. Selected children should play the chords on the piano and express their preference as to those they would like to place in a chord progression or sequence.

11 For other combined songs, see Frederick Beckman, *Partner Songs* (Boston: Ginn, 1958) and *More Partner Songs* (Boston: Ginn, 1962).

A chord is named for the note of the scale on which it is built.

Children will understand that musical sounds, like persons, must have names. Each chord may be called by either the letter name of the pitch on which it is built, or by the number of the scale step on which it is built.

Chords built on the first (I), fourth (IV), and fifth (V) degrees of the scale are particularly useful.

Through experiences in playing the Autoharp, children will discover that two or three chords are often adequate to provide an effective accompaniment. When they compare the letter names of the chords given for specific songs with the scale steps of the songs, they will also discover that these chords are most frequently built on the first, fourth, and fifth scale steps (I, IV, and V chords). Children may also experiment with producing chords vocally as a means of providing song accompaniments (see p. 159). Through experimenting with harmony, and specifically by playing the Autoharp, children will discover that most songs begin and end on the harmony of the I chord (tonic chord) and that the V chord (dominant chord) is next in frequency of use.

When in the intermediate grades children have learned to produce chords by singing and to play chords on the resonator bells, they should also be taught to play the I, IV, and V chords at the piano (treble clef, right hand only). These chords may be used separately as an accompaniment to singing or may be combined with the other instruments. Learning to play these three chords on the piano serves to reinforce concepts learned through other media, and also lays a foundation for future experiences with the piano.

With only this minimal background in piano, students might experiment on their pianos at home and endeavor to create original tunes. Children can become fascinated by the combinations of chords that they can devise, and as a result, they often develop a desire to notate their "masterpieces" for posterity. When students possess this desire they are usually more receptive to learning the mechanics of music notation.

In addition to learning to play the I, IV, and V chords on the piano, children should have the opportunity to learn the basic I, IV, V chord progression on the ukulele and guitar.

Fretted instruments, the ukulele and the guitar in particular, have particular values for use in the music class. The ukulele, although generally thought of as a recreational instrument only, is valuable in that it is relatively easy to play. Whenever possible, it is desirable for the school to purchase several of these instruments for instructional purposes, so that young children may have the opportunity to experiment with them and to play different chords. To illustrate the simplicity of ukulele fingering, the positions for three basic chords are given below. On each diagram, the

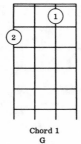

Chord 1
G

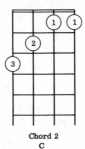

Chord 2
C

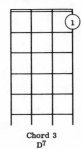

Chord 3
D7

vertical lines indicate the strings and the horizontal lines the frets. Each circle in the diagram indicates at which fret the string should be depressed and the number refers to the fingers in the left hand that should be used.

After children have become familiar with the fingering patterns for the above three chords, they should accompany the singing of specific songs. Successful early experiences will create interest and a desire to learn how to play other chords. This information should be available to the student in the form of a basic instruction book.[12]

Ft. Collins (Colorado) Public Schools

Guitar classes are a popular means of teaching children functional harmony.

[12] Various instruction books are available through local music stores. In addition to finger charts some publications also include photos of actual hand positions. See, for example, Harry Reser, *Picture Chords for Standard Ukulele* (New York: Remick Music Corp., 1960).

The guitar is more difficult to play than is the ukulele; children in the intermediate grades, however, will be more motivated to play it than they will the ukulele. It is desirable for classrooms to have available several guitars with which children can experiment and learn to play simple accompaniments. Initially, songs should be chosen that need only one or two chords. It is also highly recommended that teachers develop some facility with this instrument and play accompaniments for selected songs. A degree of authenticity is created when the guitar is used to accompany certain types of folksongs—songs of the West and of Latin-America, in particular.

Fingerings are given below for the primary chords (I, IV, and V) in C major and G major and in their related minor keys, A minor and E minor. As in the diagram on page 155, the vertical lines indicate the strings and the horizontal lines the frets; whereas the ukulele has only four strings, the guitar has six.

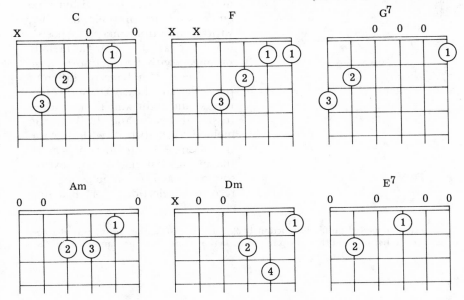

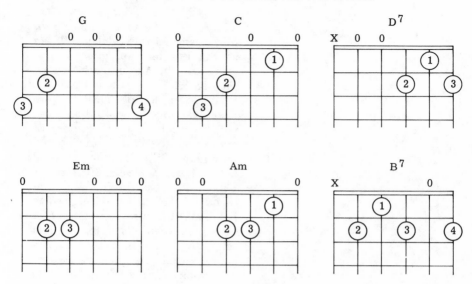

Note that, as with the ukulele, each circle indicates where the string is to be depressed and the numbers inside the circles refer to the fingers of the left hand. An X over a string indicates that it is not to be played, and an O indicates an open string.[13]

Texture refers to the "weave" of the musical structure.

Children should be helped to identify and describe the texture of the music to which they listen. To guide students in their listening, various questions may be posed: Do you hear only a single melody or music with two or more musical lines? How many different parts do you hear? Does the texture sound light and thin, or does it sound heavy and full? Is the melody embellished with decorative figures? What do you hear in the music that makes the texture sound heavier? Some suggested recorded selections for listening

---

[13] For suggested guitar instruction books, see the list at the end of this chapter, p. 178; for a list of publishers of guitar instruction books, see the Appendix, p. 287.

are: "Romanze" from *Eine kleine Nachtmusik* by Wolfgang A. Mozart (*Adventures in Music*, Grade 4, vol. 1, RCA Victor), and "Desert Water Hole" from *Death Valley Suite* by Ferde Grofé (*Adventures in Music*, Grade 4, vol. 1, RCA Victor).

Grade 5

Singing chordal accompaniments is still another way to make harmony.

The singing of chordal accompaniments to familiar songs is not only an enjoyable and satisfying musical activity, but it is also an excellent preparation for singing three-part songs.

The following chord progression may be written on the chalkboard, and each of three previously determined groups asked first to identify and then to sing the syllables in its part. In this particular case, it generally is best for each group to sing its part separately. Next, the teacher may give the pitches for the first chord and then ask the class to sing each chord it is pointed to.

	I	IV	V⁷	I
1st part:	do,	do,	ti,	do.
2nd part:	sol,	la,	sol,	sol.
3rd part:	mi,	fa,	fa,	mi.

Since chords in a song will not always occur in the precise order of the sequence written on the chalkboard, the teacher should then have the class sing the chords in varying sequences. It is also desirable in this practice to prescribe a certain meter and establish a particular tempo. The following chord progression might be sung by the class as the teacher points to the three basic chords written on the chalkboard: I, I, IV, I, I, I, V^7, I.

After the class has had a reasonable amount of experience in singing chord progressions in this manner, chords may then be used as an accompaniment for selected songs. The song melody may be played on an instrument, or a small group of students may be asked to sing it. The teacher may use one of several procedures: pointing to the appropriate chord on the chalkboard or to the column of syllables under the chords, or indicating the appropriate chord by holding up one, four, or five fingers—each signal representing the corresponding chord.

Resonator bells may be used to supplement and clarify the teaching of sung chords; that is, the I, IV, and V chords in C major may be written on the chalkboard, and the bells for the pitches in these chords may be distributed to various children in the class. Each bell is imprinted with its respective pitch, and individual children can identify their bells and then locate their pitches in one (or more) of the chords on the chalkboard. After all the children understand the relationship of their pitches to the chords, they will strike their particular bells as the teacher points to specific chords on the chalkboard. In this manner the resonator bells may be used to accompany singing or to provide tonal security for singing chords. After children have had considerable experience playing chords under the teacher's direction, they may be encouraged to listen carefully and decide where in the music their particular chords may be appropriately played. Special mallets are available for playing three bells simultaneously, and older children may be assigned a particular *chord*. They may select the tone bars for their chords from the carrying case and then determine where in the music their chords may be appropriately used. Experiences giving children the opportunity to make individual judgments may contribute substantially to their musical development.

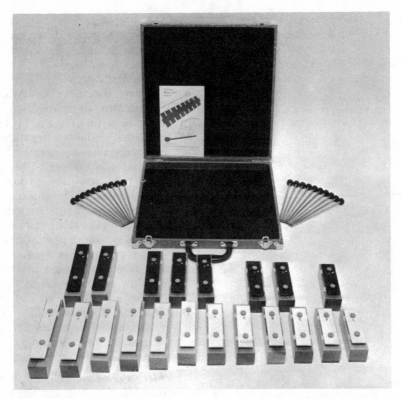

B. F. Kitching & Co., Inc.

A set of individual resonator bells, with carrying case and mallets. Bells may be arranged in the case and played as a set of melody or orchestra bells, or they may be removed from the case for individual use.

Harmonizing the final cadence of a song enhances the ending.

Harmonizing the final cadence of a song sung in unison can enhance its singing, as well as develop an interest in harmony that will lead to further experiences in part-singing. After selecting an appropriate song, the teacher may teach by rote either a two-part or a three-part harmonization of the final cadence. Initially, it is desirable to make the harmonizations as simple as possible and to present the cadence in only two parts. For example, the final two measures in "America" might be sung as follows:

As students gain experience in this activity, they may be encouraged to attempt to harmonize by ear their own song endings. With the guidance of the teacher they should also endeavor to notate the parts on the chalkboard. This experience may lead the group to an examination of the endings of various two-part songs. In many they will observe that the last two pitches of the upper, or soprano, part is often either *re, do,* or *ti, do,* and that the pitches in the lower, or alto, part may often be identified as *sol, do,* or *fa, mi.* Having analyzed a number of songs, the students will be better prepared to harmonize, and subsequently notate, endings for other songs.

After varied experiences with two-part singing, the teacher may suggest that the class harmonize certain song endings in three, rather than two parts. For example, the following version of the final cadence of the familiar song "All Through the Night" may be used in preparation for three-part singing.

Chords for harmonizing may be determined by examining the melody to see which chord includes most of the pitches in the measure.

When children hear a "wrong" chord used in a piano accompaniment they often "wince" because of the disagreeable (or unusual) sound. This response indicates a level of discrimination which should be even further developed by a knowledge of why certain chords are more appropriate in a given measure than others. Children should identify the pitches in a given measure of a selected song, and the teacher or a child may play them all together. Do these notes sound like a chord? If so, what chord do the notes spell out? Could another chord be used instead? Which chord sounds best? Through these types of experiences children may develop the ability to examine a melodic line and select appropriate chords to play on the Autoharp or the piano, depending on their level of musical maturity.

A harmony part may be created by singing or playing one or more tones of the accompanying chords.

Children should be encouraged to create a second harmony part by singing or playing. Initially, they should play the roots of the chords indicated in their song books on the xylophone, melody bells, or resonator bells. They should then be encouraged to sing a harmony part based on these chord roots or on other tones in the specified chords. Encourage the class to try singing both above and below the regular melody.

Because the root of a chord is fundamental and is the easiest part of the chord to hear, the singing of chord roots is an excellent experience for children in the intermediate grades. Initially, the teacher, as a means of introducing the procedure, may sing or play the chord roots on the piano while the class sings the song in unison. After discussing briefly with the class what was done, the teacher may ask the class to write the syllable names of the chord roots under the text of the song. (Generally, one syllable for each measure is adequate.) The entire class may then sing the syllables as the teacher plays the melody on the piano or another instrument. After this, several approaches are possible. The class may divide into two equal groups, one singing the chord roots with syllables while the other group sings the melody of the song; or a group may play the melody on instruments while most of the class sings the syllables.

As students gradually gain a feeling for harmony and for the relationship of one part to another, they will enjoy harmonizing familiar songs by ear. This is highly important to the development of the aural sense. The teacher should utilize harmonizing in the classroom and should also encourage the children to practice it whenever the opportunity provides itself (for example, at Boy Scout and Girl Scout sings). Students who develop the ability to harmonize songs "by ear" will learn more readily to translate the printed symbols on the page into actual harmony.

Songs that have a minimum of chord changes should be selected for the initial experiences. For example, in the song "Oh Where, Oh Where Has My Little Dog Gone?" an effective second part may be created by singing the pitches *do, sol,* and at the final cadence, *sol, la, ti, do.* This approach to harmonizing obviously grows out of the experience of singing chord roots and acts harmonically as a bass part (even though the voices—soprano and alto—are unchanged). Teachers will also want to help children create an alto part using largely thirds and sixths, with other intervals as passing tones.

After a reasonable amount of experience in harmonizing songs by ear, the class should endeavor, with the teacher's guidance, to notate properly their second, harmonizing, parts.

Two-part songs in basic music series are only visual representations of harmony similar to that which students have experienced, created, and notated.

Two-part songs may be introduced to students in the fifth grade, providing they have previously had adequate aural experiences with harmony, including the singing of dialogue songs, chants, descants, rounds and canons, combined songs, harmonized song endings, and harmonizations by "ear."

In addition, they should have ample opportunity to create their "own" harmony both with instruments and with voices. It is most important that the teacher encourage students to notate their creative endeavors, for at this critical point they can implement their previous learning about harmony and take a giant stride toward a fuller understanding of and sensitivity to harmony. When this occurs, the reading of part-songs will be a more meaningful and natural experience, and can be undertaken without such a struggle. (For a further discussion of part-singing and procedures for teaching part-songs, see the section at the end of this chapter, pp. 172–176.)

[The following starred (*) concepts are more advanced than others and should be introduced only to motivated students with an adequate background.]

*Harmony parts use different intervals, including thirds, sixths, fourths, and fifths.

In examining the notation of part-songs, children will discover the most frequently used intervals between parts to be thirds and sixths, with the fourths and fifths often occurring as passing tones between the thirds and sixths.

Music often begins and ends on the harmony of the tonic or I chord.

Through various experiences, children will discover that the tonic or I chord evokes a feeling of finality and repose, and that a song will usually end on this harmony. Music may also often begin with the tonic chord, but not always. On what chord does the song end? Does it begin on a I chord? If not, what is the chord?

*Chords sometimes are arranged in changed positions called inversions.

Distribute the resonator bells C, E, and G to three different children with instructions to play their bells when directed. Ask each child to play his or her pitch, notate it on the chalkboard, and

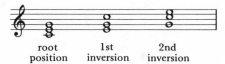

root position   1st inversion   2nd inversion

then label each tone by its letter name and by its other designation, i.e., root, third, fifth. The teacher should identify this as the C-major chord in *root* position. Next, give a resonator bell an octave above the first C distributed (third-space C) to another child, and then ask the children with the three highest-pitched bells to play their tones, then write the pitches on the chalkboard and designate them by letter name and by part in the chord. Identify this as a C-major chord in first inversion. Similarly, provide another child with a bell for the E an octave above the first E and ask the children who now have the three highest-pitched bells to play their respective tones singly, then together, and then write the pitches on the chalkboard. Again ask the students to label their pitches by letter name and part in the chord, and to identify the chord as a C-major chord in second inversion. Invite selected children to play chords on the piano in root position, first inversion, and second inversion. What effect do inverted chords have?

A major triad is made up of two intervals—a major third and a minor third, with the major third on the bottom.

By constructing intervals on the chalkboard, and by referring to the piano keyboard, help the class to see that the interval of a major third has two whole tones and that the interval of the minor third has one and a half tones.

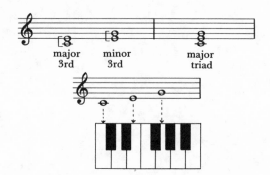

Tone clusters are chords made up of tones that are very close together—primarily whole steps and half steps.

The song "Traffic" by Francis J. Pyle (*The Magic of Music*, Book 6) uses tone clusters in the piano accompaniment—one to be played on the white keys by the left hand, one on the black keys by the right hand. After singing this song (with accompaniment), children will have a concept of tone clusters and should be encouraged to experiment on the piano keyboard, playing tone clusters on both the white and black keys and in various rhythm patterns. Encourage the class to notate their "new" sounds.

Grade 6

*Chords built on the first, fourth, and fifth degrees of the major scale are called major chords, and those built on the second, third, and sixth scale degrees are minor chords.

Write triads on the chalkboard based on each step of the C-major scale. Help children to analyze the I chord as comprising a major third (two whole steps) and a minor third (a step and a half). By analyzing all the chords in this way, the children will discover that the major chords (I, IV, and V) have the major third on the bottom and the minor third on the top, and that the minor chords (II, III, and VI) have the minor third on the bottom and the major third on the top. How might a minor chord be changed into a major chord? How might a major chord be changed into a minor chord? What intervals are in the VII chord (called a diminished chord)? Through listening and analyzing, children will come to recognize the difference in sound between major and minor chords.

"Homophonic" refers to a vertical organization of music, specifically, to a melody supported by a chordal accompaniment.

Children's initial experiences in part-singing will be with a melody supported by a second part, one primarily in thirds and sixths with some connecting intervals. Both parts will move mostly together, and, therefore, children will have a basis for understanding any discussion of homophonic music, which should be reinforced through various listening experiences. The following orchestral selections are suggested: "Saraband" from *Suite for Strings* by Arcangelo Corelli (*Adventures in Music*, Grade 6, vol. 2, RCA Victor), and "Spanish Dance No. 1" from *La Vida Breve* by Manuel de Falla (*Adventures in Music*, Grade 6, vol. 1, RCA Victor).

"Polyphonic" refers to music organized in a linear manner, specifically, to a combination of two or more melodic lines each having individual significance.

Having the class sing a familiar round or canon is a good activity prior to introducing the term *polyphonic*. It is helpful if the teacher will write the notation on the chalkboard so the children can see as well as hear the interrelationships of the various parts.

The actual experience of performing music in a linear manner will lead appropriately to listening and studying compositions written in this style. A suggested composition for listening and study is:

"Farandole" from *L'Arlésienne* Suite No. 2 by Georges Bizet (*Adventures in Music*, Grade 6, vol. 1, RCA Victor).

In this selection, the first main theme (in D minor) begins as follows:

The second time this theme is heard it is played as a canon. (If desired, the class may be divided into two groups and at this point sing along with the recorded music.) The second main theme is a gay French folk tune (in D major) which begins as follows:

Children should listen for the return of theme 1, which is interrupted by phrases of theme 2 in a type of musical dialogue. Finally, both themes may be heard together in the manner of a song and descant.

Themes 1 and 2:

After the complete composition has been heard, the class may be divided into two groups, with one singing (or playing on appropriate instruments) theme 1, and the other singing or playing theme 2. A discussion may follow on the "uniqueness" of each melody and how they both "fit" together as do partner songs.[14]

Interesting chords may be devised by adding additional thirds. The resulting chords are named according to the interval formed by the outside voices (ninth, eleventh, thirteenth)

Ask specific children to come to the chalkboard and add an additional third to each chord, beginning with a triad. Have children identify the name of each chord by determining the interval formed by the outside voices. Discuss the unique sound of each chord.

Some composers may write music with two or more different tonal centers sounding together (polytonality).

To introduce the idea of polytonality, ask two children to play on the melody bells a simple tune, for example, "Hot Cross Buns," in two different keys—C and B♭, first separately and then together. Experiment also in other keys. Next, introduce to the class the choral composition "Psalm 67" by Charles Ives (Associated Music Publishers, No. A-274). First play on the piano the treble parts, which are in C major, and then the men's parts, which are in G minor; then play a phrase or two of all voice-parts together. This will prepare the class somewhat for listening to the recorded version of the entire work (Charles Ives: *Music for Chorus,* Columbia MS 6921).

Another polytonal work suggested for listening is Darius Milhaud's *Scaramouche* Suite, first movement (London 6434).

---

[14] For additional teaching suggestions, see the *Teacher's Guide to Adventures in Music,* Grade 6, vol. 1 (RCA Victor), pp. 12–20.

TEACHING PART-SINGING

Singing in parts can be a satisfying and enriching experience for children in the intermediate grades. Two-part singing is generally introduced in the fifth grade and three-part singing in the sixth grade. The outmoded procedure of always learning each part separately by rote and then singing them together is, however, decidedly *not* the way to develop skill in part-singing. Students *are* capable of interpreting the printed symbols that represent these parts, but prior to learning to do so they must have had a variety of preparatory aural experiences with harmony. The study of harmonic notation will be relatively meaningless until the sound has been experienced. After students have had a number of successful and meaningful aural experiences with harmony, they may then be led to recognize and sing notated harmonies that they have already experienced by ear.

Preparatory Experiences

Readiness to undertake a particular task is essential if children are ultimately to be successful. To provide this necessary background, several approaches are needed. Among these it is important to include dialogue songs, chants, descants, rounds and canons, combined songs, harmonized song endings, singing chord roots, harmonizing "by ear," and singing chordal accompaniments. Many of these activities may be introduced in the fourth grade and some even in the latter part of the third grade, depending upon the maturity and background of a particular class. These activities, however, should not be considered as terminal in nature, but may be continued for as long as they are enjoyable and contribute to the musical development of the children.

Initial Experiences in Part-singing

Two-part songs are generally introduced to children on the fifth-grade level. Students who have had the advantage of preparatory aural experiences with harmony will be more likely to be successful in their first attempts at part-singing. Without a minimum degree of adequate preparation, students will find the task more difficult than it needs to be; frustration will result, and the teacher will often resort to the outmoded procedure of teaching only one part at a time and of eventually combining them.[15]

[15] For a helpful educational film on part-singing, see *Two-Part Singing* (Johnson Hunt Productions).

In presenting two-part songs to children for the first time, the teacher should endeavor to bring to bear upon the new learning activity all their previous understandings and experiences. First, the teacher should call the class's attention to the score and then ask them in what way it looks different from other songs they have sung. After the group observes that there are two vocal lines rather than one, the teacher may need to explain that in some instances both parts sing the same pitch. The pitch is indicated by only one note head with two stems—up for the soprano and down for the alto (♩). In most simple two-part songs, involving largely thirds and sixths in the same rhythmic pattern, the stems for both note heads will be in one direction. This is the case except where the two parts differ rhythmically; then the stems on the note heads for the lower part will point downward, while those for the upper part will point upward.

In a few songs, it will be noted that *all* the stems for the soprano part are up and all those for the alto part down. It is well for the teacher to point out these differences immediately before introducing the song.

Although adequate preparatory experiences prior to part-singing will facilitate the process of learning, the initial attempt will be less frustrating to the children if the teacher does utilize a semi-rote procedure. Such a procedure should be used until the children possess a degree of familiarity with part-songs and an ability to read the songs with minimum teacher assistance. This suggested procedure can be outlined as follows.

1. The teacher plays both parts on the piano, while the class listens and follows the score.
2. The students and the teacher both sing the second part, while the teacher plays both parts on the piano.
3. The class sings the second part, while the teacher sings the first part and plays both parts on the piano.
4. The high voices sing the soprano part and the low voices the alto part. (The teacher should assist the group that needs help the most.)

In general, several basic reasons exist for this process and should be given due consideration by the teacher. First, it is often desirable, in introducing new music, to provide the class with an overall view before they attempt to sing the parts (i.e., to give the children a feeling for *what the music sounds like* and *what it looks like*). This factor is highly important and should be considered unless the purpose of the lesson is only to develop increased skills in music reading. Secondly, the vocal line of the alto part is often less "melodious," somewhat more elusive, and generally a little more difficult to learn, especially when the class is familiar with the melodic part. Therefore, it is suggested that the class begin by singing first the alto or second part. This part is not learned in isolation, however, but in its relationship to the soprano part, which is played simultaneously on the piano. Finally, before the children are divided in order to sing their respective parts, it is desirable for them to have the experience of the teacher's singing one part while they sing the other. The teacher is best able to sing at a dynamic level that will provide a pleasing harmonic effect, yet will not "pull" the students away from the part they are singing. Dividing the voices into two groups assumes that the teacher knows the voice classification of each student and has previously divided the class according to parts or into high and low voices. If this has not been done, then the class may be divided arbitrarily according to left and right sides of the room.

Regardless of whether or not the voices have previously been classified as high and low, it is desirable for all the students to have some experience in singing both the soprano and alto parts. Therefore, in the above procedure a fifth step might be added, namely, to ask the two groups to switch parts periodically. Experience in singing both parts helps to develop a greater awareness of the part being harmonized, thereby facilitating more careful listening habits and cooperative endeavor.

Improving Part-singing

How does the teacher increase a class's skill in part-singing? Certainly not by merely repeating the previously mentioned semi-rote process, but by utilizing all available means to help the students to interpret the printed symbols more accurately. Children should be helped to relate their aural experiences to the harmonic notation; they should observe what the music they have sung *looks* like and, drawing upon such observation, try to determine what similar harmonic notation in unfamiliar songs *sounds* like. Broad experiences of this type are essential to the development of increased skill in part-singing.

Developing an increased understanding of harmonic notation, and of how it sounds the way it does, will contribute to the children's musical development. A knowledge of intervals, and of what they *sound* and *look* like is a good beginning point. It is helpful for a class to devote some time to analyzing the intervals in selected part-songs. The teacher might ask the class to examine a new song and identify the most frequently occurring intervals (probably thirds and sixths). Perhaps later the class can be asked to identify the intervals resulting when the voice parts move from an interval of a sixth to that of a third. Subsequently, the teacher may select a particular song and ask the class if they can remember what the intervals in the first phrase sound like. Assuming, for example, that the harmony is comprised simply of thirds, the teacher will give the lower part its pitch and ask the higher voices to sing their beginning pitch. The procedure may then be reversed. Eventually all intervals should be identified and sung in this manner. It is, of course, helpful and necessary for the teacher to guide the class carefully in understanding the sound of particular notation. A word of caution, however: too much time devoted to this procedure can result in boredom! Such analytical procedures should never be tedious, but should be approached as exciting discoveries. The activity should always be meaningful and related to music that the class is learning, never an abstract experience unrelated to actual music.

In addition to having the class analyze and sing various intervals, the teacher will also find it highly profitable to use a creative approach in studying harmonic notation. First the class can be asked to harmonize by ear a favorite song. Then, with the teacher's help, the class will endeavor to notate the "newly created" harmonization on the chalkboard. A discussion of the intervals used and why the song sounds the way it does will contribute substantially to improving eye-ear relationships. To provide further motivation, and for later study, the song should be duplicated and copies distributed to the students in order that each may possess a record of the group's creative efforts.

In addition to the study of harmonic notation, there should be continual emphasis on activities designed to improve music-reading in general.

The children should identify the meter and tonality of the song. Even before attempting to read a new song, students should be asked to observe the meter signature to see if the music swings in twos or in threes. Some physical response to pulse and accent is helpful—such as marking out the pulse (through rapping, tapping, or clapping) and accenting the strong beats in each measure. The class should also determine the tonality of the song by first locating *do* (or *la*), and then comparing this pitch with the beginning and ending pitches to see if the song is in major or minor tonality. The class may then determine and sing the syllables of the notes in the first measure (or the first phrase) to establish the tonality of the song.

Students should also be asked to scan the music and look for similarities and differences in the notation of various phrases. For example, the teacher may ask the class to examine the first phrase carefully, and then to look for other phrases that are either identical, only slightly different, or completely different. A discussion should then follow in regard to these similarities and differences. For an analysis of specifics on the printed page, the teacher may ask the class to identify certain harmonic patterns in the music. The teacher may specify a particular measure or pattern and ask the class to identify and frame a similar pattern. Or, if the pattern is repetitious, students may count the number of such patterns in the music. A variation of this procedure is for the teacher to play on the piano a particular pattern (or phrase) and ask the class to locate it in the music. This procedure and other variations of it also help to strengthen eye-ear relationships.

Through all these analytical experiences students may be helped to learn to read harmonic notation. The experience of recognizing various patterns in a wide variety of songs and different circumstances is necessary to the development of increased skill in part-singing.

Topics for Discussion

1. Formulate a sequence of concepts about harmony that moves from the general to the specific or from the simple to the complex.

2. Discuss the experiences with musical instruments that can contribute to children's understanding of harmony.

3. Recall your early experiences with part-singing. Through what means did the teacher create a feeling of anticipation for engaging in this new type of activity?

4. Outline various types of musical experience necessary and desirable as preparation for undertaking part-singing in the fifth grade. Why are these activities and experiences important?

5. Why should a rote approach to the teaching of part-singing generally be avoided and to what extent can this objective be realized?

6. What types of experience lead to the development of independence in music reading and part-singing? What factors cause some singers to be overly dependent upon others?

Suggestions for Further Study

COPLAND, AARON, *What To Listen For In Music*. New York: New American Library, 1957, chapters 6 and 8.

GARY, CHARLES, ed., *The Study of Music In The Elementary School—A Conceptual Approach*. Washington, D.C.: Music Educators National Conference, 1967.

MACHLIS, JOSEPH, *The Enjoyment of Music* (3rd ed.). New York: Norton, 1970, chapter 4.

TIPTON, GLADYS, and ELEANOR TIPTON, *Teacher's Guide: Adventures in Music*. Camden, N.J.: RCA Victor, 1961. (See guides for all albums, grades 1–6.)

Suggested Song Materials
(descants, rounds and canons, "partner songs")

ANDERSON, RUTH, *Rounds from Many Countries*. New York: G. Schirmer, Inc., 1961.

BECKMAN, FREDERICK, *Partner Songs* (1958); *More Partner Songs* (1962). Boston: Ginn.

DANIEL, OLIVER, *Round and Round and Round They Go*. Evanston, Ill.: Summy-Birchard Publishing Company, 1952.

DRAKE, JANET, *The Descant Program Book*. Melville, N.Y.: Belwin-Mills Publishing Corp., 1957.

DUNNING, SARAH L., *Fifty-five Rounds and Canons*. New York: G. Schirmer, Inc., 1936.

FOLTZ, DAVID, and ARTHUR MURPHY, *Descants to Sing for Fun*. Melville, N.Y.: Belwin-Mills.

KODÁLY, ZOLTÁN, *Choral Method: Let Us Sing Correctly*. London: Boosey & Hawkes, 1952.

KRONE, BEATRICE, and MAX KRONE, *Our First Songs to Sing With Descants* (1949); *Very Easy Descants* (1951); *Songs to Sing with Descants* (1940); *Descants for Christmas* (1949); *Our Third Book of Descants*, (rev. ed.; 1954); *From Descants to Trios* (rev. ed.; 1954); *Intermediate Descants* (1954); *Descants and Rounds for Special Days* (1962). Park Ridge, Ill.: Neil A. Kjos Music Company.

NEWMAN, HAROLD, *Round and Round Again: 50 Canons and Rounds*. New York: Hargail Music Press, 1965.

TAYLOR, MARY CATHERINE, MARGARITA WINDHAM, and CLAUDE SIMPSON, *Catch That Catch Can* (One Hundred English Rounds and Catches). Boston: E. C. Schirmer Music Company, 1945 (3 parts—advanced).

TERRI, SALLI, *Rounds for Everyone from Everywhere*. New York: Lawson-Gould Music Publishers, Inc., 1961.

WILSON, HARRY R., *Rounds and Canons*. Minneapolis: Schmitt, Hall & Mc-Creary, 1943.

All Basic Music Series. For listing of books and publishers, see the Appendix, p. 286.

Suggested Materials for Guitar Instruction

D'AUBERGE, ALFRED, and MORTON MANUS, *The New Guitar Course*. New York: Alfred Music Co., Inc., 1966.

The C. G. Conn Method of Teacher Guided Self-Instruction for Guitar. New York: Warner Bros. Music, 1971.

Learning Unlimited Audio-Visual Guitar Course. Winona, Minn.: Hal Leonard Publishing Corp., 1971 (four books, each with matching cassette tape).

SNYDER, JERRY, *Classroom Guitar Instructor*. New York: Charles Hansen Educational Music & Books, 1972.

Films[16]

Elements of Composition (NET Film Service), elementary.

Harmony in Music (Coronet Instructional Films), b&w or color, $13\frac{1}{2}$ minutes, elementary/college.

Keyboard Experiences in Classroom Music (American Music Conference), b&w, 23 minutes, college.

Let's Get Together (EMC Corporation), elementary.

The Autoharp (Johnson Hunt Productions), b&w, 19 minutes, college.

Two-Part Singing (Johnson Hunt Productions), b&w, 19 minutes, elementary/college.

---

[16] For addresses of producers and distributors of educational films and filmstrips, see the Appendix, pp. 287–288.

chapter 7

TIMBRE

Timbre, or tone color, is the unique tonal characteristic of a particular instrument or voice which enables the listener to distinguish it from others. The combination of all the varied tonal colors may be compared to the artist's palette. The composer may, through combining, blending, and contrasting these various timbres, create the musical effects he wishes.

Children are capable of identifying specific instruments through the unique sound of each, and should learn how the size and shape of an instrument and the materials used in it contribute to its characteristic sound. They should also gain some understanding of why composers utilize specific instruments and combinations of instruments to achieve certain musical effects. It is toward helping teachers achieve these objectives that this chapter is directed.

CONCEPTS OF TIMBRE FOR K–6
AND ACTIVITIES AND SKILLS
FOR THEIR COMPREHENSION

Concepts	Activities and Skills
	[The long-range goal of all activities is the development of children's musicality, i.e., *increased sensitivity and responsiveness to music.* Following each activity, the effectiveness of instruction should be evaluated. Concepts need to be reinforced through varied, but similar activities; therefore, the teacher must deter-

mine what students really have learned, as this is the critical factor in determining the specific nature of subsequent experiences.]

K–1

Men's, women's, and children's voices have high and low sounds.

Provide opportunity for children to listen to recordings of songs performed by a man's low voice (baritone or bass) and a high woman's voice (soprano). Help children to recognize the differences by the contrast in pitch (highness, lowness) and subsequently in timbre (lightness and heaviness). Introduce the words *soprano* and *bass*. Following this, compare children's voices to men's and women's voices. Which voices sound lighter? Which voices sound heavier?

Instruments each have differing pitches and durations of sounds.

Introduce selected high- and low-pitched rhythm or percussion instruments, such as the triangle and large drum; also flute and string bass.

It is highly important that the rhythm instruments used produce a reasonably good tone quality; otherwise their value is minimized. Basic sets of the instruments may be purchased from companies specializing in such equipment. Although some teachers prefer that students make their own instruments because doing so is a valuable creative effort, it is nevertheless desirable for the school to purchase a basic set to serve as a model for the "homemade" instruments and to ensure that certain instruments in the total group possess an adequate tone quality.

Rhythm instruments may best be introduced over an extended period of time, thus allowing ample

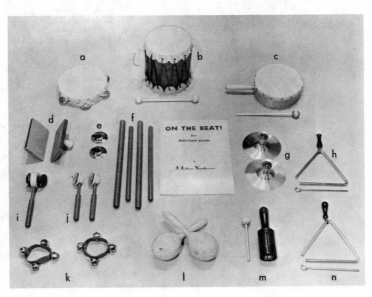

Peripole, Inc.

A basic set of rhythm instruments: (a) tambourine, (b) tom-tom drum, (c) snare drum, (d) sand blocks, (e) finger cymbals, (f) rhythm sticks, (g) cymbals, (h) triangle, (i) castanets with handle, (j) jingle clogs, (k) wrist bells, (l) gourd maracas, (m) tone block and mallet, (n) triangle.

opportunity for the exploration and discovery of each instrument's unique tonal characteristics. In this process, children may be led to understand that various instruments have differing pitches and durations of sound. They will discover, for example, that the tom-tom drum has a low pitch in contrast to the triangle, which has a higher pitch. They will also discover that the drum and triangle resound longer than do either the rhythm sticks or the jingle clogs. These understandings serve to reinforce the concepts of pitch and duration presented to young children through other means. (See pp. 60–62, 99–101.)

In the process of introducing the various instruments, each

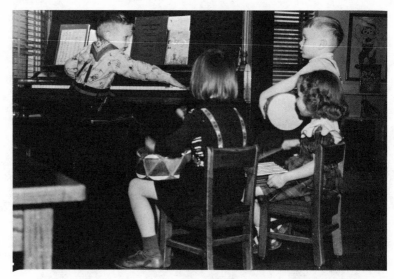

The University School, Indiana University, and
The Daily Herald-Telephone, Bloomington, Ind.

Young children enjoy the freedom of experimenting with different instruments.

may be appropriately used to accompany songs with which the class is familiar. The teacher should never dictate the use of particular instruments, but should set up learning situations where the children are allowed the opportunity to make discriminating choices. The children may choose, for example, to use the wood-block for "galloping" songs; the triangle and bells for songs depicting lightness of character, such as those about "rain" or "fairies"; and wrist bells and jingle bells to depict Christmas "sleigh bells." Instruments may also be used to accompany bodily movement. The children may wish to use the sand blocks to simulate "trains," or "shuffling feet"; the snare drum for "marching soldiers," and the tom-tom drum for Indian dances.

Interesting sounds are all about us.

A good beginning point in the development of an awareness of timbre is for the classroom teacher to help children in kindergarten and first grade explore some of the sounds that exist in everyday life. The children should discuss these various sounds, endeavor to describe their similarities to and differences from other sounds, and try to imitate them. They should then be led into a discussion of the changes of pitch and rhythm involved in each particular sound. Whereas pitch changes will often be described by children only in reference to "up and down," various rhythmic patterns may be chanted or even "tapped out" on the desk. The following are some of the many topics which may thus be explored: the wail of fire sirens, the sounds of various types of bells (church bells, school bells, cowbells, doorbells, etc.), the howl of the wind, the sounds of different automobile horns, the chant of the newsboy, the singing of birds, the patter of the rain, a singing teakettle, the "tick-tock" of large and small clocks, the rustle of leaves, the roll of thunder, the sound of footsteps, the sound of engines (automobile and steam and diesel train engines, and conventional and jet airplane engines), and various animal sounds.

Different types of materials make different and unique sounds when struck or played like a percussion instrument.

Children especially enjoy experimenting with the sounds which may be produced by various common materials—glasses, bottles, cardboard boxes, wooden boxes, metal pipes and nails, twine or cord, heavy rubber bands, flower pots, pans and other kitchen utensils, and many other materials. In addition to exploring the unique sounds of these materials, children will also be intrigued by the differences in the sounds of objects of the same material but of varying sizes. Class discussions on this topic are particularly appropriate for first-grade children and provide an excellent preparatory experience to the later playing of other simple instruments.

Water glasses, for example, may be utilized for the playing of simple melodies. They may be tuned to different pitches by varying the amount of water placed in them. The pitch of each glass may be sounded by striking it lightly on the side with a spoon or a nail. For the initial experiences for first grade children, three glasses will suffice to play simple tunes, involving, of course, only three pitches. Glasses should be carefully selected and those utilized should produce a reasonably clear tone. (A thin glass is generally preferable to a thicker one.) Glasses without water will produce varying pitches when struck with an object. Therefore, first test the glasses and use the one that gives the highest pitch for the top note. This is especially important if an entire scale of eight tones is to be prepared. When water is added to the glass the pitch will descend—that is, the more water, the lower the pitch. For the tuning process it is desirable to have available a pitcher of water, so that small amounts may be added to the glass at a time. First, add sufficient water to the first glass to give it the desired pitch. This will be considered *do,* or the first scale tone. Next add a sufficient amount of water to the second glass until it sounds a whole step up, or *re.* Likewise, tune the third glass to *mi,* a whole step up from the second glass. It is a good idea to place a small piece of tape on each glass to indicate the desired water level so that the glasses can be kept "in tune" during continual use and prepared more easily for subsequent use. The teacher may, at first, briefly demonstrate how the glasses are tuned. The children should note that when water is added the pitch lowers, and when water is removed from the glasses the pitch rises. (The pitch becomes higher as the vibrating body becomes smaller, lower as the body grows larger.) A simple explanation may accompany the demonstration if the teacher feels that the children will be able to comprehend the information. In general, however, it is better to tune the glasses prior to the lesson. The children are liable to become restless with the delay of a long tuning demonstration.

For initial experiences with the water glasses it is best to select simple tunes involving only three pitches. Suggested examples are "Hot Cross Buns" and "Mary Had a Little Lamb" (alter the fifth scale step to a third).[1] Both these tunes are familiar to most first graders, having been learned in kindergarten or during their pre-school years. After the teacher has played the tune at least once, it should be repeated with the entire class singing. A few children may then be asked to play the glasses. Some

[1] Other suggested songs are "Night Song" (German folk tune), *Birchard Music Series,* Book Two, p. 110; and "Pierrot's Door" (first part).

first graders may accomplish this task perfectly—others may have some difficulty, but only by trying will they learn.

Exploring the sounds made by striking together various types and sizes of wood is a worthwhile project of considerable interest and value to children. There are differences in *pitch* between small and large sticks as they are struck together, and differences in *quality* between small and large blocks of wood as they are clapped together, and between varieties of soft and hard wood of similar-sized objects —all of these are sounds which should be explored.

Varying sizes of wooden and cardboard boxes may be struck in the manner of a drum, with a mallet or beater or with the hand. The differences in pitch and in quality should be observed. Children should also experiment by striking the boxes in various places—in the center and near the edges. Various rhythmic patterns may be played on the sticks, boxes, and blocks.

The sounds made by striking various types and sizes of metal together should also be explored. Large nails, railroad spikes, and pieces of metal pipe may be struck together and the differences in quality of sound noted. Metal triangles may be made from heavy wire (or coathangers), metal tubing, small piping, and solid iron bars (for reinforcing concrete). These materials may be placed in a vise and without too much difficulty shaped into a triangle. They should be suspended with a cord or string so that the sound is not damped. A large nail makes an excellent beater.

Young children will also enjoy investigating the sounds that can be made by plucking a taut cord or a heavy rubber band. The cord or rubber band may be lengthened or shortened and the subsequent difference in pitch noted. Such a demonstration may provide a reasonably simple and straightforward explanation as to how string instruments work, i.e., pitch depends upon the tension and length of the vibrating body.

Grade 2

Men's, women's, and children's voices all have different qualities.

Children should have the opportunity to listen to, identify, and verbalize the differences in the sounds of men's, women's, and children's voices. Help them to recognize differences between women's high voices (soprano) and women's low voices (alto) and men's high voices (tenor) and low voices (baritone, or bass). Help children to apply the proper labels (soprano, alto, tenor, baritone or bass). Compare children's voices to adult voices. Comparisons in timbre can be made on the degree of lightness or heaviness of the voices.[2] Which voices sound lighter? Which voices sound heavier?

Instruments each have unique and expressive sounds.

Experiment with a variety of percussion instruments and have children analyze and verbalize the unique tonal characteristics of these instruments. Describe differences and similarities in sounds of various instruments; encourage

---

[2] In the classification of adult voices, there are more subtle characteristics involved than simply heaviness and lightness; however, they are usually too complex for consideration at this age level.

children to select specific percussion instruments for certain song accompaniments and explain reasons for their choices; listen to and identify selected orchestral instruments, for example, trumpet, flute, clarinet, violin; continue exploration of the Autoharp, melody bells, and resonator bells.

Development of children's ability to recognize the timbre or distinctive tonal characteristics of various

Cincinnati Public Schools

Displays relating to children's listening topics provide interest and may clarify the learning of concepts.

instruments can contribute substantially to their enjoyment of recorded instrumental music. The recording *Child's Introduction to the Orchestra* (Golden Record LP–1) is suggested for these beginning experiences.[3] The first part of the section devoted to each instrument utilizes a story sung by a singer who describes the characteristics of the instrument and the position each holds in its respective family in the orchestra. The second part of each section features the instrument in a presentation of music from the standard solo or orchestral literature. After the children are reasonably acquainted with the instruments from listening to the record and through seeing pictures or demonstrations of actual instruments, they may be asked to identify particular instruments as the second part only of the record is played. Later, after the children have progressed in their ability to recognize these various instruments, the teacher may select at random instruments from the series and ask the children to identify them.

Grade 3

Certain types of tone quality are appropriate for the songs we sing.

In the process of learning a song, children should examine the words to determine the overall mood as it affects the tempo, dynamics, and particularly the tone quality. Children should verbalize their thoughts and the class should reach some agreement as to the tone quality desired, i.e., light, or dark and heavy.

[3] Available through local dealers or through AA Records, Inc., 250 West 57th Street, New York, New York 10019.

String instruments produce a sound when a bow is drawn across the strings or when they are plucked; the longer and thicker the strings, the lower the pitch, and the shorter and thinner the strings, the higher the pitch; the pitch of a string is raised when its vibrating portion is shortened.

By plucking a taut cord or rubber band, children may be introduced to the concept of pitch as it is related to the vibrating portion of a string. As a class project they may wish to construct a "monochord" so as to be able to experiment with changing pitch as it relates to the length of a string.

At this level it is desirable to introduce the violin and the string bass (a high- and a low-pitched instrument) to the children. If possible, it is desirable to demonstrate actual instruments. Children can comprehend best how sound is produced if they have an opportunity to hold an instrument (violin) and draw a bow across one of the open strings. They should also be helped to understand how a player shortens the vibrating portion of a string by depressing it against the fingerboard. (In lieu of actual instruments, photographs should be shown to the class.) The following recordings are suggested as a means of reinforcing the previous experiences: *The Wonderful Violin* (Young People's Records, YPR 311); "Violin" (band 1, side 1), *The Instruments of the Orchestra* (RCA Victor); and any recording of "The Elephant" from *The Carnival of the Animals* by Camille Saint-Saëns.

Sound on the brass instruments is made by blowing into a cup-shaped mouthpiece to create a vibrating column of air; the longer the tubing, the lower the pitch.

Children may be introduced to the concept of how sound is produced on brass instruments by first "pursing" their lips and trying to make a sound by steadily vibrating the lips. Understanding of the concept of the relationship of pitch to the length of tubing may be achieved by having them blow into two lengths of old garden hose (4-

ft. and 8-ft. lengths). Is the pitch different? Which length is higher? (Try experimenting with different lengths as well as different sizes of hose.) The quality of the tone can be improved somewhat if a trombone mouthpiece is inserted into the end of the hose. Does the pitch sound better with a mouthpiece? Why? Try inserting a funnel in the end of one of the hoses. Does this change the quality?

After the previous experience, children may be introduced to high- and low-pitched brass instruments, preferably the trumpet and the tuba. An actual demonstration of a trumpet by the teacher or an older student is desirable, so that children can not only achieve a concept of its sound, but also can comprehend that the pitch can be changed by depressing combinations of valves which affect the length of the tubing. Suggested recordings to reinforce the beforementioned concepts are: *The King's Trumpet* (Young People's Records); "Trumpet" (band 1, side 3), *The Instruments of the Orchestra* (RCA Victor); "Tubby the Tuba" (Columbia or Decca Records); "Tuba" (band 4, side 3), *The Instruments of the Orchestra* (RCA Victor).

Sound on the woodwind instruments is produced by blowing across a hole in a mouthpiece (flute, piccolo), into a mouthpiece with a reed attached (clarinet, saxophone), or into a double reed (oboe, English horn, bassoon) to set into motion a vibrating column of air. The longer the vibrating column of air, the lower the pitch.[4]

To illustrate the way sound is produced on a flute, children may blow across the top of a bottle, and varying amounts of water may be used to change the column of vibrating air and the pitch. A single-reed mouthpiece (clarinet or saxophone) may be shown to a class, and the manner in which it produces sound can be rather easily

---

[4] For information on simple wind instruments, and techniques of teaching them, see pp. 201–205.

demonstrated. To illustrate the concept that the longer the vibrating column of air the lower the pitch, a teacher (if not proficient on a single or double reed instrument) may use a simple wind instrument, such as the Flutophone or the recorder. Children can observe that as a C major descending scale is played, each tone hole covered by a finger extends the vibrating column of air and makes the pitch lower. Of the instruments mentioned above, it is desirable to demonstrate to children one of each type, preferably the flute, clarinet, and oboe (or bassoon). Suggested recordings to reinforce the concepts presented are: "Flute" (band 1, side 2), "Clarinet" (band 5, side 2), and "Oboe" (band 3, side 2), *The Instruments of the Orchestra*, RCA Victor.

Percussion instruments are played by striking or shaking, and there are two types: those that produce a definite pitch and those that have an indefinite pitch.

Most children will have had some prior experience with various rhythm and percussion instruments and will have some concept of how they are played and how sound is produced. These understandings, however, need to be strengthened and reinforced through further experiences and subsequent discussions. Provide children, if possible, with a number of percussion instruments, such as snare drum, tambourine, wood block, temple blocks, triangle, orchestra bells, and xylophone. Which instruments are played by striking? By shaking? Which instruments produce a definite pitch? Which instruments produce an indefinite pitch? Selected instruments may then be used to accompany classroom singing, with the children determining the rhythmic and/or tonal patterns and effects they feel are most appropriate.

If actual instruments are not available for demonstration purposes, then as an alternative, pictures of the instruments may be shown, and the sounds illustrated through a recording, such as "Percussion" (band 14, side 4), *The Instruments of the Orchestra* (RCA Victor).

Following these experiences, children should have many other opportunities for listening and identifying percussion instruments in selected orchestral recordings.

Jefferson County (Colorado) Public Schools

One of the best ways to familiarize children with the different types of percussion instruments is to provide opportunity for them to be used in the accompanying of class singing.

Grade 4

Latin-American instruments have unique tonal characteristics and are effective instruments for song accompaniments.

The basic Latin-American instruments are: maracas, tubo, claves, cowbells, guiro, bongo drums, and the conga drum.

Maracas, played in pairs, are made either from carved wood or from gourds. They are approximately four inches in diameter and are equipped with handles. Each of the pair is filled with either pebbles, lead shot, or dried seeds. The maracas are shaken—one in each hand—in a short, precise, up-and-down movement. Perhaps a slightly simpler procedure for young children is to play only one maraca by rapping it against the palm of the hand.

The *tubo* (or shaker) is a long cylinder made from either metal or wood and filled with pebbles, lead shot, or dried seeds. It is played by being held at each end and shaken either up and down or

Rhythm Band, Inc.

A basic set of Latin-American instruments: (a) cowbell, (b) tambourine, (c) conga drum, (d) bongo drums, (e) guiro, (f) maracas, (g) claves, (h) tubo or shaker.

back and forth. The tonal effect is similar to that of the maracas.

The *claves* are two hardwood sticks approximately six inches in length and an inch in diameter. When struck together, they produce a sharp, yet resonant quality. One of the claves is held lightly in the left hand between the palm and the cupped fingers, while the other is held in the right hand between the thumb and the forefinger. When the claves are played, the one held in the right hand is used to strike the one in the left, which is held in a stationary position.

The *cowbell* is struck with a mallet and produces a dull, metallic tone. Cowbells are available in a variety of sizes ranging from four to seven inches. If a more muffled tone is desired, a small piece of adhesive tape may be placed inside the instrument.

The *guiro,* although generally made from carved wood, may also be made from a long-shaped gourd. Two small openings for securely holding the guiro are located on the bottom side—one for the thumb and one for the index finger. The top side has a number of grooved notches. When the guiro is played, these notches are "scratched" with a stick in a rhythmical manner.

The *bongo drums* are relatively small and are joined together with a wooden brace. One of the drums is slightly higher in pitch than the other. The drums should be placed between the knees and played by striking one or more fingers against the drum heads.

The *conga drum* is a larger, barrel-type drum and possesses a much deeper resonant tone than either of the bongo drums. It may be held between the knees while seated or suspended by a sling from the shoulder while standing.

Perhaps the best way to introduce the students to all these instruments is to utilize one or two as an accompaniment to a Latin-American folksong. The teacher should first demonstrate each instrument, emphasizing the manner in which it is held, describing the type of tone quality desired and the rhythmic patterns most appropriate to the particular instrument. These rhythmic patterns may be written on the chalkboard, analyzed and discussed, and then played. It is essential that the entire class participate actively in the study of these rhythmic patterns—they should rap, tap, or clap the patterns together. Certain students may then be designated to play the rhythms as an accompaniment to a particular song. The teacher might ask the class to examine the song carefully and to determine which of the patterns on the chalkboard seems to fit best. It is important that the teacher select rhythmic patterns for the initial demonstration that *will* be adaptable to the chosen songs. In some instances, suggested rhythmic patterns for these instruments are included with the songs. In such cases, the teacher might play the song on the piano and ask the class to make a choice of rhythmic patterns before they open their books. In other instances, the class may be asked to examine carefully the rhythm of a song and to see if particular patterns inherent in it might be used effectively as an instrumental accompaniment.

After the class has had considerable experience in using the various Latin-American instruments, the entire group of instruments may be utilized as an accompaniment for selected songs. In addition, the instruments can form a percussion ensemble, which can be used as a rhythmic background for interpretive bodily movement. The following partial rhythm score may be duplicated or placed on the chalkboard for the entire group to study.

An alternate rhythmic pattern for the bongo is:

Orchestral instruments are grouped into families—strings, brass, woodwinds, and percussion, and each may be identified by its unique sound.

Methods of sound production for string, brass, woodwind, and percussion instruments should be reviewed, and all instruments in each family should be discussed. Whenever possible, demonstrations of each instrument by older students are highly desirable. Recordings of all the instruments in one of the following albums should be played for the class, and the unique characteristics of each instrument identified and described. Each instrument should then be made a focal point for later listening to orchestral excerpts.

> *Instruments of the Orchestra* (Columbia, Decca, RCA Victor)
>
> *Meet the Instruments* (Bowmar Records; filmstrips also available).
>
> *Young Person's Guide to the Orchestra* by Benjamin Britten (Capitol)

Recordings that present a story about musical instruments are excellent for motivational as well as for instructional purposes. Although they may be considered as supplementary to the previously mentioned records, they are essential to a well-rounded listening program. Some of these titles are as follows:

> "Tubby the Tuba" (Decca)
>
> "Pee Wee the Piccolo" (RCA Camden)
>
> "Rusty in Orchestraville" (Capitol)
>
> "Said the Piano to the Harpsichord" (Young People's Records)
>
> "The Wonderful Violin" (Young People's Records)

Several filmstrips, with recordings, are available on the instruments of the orchestra, and their use is most helpful, particularly when actual instruments are not available for demonstration. For a listing of titles and producers, see page 207 at the end of this chapter.

Playing simple wind instruments increases a child's sensitivity to timbre and develops a clearer understanding of intervallic relationships.

(See special section at the end of this chapter, pp. 201–205.)

Grade 5

Sounds are created by vibrations; vibrations of musical tones are even, and vibrations of noise are uneven.

If possible, borrow an oscilloscope (an instrument that shows sound waves visually on a cathode-ray tube) from a high-school science department, and have the children observe the screen as various sounds are produced. They will note that the sound waves of the various musical instruments are different, but nevertheless even and regular, whereas the waves of such noises as "banging on a pan" are uneven and irregular.

Various objects vibrate at varying speeds or frequencies (number of vibrations per second). The speed at which an object vibrates determines its pitch.

Have a child place a piece of wax paper over a comb and hum a familiar song. The child will note that the lips vibrate more rapidly on the higher pitches than on the lower pitches. With this experience as a background, children may be helped to understand the concept that when the vocal cords, or the strings of a violin or piano vibrate faster, the pitch will be higher. Have children observe and touch high and low strings on the piano as they vibrate.

Instruments have unique tonal characteristics that prompt composers to use them singly and in combinations to express various musical ideas.

In listening to orchestral excerpts, identify specific instruments and discuss the effect this instrument, or combination of instruments, achieves. (For example, the tone of the trumpet has been described as brilliant and triumphant, and the instrument has been called the "herald" of the orchestra.) Does the use of a specific combination of instruments seem to fit a composer's expressive ideas? What effect would the use of other combinations of instruments have? Is not the use of specific instruments an important part of the total creative effort of a composer?

Grade 6

Voices and instruments will vary in quality according to the range in which they are sounding.

It is highly desirable, whenever possible, to have all the orchestral instruments demonstrated for all children in a particular classroom, either by students in the same elementary school or by those from a nearby junior high school. These students should endeavor to demonstrate the differences in quality of sound between the various registers of an instrument. For example, the quality of the clarinet in the lower range is full and mellow, whereas in the upper register the quality takes on a harsher sound. Yet although there are differences in quality of sound, the differences are less than those among different instruments.

Children should also recognize that when they sing in the upper range, their voices can sound forced and strained unless their tones are properly supported by the breath. They should attempt to minimize the extreme differences in vocal sound that can occur when correct vocal production is not achieved.

Composers of electronic music use a variety of different means to produce their music and to achieve their musical objectives.

Since the beginning of the present century, composers have experimented with electronic devices to produce musical sounds and effects. Electronic music had its beginnings in Europe about 1948.

One method is to record different sounds in the environment and to alter them in various ways before combining them in interesting and meaningful ways.[5] This is called *musique concrète*. What would be some interesting sounds to record? Suggested examples of *musique concrète* for student listening are "Dripsody" by Hugh Le Caine and "Pinball" by Jean Eichelberger Ivey (*Electronic Music,* Folkways Records FMS 33436).

Another approach to electronic composition is to use only sounds produced by an electronic instrument called a *synthesizer,* which can imitate regular traditional instruments, as well as voices, and can also produce a variety of other sounds. For examples of music composed by means of a synthesizer, see the recording *Columbia-Princeton Electronic Music Center* (Columbia MS 6566).

TEACHING SIMPLE WIND INSTRUMENTS

Through their experiences with simple wind instruments, children's awareness of *timbre* is increased considerably, and their study of orchestral instruments thus becomes more meaningful. In addition, experience with these instruments provides children with the opportunity to develop a clearer understanding of intervallic relationships and can contribute to their comprehension of concepts of *melody, rhythm,* and *harmony.*

The best-known and least expensive of the simple wind instruments are the Flutophone, the Songflute, and the Tonette. When they were first introduced, their value was thought of primarily as a preparation for the playing of regular band and orchestral instruments. Today these instruments are considered to have a broader and more basic educational

---

[5] For detailed procedural information, see Anne D. Modugno, *Creating Music Through the Use of the Tape Recorder* (New Haven, Conn.: Keyboard Jr. Publications, Inc., 1972; textbook, LP recording, and two filmstrips).

value. The playing of such instruments requires each child to give thoughtful consideration to the proper manipulation necessary for effective playing. Experience with such instruments also assists in the improvement of music-reading by reinforcing the response established through the use of syllables and/or numbers. The recorder may also be considered as a simple wind instrument.[6] Although slightly more expensive in initial cost and somewhat more difficult to play, it does have the advantage of a more extensive range (two octaves versus a ninth). Some teachers prefer to use the recorder exclusively, whereas others prefer to use the simpler instruments. Still other teachers like to use both, with the recorder being introduced after the children have had a year or so of experience with one of the simpler instruments.[7] Since it is desirable that students own their own instruments, the teacher, in making a choice to

Cincinnati Public Schools

Playing the recorder or other simple wind instruments increases children's awareness of *timbre,* and develops a clearer understanding of intervallic relationships.

[6] The following soprano recorders are moderately priced and have proven practical for school use: Dolmetsch (plastic), Corelli (wooden), Ideal (wooden), Hohner Educator (wooden), and Aulos Standard—Toyama (plastic).

[7] A recommended plan is to use either the Flutophone, Songflute, or Tonette in the fourth grade and follow-up with the recorder in the fifth and sixth grades.

use these instruments, should consider the children's socio-economic backgrounds, as well as their previous musical experience and basic musical aptitudes.

Introducing the instrument. In introducing a simple wind instrument, the teacher should first demonstrate it by playing a simple tune, and then discuss with the class its principle of operation. (That is, the sound is caused by a vibrating column of air, and the longer the column, the lower the pitch.) The teacher should demonstrate to the class that as the holes are covered by the fingers from top to bottom, the resonating column of air becomes longer and the pitch lower.

The correct manner of holding and blowing the instrument should also be stressed. The instrument is supported by placing the thumb of the right hand under the thumb rest, and should be held steady by the first finger of each hand. The left thumb should cover the hole on the back of the instrument. The remaining three fingers of the left hand are used to cover the top three holes on the front of the instrument and the four fingers of the right hand to cover the bottom four openings. If this point is not stressed, some students will invariably try to place the right hand above the left. This leads to a variety of problems and, therefore, the hand position of each child should be checked by the teacher at the outset. The mouthpiece should rest on the lower lip, with the upper lip placed on the top of the mouthpiece. The teeth should not touch the mouthpiece. Only about half of the mouthpiece should be between the lips. As some students are inclined to insert too much and some too little of the mouthpiece, each individual student should be checked for the proper position.

In blowing the instrument, only a minimum amount of air is needed. When children blow too hard (overblow), false notes and noises are produced, which are generally a disrupting influence to the teaching procedure. To avoid this, the teacher should stress from the outset the importance of blowing easily. When the instrument is blown, each note should be started as if saying the word "too"; that is, the tip of the tongue touches the end of the mouthpiece lightly and then is drawn sharply back.

It is important that children have some facility with an instrument before they endeavor to begin reading; therefore, a semi-rote procedure is suggested in the beginning. Introduce "B" (third line, treble clef) as played with the thumb and first finger of the left hand and have the class play in the manner suggested above. Next, introduce "A" (thumb and two fingers in left hand) and then "G" (thumb and all three fingers in left hand). It is essential, at this point, for the teacher to stress the importance of carefully covering the necessary holes in order to play each note. A procedure helpful in developing awareness of the function of the fingertips is to ask the class to press their fingers securely for several seconds on the finger holes, and then to look at the imprints on their finger tips. The teacher may play one of several simple tunes, such as "Hot Cross Buns" or "At Pierrot's Door," that requires the use of only these three tones. Following this experience, the teacher may introduce by rote the remaining tones in the upper and lower register (C, D, and F, E, D, and C), and, at the close of this initial lesson, encourage the students to practice at home the tunes which they learned in class and to familiarize themselves with the other tones on the instrument.

Introducing notation.   At the beginning of the subsequent lesson, the teacher may place on the chalkboard the notation of the simple tunes which the class learned to play previously. The class may then be asked if they can identify the music. If they are unable to do so, the teacher should play the tune for them, after which it should be explained that this is simply the notation for the music they have already learned to play. The letter names and the position of the notes on the staff should then be reviewed for the children's benefit; e.g., "This note is B, and is played with the thumb and the first finger; this note is A; and so on." Following this review, the students should play the tunes as the teacher points to each note. After these initial experiences, the students may be provided with instruction books that include a progressive sequence of tonal and rhythmic studies.

Teaching procedures.   The teacher will want to use a variety of procedures in teaching simple wind instruments. In encountering a new musical selection, the students should examine it carefully, looking for familiar and unfamiliar elements in the music. The teacher, after playing the music for the class, will explain the fingerings for new notes and clarify unfamiliar rhythmic patterns. After this, the class should attempt to play the music. When difficulties arise, a combination of the following procedures may be used.

1. The students may be asked to sing the letter names of the music, while the teacher plays the instrument. This orients the group to the over-all configuration of the music, and also provides practice in the identification of letter names.
2. The class may count the pulse of the music (1, 2, 3, 4, etc.) as the teacher plays. This procedure helps those students who forget to count to themselves while playing.
3. The class and the teacher may clap the rhythm of the notation together. (In general, rhythmic difficulties are a greater stumbling block than are fingering patterns.)

4. Half of the class may alternately play, while the other half either counts the pulse, claps the rhythm, or concentrates on the fingering patterns.

As previously mentioned, the playing of simple wind instruments will facilitate the improvement of skills in vocal music reading. If playing simple wind instruments is to be of optimum value, a variety of supplementary materials should be used. After the basic instruction book has been completed, the teacher may utilize reading materials from the basic music series. The students may benefit in several ways when instrumental study is correlated with the singing program. Half the class may alternately play their instruments while the other half sings. Not only do the basic series provide a rich source of reading materials for the instrumentalist, but improved tonal security and vocal quality often also result when the two activities are combined.

Topics for Discussion

1. Formulate a sequence of concepts about timbre that moves from the general to the specific or from the simple to the complex.

2. How may varied sounds in the environment be related to classroom discussions on timbre?

3. Discuss the importance of children's experimenting with and playing various instruments as a prerequisite to comprehending timbre.

4. Discuss the merits and advantages of having children construct their own simple rhythm instruments, as opposed to having them play only factory-made ones.

5. What advantages and disadvantages exist in asking students to purchase their own simple wind instruments, as opposed to using school-owned instruments? What procedures should the teacher follow in asking students to purchase instruments?

6. Discuss combinations of instruments that may be used for accompanying singing. What factors should determine one's choice of certain instruments?

Suggestions for Further Study

BENADE, ARTHUR H., *Horns, Strings, & Harmony*. Garden City, N.Y.: Anchor Books, Doubleday, 1960.

BUNCHE, JANE, *Introduction to the Instruments of the Orchestra*. New York: Golden Press, 1962.

COPLAND, AARON, *What To Listen For In Music*. New York: New American Library, 1957, chapter 7.

GARY, CHARLES, ed., *The Study of Music In The Elementary School—A Conceptual Approach*. Reston, Va.: Music Educators National Conference, 1967.

MACHLIS, JOSEPH, *The Enjoyment of Music* (3rd ed.). New York: Norton, 1970, chapters 8–10.

MANDELL, MURIEL and ROBERT E. WOOD, *Make Your Own Musical Instruments*. New York: Sterling Publishing Company, 1957.

MODUGNO, ANNE D., *Creating Music Through the Use of the Tape Recorder*. New Haven, Conn.: Keyboard Jr. Publications, Inc., 1972.

MORALES, HUMBERT, *Latin American Rhythm Instruments*. New York: H. Adler Publishers Corp., 1954.

TIPTON, GLADYS, and ELEANOR TIPTON, *Teachers Guide: Adventures in Music*, Camden, N.J.: RCA Victor, 1961. See guides for all albums, grades 1–6.

WALTON, CHARLES, *Teaching Guide: Instruments of the Orchestra*. Camden, N.J.: RCA Victor.

Suggested Materials for Simple Wind Instruments

BECKMAN, FREDERICK, *Classroom Method for Melody Flute*. Laurel, Maryland: Melody Flute Company, 1952.

BRADFORD, MARGARET, and ELIZABETH PARKER, *How to Play the Recorder*, Books I and II. New York: G. Schirmer, Inc., 1938.

DAVIS, HENRY W., *Tonette Tuner and Technic*. Chicago: Rubank, Inc., 1941.

EARLE, FREDERICK, *Music-time for Flutophone and Other Pre-Band Instruments*. Cleveland: Trophy Products Company, 1961.

GOLDING, SALLY, EUGENE LONSTEIN, and JERROLD ROSS, *Melodies for Music Makers* (2nd ed., rev.). Far Rockaway, N.Y.: Carl Van Roy Company, 1964.

GOODYEAR, STEPHEN, *The New-Recorder Tutor*, Books I and II. Melville, N.Y.: Belwin-Mills, 1956, 1957.

LANAHAN, WALTER D., *Melody Method for the Recorder*. (rev. ed.). Laurel, Maryland: Melody Flute Company, 1956.

PRIESTLY, EDMUND, and FRED FOWLER, *The School Recorder*, Books 1 and 2. London: E. J. Arnold & Son Limited Leeds, 1962. (Available through Hargail Music Press, New York.)

Trapp Family Singers, *Enjoy Your Recorder*. Sharon, Conn.: Magna-music Distributors, Inc., 1954.

Van Pelt, Merrill B., and Leon J. Ruddick, *Flutophone Classroom Method* (rev. ed.). Cleveland: Trophy Products Company, 1948.

Weber, Fred, *Pre-Instrument Method*. Melville, N.Y.: Belwin-Mills, 1950.

Films and Filmstrips[8]

Instruments of the Orchestra (Jam Handy). Series of six filmstrips.

Listen to a Rainbow (EMC Corporation). Filmstrips on timbre, elementary.

Meet the Instruments (Bowmar Records). Two filmstrips, elementary.

Move to Music (Modern Talking Picture Service), 25 minutes, elementary.

Musical Books for Young People (Society for Visual Education), elementary. A series of six filmstrips on orchestral instruments.

Pretty Lady and the Electronic Musicians, The (Xerox Films), color, 15 minutes, elementary.

Rhythm and Percussion (Encyclopaedia Britannica Films), b&w, 12 minutes, elementary/college.

Sounds of Music, The (Coronet Instructional Films), b&w or color, 10 minutes, elementary. Discusses the physics of sound.

Toot, Whistle, Boom, and Plunk (Walt Disney Productions), elementary.

What Does Orchestration Mean? (McGraw-Hill Films), one hour, elementary.

[8] For addresses of producers and distributors of educational films and filmstrips, see the Appendix, pp. 287–288.

chapter 8

FORM

Musical form refers to the general shape or architecture of music. It has sometimes been referred to as the skeleton of music—that which gives it its overall shape. The possibilities for learning situations on this topic are considerable, for all music has form which can be analyzed by some means or another.

An understanding of form provides children with increased insight into the structure of music and establishes a further basis for musical growth. This chapter includes concepts of form suitable for presenting to children, and activities and skills leading to their comprehension.

CONCEPTS OF FORM FOR K–6
AND ACTIVITIES AND SKILLS
FOR THEIR COMPREHENSION

Concepts	Activities and Skills
	[The long-range goal of all activities is the development of children's musicality, i.e., *increased sensitivity and responsiveness to music.* Following each activity, the effectiveness of instruction should be evaluated. Concepts need to be reinforced through varied, but similar activities; therefore, the teacher must determine what students really have learned, as this is the critical factor in determining the specific nature of subsequent experiences.]

K–1

A phrase expresses a musical idea.

The use of musical questions and answers can help children to understand that a phrase expresses a musical idea. Musical questions may be sung by the teacher or played on an instrument such as the resonator bells. When children have had the opportunity to express their thoughts through song, and when their expression is natural and spontaneous, then they are more likely to be responsive to this activity. Stated simply, the teacher sings a question and a designated pupil responds in a way he or she feels is appropriate. For this procedure to be effective, the answers to the questions must be readily understood by the children. To determine a child's comprehension, the teacher may ask the question verbally, and then after the child has responded, repeat the question by singing it. In addition to a vocal approach, instruments, such as the resonator bells, should also be used. Using a few selected pitches from the set, children may improvise musical phrases with one child playing the question and another, a response.

The question-and-answer type of activity may be begun in the kindergarten or first grade and continued throughout the intermediate grades by adjusting the word-content of the questions and by singing or playing more intricate musical questions. In the initial stages, the questions should be relatively short and phrased in such a manner as to require a simple and rather direct answer. The following are some typical questions

that could be sung, and some prob-
able answers:

Through their expression of musical ideas which they comprehend
as meaningful, children will come
to attach the word "phrase" to
such ideas. Whether the "tag" is
immediately verbalized is of less
importance than is the opportunity
for creative musical expression.

Phrases can be of different lengths.

Children should be encouraged to
experiment with musical questions
and responses of varying lengths.
To stimulate thinking concerning
differences, various questions may
be posed: "Are all questions and
answers the same or are they of
different lengths?" "Is there a rea-

son for long or short questions or answers?" "Which do you prefer and why?"

Grade 2

Some phrases are the same and others are different.

The basis for understanding form lies in the children's ability to recognize similarities and differences in music. After experiences in which children can recognize the differences between phrases, the term *binary* form may be introduced and described as music with two contrasting sections that are different but related. *Bi*nary may be compared to the word *bi*cycle and the similarities in meaning identified by the class.

To reinforce the concept of binary form, children should engage in a variety of activities to stress or highlight the differences between phrases. For example, children may "act out" differences by: sitting on one phrase and standing on another, walking in one direction for one phrase and then changing direction, playing different kinds of instruments on different phrases (let children select instruments they feel are appropriate), having the left side of the room sing the first phrase and the other side sing the contrasting phrase. The following songs, in simple binary form, are suggested for listening and study:

"America" by Henry Carey(?)
"Santa Lucia" (Italian folksong)
"Go Tell Aunt Rhody" (American folksong)
"Lullaby" by Johannes Brahms

After appropriate listening experiences, children should examine the forms of various songs and be asked to look for phrases that look alike and for those that look different.

First, the teacher may ask the class to look closely at the first phrase. They may then be asked to look for another phrase that is just like the first one and to "frame" it. Framing simply involves using the index fingers of both hands to surround on both sides a particular musical phrase or melodic pattern. Framing has two advantages: it sets apart the particular phrase or melodic pattern so that it bears closer scrutiny; and it enables the teacher, by walking up and down the aisles, to determine rather quickly whether or not the students understand the directions and if they are learning the idea or process involved. As children mature and develop in their skill of comprehending the printed page, they may be asked to identify many things about the musical score. As previously suggested, they may be asked to examine the first phrase of a song carefully, and then to look for a phrase that is like it; then one that is different. The teacher may write a pattern on the chalkboard, ask the class to frame the first such pattern in a particular song, and then ask them to count the number of such patterns in the song.

Repeat signs indicate that all the notes between the signs are to be sung or played again.

Locate repeat signs in the music and ask the class to explain what happens between these repeat signs.

‖: :‖

To make certain the class understands, ask them when singing a

Different phrases provide variety and contrast.

particular song to raise their hands when they reach the repeat sign.

Bodily movement or actions expressing ideas in each phrase help to highlight the contrasts. For example, while singing the simple song "Hot Cross Buns," children may raise one and then two fingers on the short contrasting phrase "one a penny, two a penny"; children may be asked to identify the B section of an AB form by raising their hands when they hear the "new" section, or by associating various sections with colors or geometric shapes. For example, a sheet of yellow paper may represent the first phrase and a sheet of green paper the "new" or contrasting phrase. Two or more children may be selected to stand in front of the class, hold the colored sheets of paper and raise them at arms length when "their" part of the song is sung. The use of geometric shapes to represent different sections can serve to further highlight the contrasts. For example,

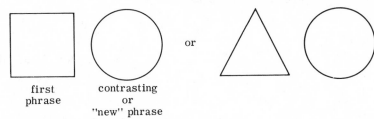

first phrase   contrasting or "new" phrase   or

Grade 3

A contrasting phrase (B) provides variety, and a return to an original phrase (A) creates unity.

Ask children to relate how the contrasting phrase (B) sounds different; i.e., how it provides variety or a change (rhythm, melody). Why does a return to theme A result in a satisfying effect? Search in song notation for phrases that look alike and that look different. When listening, ask children to raise their hands when they hear a phrase that is different.

After children have demonstrated some understanding of *variety* and *unity,* the term *ternary* form may be introduced and described as a musical form in three parts, generally outlined as ABA.

The first section (A) is followed by a contrasting middle section (B), in turn followed by a restatement of the original section (A). Examples of this form may be found in music ranging from folk and popular songs to more extended works.[1] In songs, the first part is generally repeated, followed by a contrasting section, and ending with a repetition of the first part. Examples of music to use with students are as follows:

"The Ash Grove" (Welsh folk-song)

"Drink to Me only with Thine Eyes" (old English air)

"Circus Music" from *The Red Pony* by Aaron Copland (*Adventures in Music,* Grade 3, vol. 1, RCA Victor).

"Children's Symphony," First Movement, by Harl McDonald (*Adventures in Music,* Grade 3, vol. 2, RCA Victor).

"March" from *Ballet* Suite by Jean-Baptiste Lully (*Adventures in Music,* Grade 3, vol. 2, RCA Victor)

"Hoe-Down" from *Rodeo—Ballet* Suite by Aaron Copland (*Adventures in Music,* Grade 5, vol. 2, RCA Victor).

[1] Songs listed as examples of simple binary and ternary forms may be found in *Songs for Every Purpose and Occasion* (Minneapolis, Minn.: Schmitt, Hall & McCreary, 1938).

In a rondo, the main theme returns or is repeated after each new theme.

Rondo is a form in which the original theme "returns" following a number of "digressions" or statements of contrasting melodic material. Various rondo forms may be outlined as **ABACA, ABACADA,** or **ABACABA.** In presenting this particular form the teacher should first make sure that the students are familiar with the principal theme. This process is often facilitated if the theme is written on the chalkboard and sung by the class. Before playing a particular composition, however, the teacher should ask the class to keep track of the number of times the main theme returns following a digression. They may be asked to raise their hands upon the "return" or simply to "keep score" by themselves. The procedure used, of course, will depend upon the general ability of the class. Subsequent discussion may focus upon the nature of the digressions. The following are some examples of rondo form that may be used with young children.

"Waltz on the Ice" from *Winter Holiday* by Sergei Prokofiev (ABACA Coda) (*Adventures in Music,* Grade 3, vol. 2, RCA Victor)

"Grand Walk-Around" from *'Cakewalk'* Ballet Suite by Louis Moreau Gottschalk (ABABACA Coda) (*Adventures in Music,* Grade 5, vol. 1, RCA Victor)

"Rondo for Bassoon and Orchestra" by Carl Maria von Weber (Young People's Records 1009)

"Rondo" from Sonata in D Major for piano by Franz Joseph Haydn (ABACA)

A phrase is a complete musical thought.

As children develop facility in reading, they soon learn that a sentence is a group of words expressing a thought or an idea. Children should also be helped to find musical sentences or phrases in the songs they are singing. This will be comparatively easy, because the phrases in many of the songs in the basic series are written on separate staves. Of course, this doesn't occur with all songs. Therefore, other means of identifying phrases should also be used. Children may find clues by examining the text of the song and looking for commas and periods. More important, however, is for children to develop an awareness of the rise and fall, or melodic contour of phrases. Also, after examining carefully the first phrase of a song, the class should scan the song and look for phrases that are identical, similar, or different.

Children's understanding of phrases, while vague and hazy at the outset, may also be clarified through appropriate bodily movement. For example, to indicate the rise and fall of the phrase they may slowly raise and lower their arms, move the arms in a slow circular motion, or move their right arm from left to right in a curved pattern. If the tempo of a song is moderate, they may walk in time to it and reverse directions at the beginning of each new phrase.[2]

---

[2] Another related procedure of teaching understanding of phrases is simply to divide the class into two groups and have them alternately sing each phrase. Still another means is through playing different groups of rhythm instruments on each phrase.

As children's understanding of phrases is clarified through the procedures mentioned above, they will gain a concept of unity and variety as an essential of musical form. The ternary form ABA, for example, will take on greater meaning. Bodily movement may also be utilized to clarify the concept of ternary form in more extended musical works. Again, if the tempo is moderate, students may walk in time to the music and reverse directions when the contrasting musical material is introduced. During the reiteration of the first section, they may again reverse directions. Some selections written in ternary form are more obvious than others because of a

Cincinnati Public Schools

Arm movement is one method for clarifying and checking children's comprehension of phrasing.

distinct change in mood, tempo, or both. For this reason, the selection "Run, Run" from *Memories of Childhood* by Octavio Pinto (*Bowmar Orchestral Library*, Bol #68) is particularly recommended for the initial use of this approach. In this selection the tempo of the first and last parts would require a quick running movement, while the middle section would demand a slow walk.

Opportunity should also be allowed for more creative bodily movement that depicts the mood of the music. For example, in the Chopin Prelude No. 15 ("The Raindrop"), the children might move gracefully and lightly to the first and last sections and in a stalking manner on the somewhat sombre middle section. After listening to particular musical selections, children should discuss various possible movements and select those that they feel are most appropriate. Through making considered choices and then evaluating their effectiveness, children are allowed further opportunities for musical growth.

Some phrases in songs are similar but not identical.

Have children examine carefully each phrase of a song, look for those phrases that are similar but not identical, and identify the similarities and specific differences. Are one or more pitches in the similar phrases different? Is the rhythm different?

Some sections in larger compositions are similar but not identical.

Endeavor to compare aurally the similarities and differences between sections of larger compositions. Ask children to listen carefully and to raise their hands when they detect a difference. Describe the differences.

Grade 4

A motive is a short rhythmic or melodic pattern.

When they are scanning songs, ask children to search for short melodic patterns or rhythmic figures that provide a nucleus or "germ" to the phrase and melody. These are called motives.

Later, children may be helped to discover how several motives can be combined to make a musical phrase or sentence.

Phrases may be combined to make a section.

Ask children to listen for repeated phrases that make a section. When a song with three sections is diagrammed, the phrases are designated with lower case letters and the sections with capital letters. For example:

A		B		A	
a	a	b	b	a	a

In the form theme and variations, each variation will be somewhat different.

Theme and variations is a form utilizing a statement of a theme followed by a number of variations of this theme that are still recognizable, but altered by changes in melody, rhythm, harmony, or a combination of these. The number of variations may range from two (as in the first example below) to thirty or more. Students should be reasonably acquainted with the principal theme before the music is played. Prior to listening, they should be asked to keep track of the number of variations and to be prepared to describe the manner in which the main theme was changed in

each. The works listed below are
good examples for use with intermediate-grade children.

"Theme and Two Variations"
by Enrique Granados (*Meet
Modern Music,* Part Two.
New York: Mercury Music
Corporation). Excellent for the
initial demonstration of this
form.

"Variations on the Theme 'Pop
Goes the Weasel' " by Lucien
Cailliet (*Adventures in Music,*
Grade 4, vol. 1, RCA Victor).

"American Salute" by Morton
Gould (*Adventures in Music,*
Grade 5, vol. 1, RCA Victor).

"Symphony No. 94 in G" ("Surprise" second movement) by
Franz Joseph Haydn.

Grade 5

*In contrasting sections, a composer
will often change the melody,
rhythm, harmony, or all of these
to provide variety.*

As children grow older, their maturity and experience enable them
to benefit from listening to and
understanding more extended orchestral compositions. Therefore,
their attention should increasingly
be directed toward the specific
ways in which composers achieve
variety in their music. To assist
teachers in this process, the
Teacher's Guides to the RCA Victor Adventures in Music Series are
particularly recommended (10 albums and a separate guide for each).

*A good way to determine the form
of a song is to examine its phrases
carefully.*

In the process of learning a song,
children should comprehend its
form or structure. Some phrases
may be the same, some almost the
same but slightly different, and
some entirely different. Phrases
that are different provide variety,
and phrases that are the same provide unity. Help children to hear

each phrase and to identify it with a letter name, i.e., A for the first phrase or theme, and B for a new phrase or theme, and so forth.

Grade 6

An overture is an instrumental introduction to an opera.

As an introduction to an opera, the overture may contain a "potpourri" of tunes from the opera, or a free "Vorspiel" leading directly into the opera. For the first type, children should be introduced to the melodies from an opera in the context of their settings in the opera. Then, in listening to the overture, they will more readily identify the tunes and appreciate their use in the overture. Suggested listening for this type of overture is as follows: *Carmen* by Bizet, *The Flying Dutchman* by Wagner, *Pagliacci* by Leoncavallo, *Tannhäuser* by Wagner, *La Traviata* by Verdi. For examples of a free "Vorspiel" type of overture, which generally does not include excerpts from the opera and can stand alone as an individual composition, listen to: *Marriage of Figaro* by Mozart, *Fidelio* by Beethoven, *The Barber of Seville* by Rossini, and *Die Meistersinger* by Wagner. How does listening to an overture prepare one for an opera? Does it build anticipation?

A coda is a concluding section of a composition which is added to the form proper.

Help the class to discover that the *coda* is but an extension of the musical ideas presented and that it helps to achieve a feeling of "completeness" and finality. When playing a selected recorded work, pick up the needle just before the coda. Was the ending abrupt? What effect does the coda have upon a listener. Are codas all the same length? What do we call a short coda? (codetta) What kind of musical ideas do you hear in a coda?

In contrasting sections, a composer will often change the key. Hearing the key changes can help one to understand the form of a piece.

In contrasting sections of music, particularly in ternary form (ABA), the key will often change, in addition to the melody and rhythm. Combined, these factors make the change easier for children to identify. When the students listen to various recorded works, ask them to raise their hands when they hear a contrasting section. After playing the new section briefly, lift the needle and ask the class to discuss what they heard. Did the key change, or did only the melody and rhythm change? If the key did change, what was the effect on the listener? Suggested compositions for listening are as follows: "Hoe-Down" from *Rodeo*—Ballet Suite by Aaron Copland (*Adventures in Music,* grade 5, vol. 2); "Menuetto" from Divertimento No. 17 in D, K. 334, by Mozart (*Adventures in Music,* grade 5, vol. 2).

A fugue is a style of composition in which a subject or musical idea is introduced in one part and developed in the other parts in contrapuntal style.

Help children to identify the voice part or instrument that introduces the subject in a *fugue* and the instruments that take up the theme in the other parts. Do some voices seem to answer or imitate others? Can you describe the texture of a fugue? Suggested listening: "Little Fugue in G Minor" by J. S. Bach (*Adventures in Music,* grade 6, vol. 1).

Sonata-allegro form is a movement which falls into three large sections called exposition (usually repeated), development, and recapitulation (AABA).

The *sonata-allegro form* is an extended type of composition in three parts, with a statement of two different themes (exposition) followed by a contrasting section in which the themes are developed (development) and concluding with a restatement of the themes (recapitulation) to provide unity to the composition. Children should be helped to identify the differences in the two main themes of the exposition and to describe the ways in which the themes are developed in the development section. Suggested listening: Symphony No. 5 (first movement), by Schubert (*Adventures in Music,* grade 5, vol. 1); Symphony No. 40 (first movement), by Mozart (Columbia MS-7029).

A tone poem or symphonic poem is quite free in structure and allows the composer to create imagery in his music.

A tone poem or symphonic poem is based on some extra-musical idea, either poetic or descriptive. This type of composition is referred to as "program music," in that it is either suggestive of, or tells, a story. The notes on the record jacket or album generally summarize the story, which may be related to the children prior to listening. Suggested listening: *Grand Canyon* Suite by Ferde Grofé; *From the Steppes of Central Asia* by Alexander Borodin; *Till Eulenspiegel's Merry Pranks* by Richard Strauss; *The Sorcerer's Apprentice* by Paul Dukas; *Le Mer* ("The Sea") by Claude Debussy; *The Fountains of Rome* by Ottorino Respighi; *Pacific 231* by Arthur Honegger.

Interesting variations on any theme can be devised by changing the melody, the rhythm, the harmony, or a combination of these elements.

Write the main theme on the chalkboard and have the children thoroughly familiarize themselves with it through singing it (on a neutral syllable), playing it on the melody bells or recorders, and by analyzing its melodic contour and underlying chord structure. In each variation help the class to identify and describe the specific changes that occur in either the melody, the rhythm, or the harmony, or in a combination of these elements. Additionally, help children to determine if, for example, the character of the music has been altered by changing the meter, or such expressive elements as the tempo and the dynamics. Suggested listening: "Brazilian Dance" from *Three Dances for Orchestra* by Camargo Guarnieri (*Adventures in Music*, Grade 6, vol. 2); "The Girl I Left Behind Me" from *Irish Suite* by Leroy Anderson (*Adventures in Music*, Grade 5, vol. 2).

Topics for Discussion

1. Formulate a sequence of concepts about *form* that moves from the general to the specific or from the simple to the complex.

2. What is the practical effect of a child's "framing" with his or her index fingers a particular musical phrase or melodic pattern?

3. How can visual shapes be used to clarify concepts on form?

4. How can bodily movement be used to clarify concepts on form?

5. What is meant by *unity* and *variety?*

6. Discuss how an understanding of form can serve as a guide to the listening of music.

Suggestions for Further Study

COPLAND, AARON, *What To Listen For In Music.* New York: New American Library, 1957, chapters 9–14.

GARY, CHARLES, ed., *The Study of Music in the Elementary School—A Conceptual Approach.* Reston, Va.: Music Educators National Conference, 1967.

MACHLIS, JOSEPH, *The Enjoyment of Music* (3rd ed.). New York: Norton, 1970, chapter 11.

TIPTON, GLADYS, and ELEANOR TIPTON, *Teacher's Guide: Adventures in Music.* Camden, N.J.: RCA Victor, 1961. (See guides for all albums, grades 1–6.)

Films[3]

Design to Music (International Film Bureau), color, 6 minutes, elementary/college.

Forms of Music: Instrumental (Coronet Instructional Films), 10 minutes, elementary.

Let's Dance to Design (EMC Corporation), elementary (age 10 and up).

What Is a Concerto? Young People's Concert Series, Leonard Bernstein (McGraw-Hill Films), 1 hour, elementary.

What Is Sonata Form? Young People's Concert Series, Leonard Bernstein (McGraw-Hill Films), 1 hour, elementary.

What Makes Music Symphonic? Young People's Concert Series, Leonard Bernstein (McGraw-Hill Films), 1 hour, elementary.

---

[3] For addresses of producers and distributors of educational films and filmstrips, see the Appendix, pp. 287–288.

chapter 9

TEMPO, DYNAMICS, AND EXPRESSION

Artistic musical expression requires a careful interpretation of a composer's music and is dependent upon a knowledge of the overall style of the music, a sensitivity to the variables of tempo and dynamics, and an awareness of various musical markings in the score. This chapter includes basic concepts of expression and suggests activities and skills leading to their comprehension.

Effective interpretation of a song text requires an understanding of the meaning of the words and a sensitivity to the nuances inherent in them. A section on choral speaking, therefore, is included for the purpose of helping children to develop greater sensitivity to the subtle meanings of words. In addition, information is provided on procedures for encouraging creative expression, including initial experiences utilizing musical questions and answers, creating new verses to familiar songs, and composing songs.

CONCEPTS OF TEMPO, DYNAMICS, AND EXPRESSION FOR K–6 AND ACTIVITIES AND SKILLS FOR THEIR COMPREHENSION

Concepts

Activities and Skills

[The long-range goal of all activities is the development of children's musicality, i.e., *increased sensitivity and responsiveness to music.* Following each activity, the effectiveness of instruction should be evaluated. Concepts need to be reinforced through varied, but similar activities; therefore, the teacher must determine what students really have learned, as this is the critical factor in determining the specific nature of subsequent experiences.]

K–1

Music can be loud and music can be soft.

Relate dynamic levels to known sounds, such as "soft as a whisper" and "loud as a siren"; let children determine dynamic levels (loud–soft) that are appropriate to the texts of particular songs.

Music can be fast and music can be slow.

In assisting children toward an understanding of tempo, the teacher should relate concepts to familiar aspects of the child's background. For example, "the tempo of music can be fast like running deer, or slow like a lazy turtle." "Is the tempo fast or slow?"

Or, ask the children if the tempo of the music sounds fast, as in running, or slower, as in walking. In the initial listening experiences, comparing tempo to running or walking provides the child with a more concrete basis for making a judgment. Although such knowledge seems quite elementary to the experienced musician, it is not always so with a young child, and a reasonable amount of time devoted to this topic will provide the child with a basis for making more subtle judgments about tempo during subsequent lessons.

Thoughts and ideas may be expressed through singing as well as through speech.

The creative process may flourish best as an outgrowth of the ongoing class activity. With this thought in mind, the teacher should periodically encourage the children to sing their thoughts rather than speak them. If children are enthusiastic about their class work and have something they would like to express about the topic of study, then this type of creative expression is more readily achieved.

Grade 2

Music can be loud and music can be soft, and certain symbols are used to indicate the composer's intentions.

   f = forte or loud,
   p = piano or soft.

Children may "act out" certain loud and soft sounds, such as shouting, echoes, and whispers, and have their classmates guess the answer. Using the pentatonic scale, they may improvise tunes on the resonator bells or the xylophone and experiment with different dynamic levels, first loud, then soft. As "composers," they should express their dynamic preferences for the melody they improvised and endeavor to verbalize their reasons. Children should be asked to search out dynamic markings for loud (*f*) and soft (*p*) in specific songs.[1]

Dynamics *means the degree of loudness or softness.*

The teacher should use the word *dynamics* when referring to degrees of loudness or softness.

Tempo *means the rate of speed.*

Use the word *tempo* when referring to degrees of speed of a composition. Continue to relate tempo to familiar experiences with movement, for example, "Is the tempo fast, as in running, or slower, as in walking?"

The words of a song give a clue to the proper dynamics and tempo.

Examine the texts of familiar songs; identify the prevailing mood and intent of the text, and let

[1] For other related activities on dynamics appropriate for this grade level, see Ronald B. Thomas, *MMCP Synthesis: A Structure for Music Education* (Bardonia, N.Y.: Media Materials, Inc., 1970), p. 44.

children discover the appropriateness of certain tempi for specific songs. For example, with a lullaby, have children sing at fast, medium, and slow tempi and then choose the most appropriate speed. Experiment also with different dynamic levels, and then have children explain their choices. (See also the section on choral speaking, pp. 238–242).

⌢ *means fermata or hold.*

Use the term *fermata,* meaning "to hold," and ask children to look for the symbol ⌢ in the notation of specific songs. Ask children to "use" a fermata in the music they improvise.

> *means accent or stress.*

> is a symbol meaning to accent or stress a note not normally stressed; ask the class to search for accent markings in the notation of songs or instrumental selections.

Grade 3

The mood of the words of a song is reflected in the melody and harmony.

Examine various songs, and look for places where the melody meets the demands of the text. For example, "reaching upward" suggests an ascending scale. Also, note that stepwise movement creates a more peaceful, restful mood, whereas wide melodic leaps create tension and excitement. Also, chord changes, when few, contribute to a quieter mood, and numerous chord changes create tension.

Some passages in music are somewhat louder (or softer) than others.

Children will observe dynamic markings which indicate levels desired by the composer; more basic, however, is the development of their sensitivity to slightly changing dynamic levels as suggested by the text or the melodic line. As-

The tempo, or speed, can vary slightly within a piece.

Italian words are often used to indicate the tempo and dynamics of a piece. Allegro *means fast and* andante *means at a medium walking speed.*

Making up new words to a familiar song is another means of creative expression.

cending passages often require a slight crescendo and descending passages a slight decrescendo.

Children should examine the words of a song and search for those places that seem to say "just a little bit faster" or "just a little bit slower." For related suggestions, see the section on choral speaking, pp. 238–242.

When observing the marking *andante* on a song or other musical composition, ask the children before singing to think of a medium walking tempo and to tap their fingers lightly on the desk at this tempo. Concerning the marking *allegro,* ask the children to think of a running speed and to respond at that tempo.

Creating new or additional verses to a familiar song is an activity which may be utilized on all grade levels beginning in about the second or the third grade, depending upon the children's background and development. The following is a generalized procedure which is recommended for this activity:

1. Ask the class to think of words and ideas they are reminded of as they sing a particular familiar song.
2. Write the list of suggested words on the chalkboard.
3. Ask the students to think of complete sentences or phrases (using the list of words or related ideas) that will fit with the first phrase of the song.
4. Write the suggestions of the class on the chalkboard. (If there is more than one suggestion, let the class select the

line or phrase they like best.)

5. Repeat steps 3 and 4 for the remaining phrases of the song.

Children enjoy creating new words to songs when the topic is within the realm of their own experiences. The following is an additional verse which one third grade class created for the song "America, the Beautiful."[2]

George Washington was President in seventeen eighty-nine,
He helped design our country's flag, our symbol for all time.
Oh, Betsy Ross made our first flag, with stars and stripes so new,
She stitched our banner carefully, the red, the white, and blue.

Children are capable of devising unique and clever additional verses to familiar songs. As in the previous example, the new verses will grow out of, and elaborate upon, the already familiar existing verses. In other cases, children will simply use a favorite tune and devise verses entirely unrelated to the existing text.

The following verse, as well as the title, was devised by a fifth-grade class as part of a school project called "Clean Up Week," held in both the spring and the fall.[3]

Tune: "Clementine"; title: "The Can Can"

Pick up paper,
On the school ground,
Put it in the nearest can.
It will soon become a habit,
To use the trash can.
This is a rule,
Don't break it,
Obey it all the time.
It will soon become a habit
To use the trash can.

[2] Written by a third-grade class at Losantiville School, Cincinnati, Ohio; Natalie Skurow, teacher.

[3] Written by fifth-grade students at Pleasant Ridge Elementary School, Cincinnati, Ohio; Sara McSpadden, teacher.

Children often enjoy creating verses on their own. One fourth-grade student, after encouragement from his teacher, created the following, which was an outgrowth of a unit of study on library resource materials.

Tune: "Pepsi-Cola Hits the Spot"

The Encyclopedia's a good, good book!
One glance at first was all we took,
Now we definitely do agree,
The Encyclopedia's for you and me!

In addition to encouraging individual creative efforts, the teacher will often find it desirable to arrange for children to work either in small groups or in pairs. The following verse, by two second-grade children, was written during the last week of school. It reflects the children's thoughts and reveals their unique sense of humor.[4]

Tune: "I've Been Workin' on the Railroad"

I've been workin' in the classroom,
All the live-long day.
I've been workin' in the classroom,
Just to pass this term away.
Can't you hear the parents singing,
"Teacher, don't blow your top.
Hang on a little bit longer,
It's June and school will stop!"

Children, go home; Children, go home;
Children, go home, Hooray! Hooray!
Children, go home; Children, go home;
Children, go home, Hooray!

No one's in the classroom with teacher,
No one's in the classroom, you see.
No one's in the classroom with teacher,
No one's here but me!

Composing a song is a means of musical expression in which all the elements of music may be integrated.

(See the section on creating songs at the end of this chapter, pp. 242–246.)

[4] Written by second-grade children at the Westwood Primary School, Cincinnati, Ohio; Joy Roof, teacher.

Grade 4

[Children at this age level should observe musical markings whenever they occur, relate what they mean, and then discuss the reasons why they feel a composer used a particular marking.]

Accelerando *means gradually getting faster;* Ritardando (ritard.) *means gradually getting slower.*

Young children should learn to identify gradual changes in tempo —either faster or slower (*accelerando* and *ritardando*). The teacher should begin by asking the children to "listen carefully and decide if the music gradually gets faster or gradually gets slower." These tempo changes may be compared to the gradual speeding up of a merry-go-round and the gradual slowing down at the end of the ride. Using the piano or another instrument to illustrate changing tempi is preferable to using recordings; the initial experience should be made somewhat obvious to young children if they are to comprehend the concept, as in most cases the changes in recorded music are likely to be somewhat subtle. Once the children fully understand the concept, however, a variety of recorded music may be utilized. The "Acceleration Waltz" by Johann Strauss (RCA Victor LSC-2745) is a good beginning point. The slight *ritardandi* at the end of certain musical selections also provide desirable focal points for listening lessons. A most interesting example, containing *accelerando* and *ritardando,* as well as some abrupt changes in tempi, is the Brahms *Hungarian Dance* No. 1 (*Adventures in Music,* Grade 5, vol. 2, RCA Victor).

The word *accelerando* may also be related to the meaningful word accelerator in an automobile and a discussion held as to what happens when one's parents gradually press a foot on the accelerator.

Discuss with the children what happens when one's parents press easily on the brake pedal of the family automobile. Also, have several children "act out" the meaning of *ritardando*.

A tempo *means to return to the original tempo.*

Have several children "act out" the word *accelerando,* and when at the fastest point, suddenly return to the tempo at which they began. Select children to improvise melodies on the resonator bells or the xylophone and ask them to create an *accelerando* section followed by a return to the original tempo. What effect does this sudden change create? Ask children to use the marking *a tempo* on compositions they write.

━━━━━▶ *means* crescendo, *or gradually growing louder;* ━━━━━ *means* descrescendo, *or gradually decreasing in volume or loudness.*

Have several children play a steady pulse on a drum, beginning as softly as possible, gradually growing louder, and then gradually growing softer. Ask the class if they can devise a way to illustrate on the chalkboard what they did. Show them the symbols that composers use (━━━━━▶━━━━━) and introduce the words *crescendo* and *descrescendo*.

An excellent example illustrating gradual *crescendo* and *decrescendo* is "Norwegian Rustic March" from *Lyric* Suite by Edvard Grieg (*Adventures in Music,* grade 4, vol. 1, RCA Victor). A composition illustrating the use of a gradual *crescendo,* from the beginning to the climax of the music, is "Bolero" by Maurice Ravel (Columbia MS-6011).

Mezzo forte (*mf*) *means half loud (or a degree softer than* forte); Mezzo piano (*mp*) *means half soft (or a degree louder than* piano).

Introduce the word *mezzo*, meaning "half," to the class and use it in connection with *forte* (loud) and *piano* (soft), with which they are already familiar. Discuss with the class why the composer might wish to modify the dynamic marking by including the word *mezzo*.

Presto *means very fast;* largo *means slow and broad.*

The tempo indicated by *presto* is much faster than *allegro* and moves more rapidly than perhaps children could move. Discuss with them animals that move *presto*. Also discuss with them an animal that moves *largo,* which is the slowest tempo marking (elephant). Then provide children with the opportunity to hear orchestral music with these two very contrasting tempi. *Presto: Capriccio Italien* (2nd section) by Peter Ilich Tchaikovsky (Columbia MS-6258), and *Largo:* Symphony No. 9 (*From the New World*), 2nd movement, by Anton Dvořák (Columbia MS-6393).

A slur is a curved line connecting two or more notes of different pitch and indicating they are to be sung or played in a connected manner; a tie connects two notes of the same pitch and indicates the note is to be sounded once and held for the duration of both notes.

Ask the class to look for slurs and ties in a song, and review with them the meaning of these markings. Would the effect be different without these markings? Try it another way! Which seems most appropriate? Why?

Grade 5

// means to stop for a short time.

Remind the class that the symbol // looks like a railroad track, and one should always stop at this symbol. What effect does such an indefinite pause create? Ask children to experiment using the

Legato *means smooth and connected.*

Staccato *means short and detached. Notes are often marked with a dot underneath to indicate staccato style* ♩ ♩ ♩ ♩ .

Marcato *means marked or with emphasis. Notes are marked with the symbol* ♩ ♩ .

marking on compositions they write.

Legato, staccato, and *marcato* are all distinctly different types of musical articulation, and when in performance each should be distinctly clear—no halfway attempts. To reinforce the meaning of each marking, it is suggested that the class learn three different songs, each with one particular manner of articulation. Then, on each song endeavor to sing it also in the two other styles of articulation. The obvious inappropriateness of certain articulations serves to reinforce the meaning as well as the appropriateness of these markings for certain types of songs. Why is one type of articulation preferable? Which seems best to fit the intent of the textual message?

Jefferson County (Colorado) Public Schools.
Photograph by Nancy J. Pitz.

Wall displays of expression markings and other music symbols provide familiar reference points in the study of music.

The metronome is a device to help a performer determine and maintain a tempo indicated by a composer on his music.

Let the children become familiar with the purpose of a metronome by setting the appropriate marking and responding to the metronome's tempo by tapping their fingers before singing a particular song.

Do all orchestra conductors follow exactly the tempo markings on their score? Select several recordings of a well-known symphony and make comparisons. Are they the same or different? Which do you prefer most and why?

Grade 6

When metrical grouping changes, the tempo remains the same unless the composer indicates otherwise.

Rhythmic insecurity is likely to occur when children are singing or playing music with changes in meter; however, this difficulty can be minimized when they fully comprehend that the tempo generally remains the same. Prior to performing music with such meter changes, the class should clap or tap the basic pulse while the teacher plays the melody. Suggested materials: "Katie Moore," and "Hungarian Folk Song," (*Making Music Your Own*, Book 6).

The way that melody, rhythm, and harmony are combined gives music its special character or uniqueness.

Help children to identify the unique character of two specific orchestral compositions, and then contrast their differences in melody, rhythm, and harmony. For a variety of appropriate and worthwhile selections for listening and analysis, see the *Adventures in Music*, Grade 6, vol. 1 and 2, RCA Victor.

As the tempo changes from slow to fast or fast to slow, the dynamics may or may not change.

There is a natural tendency for children to sing or play louder as the tempo increases. This is not, however, necessarily always the intent of a composer. To help children understand this point, as well as the interrelationships between tempo and dynamics, ask them to improvise on selected percussion instruments in several songs: (1) increase the tempo and the dynamics; (2) increase the dynamics and decrease the tempo; (3) increase the tempo and keep the dynamics the same.

Ritards may signal an oncoming cadence or a climax.

Ask children to listen closely for ritards in music and relate what they hear immediately following. A cadence? A climactic high point in the music? What is the effect that is achieved?

Accelerandi create excitement and may build toward climaxes.

Discuss with children their reactions to music with gradually increasing tempo. What do you suppose was the composer's intent?

Instruments may be played in various ways: legato, staccato, pizzicato, etc.

Review the meaning of these words and, as a focal point for a listening lesson, ask the class to identify the type(s) of articulation being used.

CHORAL SPEAKING AND MUSICAL EXPRESSION

Choral speaking is utilized by many classroom teachers as a means of fulfilling certain objectives of the language arts program. Choral speaking has numerous values that also contribute substantially to the objectives of the music program. Although choral speaking is not within the realm of responsibility of music teachers, they should nevertheless understand fully the relationship between this activity and music and should encourage its inclusion in the curriculum whenever possible.

Children display a natural liking for rhyme and rhythm. Through choral speaking, they develop an increased awareness of rhyming words and a feeling for meter (measured rhythm).[5] Choral speaking, in general, assists children in developing a sensitivity to beauty in thought, word, and tone. It increases the child's vocabulary, facilitates understanding of the dramatic qualities of words, and improves habits of speech as regards enunciation and pronunciation.

[5] Finger plays for young children can be another way of expressing rhythm and getting experience in choral speaking.

An awareness of nuances in music—subtle or delicate gradations in musical expression, either in tone, tempo, color, or volume—is basic to artistic musical performance. Choral speaking provides children insight into this important aspect of music interpretation, and also offers a background for understanding the relationship between words, and rhythm, tempo, tone quality, and phrasing.

For the purpose of achieving tonal contrast in choral speaking, the voices of children are grouped in various ways. In the primary grades the voices of younger children are often uniformly high. Differences in pitch level are not distinct enough to warrant classifying the voices into such categories as high, medium, and low. Therefore, a desirable procedure is to divide the class into two groups—either boys and girls, or left and right sides of the room. Reciting certain phrases in unison and utilizing solo voices on others provides a further means of achieving tonal variety with this age group.

The following poems illustrate the division of voices appropriate to the primary grades.[6]

The Little Stone
by Ethel Mahler

Boys: How quiet is the little stone
 Just sitting there all day.
Girls: It has no arms or legs
 To run about and play.
All: Sometimes I wish I were a stone
 When I am tired and sit alone.

The Fly and the Elephant
by Adelyn Richards

All: The elephant teased,
Solo boy: "Why, you are so small
 That really, a fly
 Means nothing at all!"
Solo girl: "Your feet,"
All: Said the fly
Solo girl: "Cover half of the lawn,
 But how many ceilings
 Have they walked on?"

In the intermediate grades greater variety and more subtle tonal differences may be achieved by classifying the students' voices into three categories—high, medium, and low. Continued and refined use of unison

[6] Reprinted with permission of Macmillan Publishing Co., Inc. from Clifford E. Barton, *Verse Choir in the Elementary School,* Revised Edition. Copyright © 1954, 1958 by Macmillan Publishing Co., Inc.

speaking and solo voices is also recommended. The following are suggested steps for classifying students' voices.

1. Write the three categories (high, medium, and low) on the chalkboard.
2. Ask each child to read aloud a short poem, selected previously by the teacher.
3. Let the class determine if each person's voice sounds high, low or medium.
4. Write each student's name under the appropriate category.
5. When in doubt about particular students, write their names on the chalkboard between the two closest categories. Then select from each of the two nearest categories a student whose classification is rather obvious. Ask each child separately to read aloud the poem, followed by the student whose classification is in question. This approach should be preceded by the remark "Listen carefully and see if you feel Mary's voice sounds in pitch more like Ruth's voice (high) or more like Jane's voice (medium)?"

The following poem for intermediate grade students illustrates the use of particular voice groupings appropriate for expressing different phrases in the text.

What Will I Do With My Horse?[7]

Med: Grandfather gave me a horse,
      A clippety, cloppety horse;
High: A puffy, white kitty
      Can live in the city
Low: And so can a doggy
      Or Johnny's pet froggy;
All: But what will I do with a horse?

Med: What shall I do with my horse,
      My clippety, cloppety horse?
Low: My horse is so balky
      And so big and gawky;
High: I've no barn to sleep him
      And no way to keep him;
All: Oh, what will he do with his horse?

Med: Guess what I did with my horse?
      My clippety, cloppety horse;
High: The part that needs feeding
Low: I gave to my mother,
High: At night when he's tired,
Low: He belongs to my brother,
High: Dad's is the share to be pastured and driven,
Low: What's left is for me and needs nothing but loving;
Med: Now Mother and Father and Brother and I
All: Have a clippety, cloppety . . . Balky and gawky
      But oh, such a very nice horse!

[7] Reprinted with permission of Macmillan Publishing Co., Inc. from Clifford E. Barton, *Verse Choir in the Elementary School*, Revised Edition. Copyright © 1954, 1958 by Macmillan Publishing Co., Inc.

The teacher should first read aloud the poem, with the class listening and following in their books.[8] The children should then identify new words and discuss the meaning and mood of the poem. The teacher should assist the children in relating their ideas of the poem's meaning and mood to previous experiences. The teacher should then point out and demonstrate the rhythmic flow of the words. Finally, the class should practice reading the poem aloud together.

After a new poem has been introduced and the children have a general conception of it, the teacher may wish further to clarify meanings and to improve the effectiveness of the choral speaking in general. To this end the teacher might suggest that the children use a vocal tone quality which assists in portraying particular word meanings. Words such as "softly," "thunder," "fluffy," "roaring," and so forth, are a natural beginning point. In conjunction with this the children's attention should be directed toward the different dynamic levels—loud, quiet, or medium—which are called for by particular words and phrases. The children should also be made aware of the different characteristics of high, medium, and low pitches and should endeavor to retain these qualities when reciting the poem. Mood, dynamics, and pitch all tend to blend together, and in the final recitation they should be completely integrated. In the beginning, however, they are best approached as distinct elements.

Generally, the next step is to ask the class to emphasize what they think are the important words and phrases of the poem. The children might clap their hands at each point of stress until they are familiar with this concept. They should also look for phrases which seem to say "please hurry" or "slow down."

Culminating activities are important in any learning sequence. A short program or school assembly arranged around such classroom work will give motivation and direction for future learning experiences in this area.

The following are publications suggested for those who seek further information on choral speaking and poems suitable for various grade levels.

ABNEY, LOUISE, and GRACE ROWE, *Choral Speaking Arrangements for the Lower Grades*. Magnolia, Mass.: Expression Company, 1973.

ABNEY, LOUISE, *Choral Speaking Arrangements for Upper Grades* (rev. ed.). Magnolia, Mass.: Expression Company, 1973.

BARTON, CLIFFORD E., *Verse Choir in the Elementary School*. Darien, Conn.: Educational Publishing Corp., 1954.

8 Choral speaking may also be done on the kindergarten—first-grade level, before children have learned to read. They may simply learn the poem by rote from the teacher.

ENFIELD, GERTRUDE, *Holiday Book for Verse Choirs*. Magnolia, Mass.: Expression Company, 1973.

————, *Verse Choir Technique*. Magnolia, Mass.: Expression Company, 1973.

CREATING SONGS

Creating songs as a group or individual endeavor has a number of values. Such activities facilitate the development of the imagination and individual resourcefulness, and they contribute to the development of *esprit de corps* within a class. The end product becomes "our song." Perhaps most important is that the activity increases the children's insight into the inner workings of music; an increased understanding is gained of how a song comes into being, how the words are related to the melody, and of how subtle nuances come to exist in a creative product. In addition, the class gains an appreciation of the efforts that others have made in the creative process. Some of these important understandings can be gained in no other way than through the experience of actually creating a song.

The creation of songs is generally more successful when writing the poem and composing the music are a single, unified creative act that grows out of a topic for which there is a high degree of enthusiasm. The following generalized procedure is recommended for composing songs. If, however, the teacher wishes to utilize a poem written by someone other than the class, then steps one through five would be omitted. In this case, it is essential that motivation be provided through adequate discussion of the poem prior to setting it to music.

1. Motivation is important. A topic or idea growing out of a unit of work, a specific holiday, or special event is more likely to provide the motivation necessary for successful completion of a creative act than teacher-selected and -imposed ideas.

2. Question the children. For example, "What events happen in the fall of the year that you particularly enjoy?" Write list of topics on the chalkboard:[9]

    football games
    falling leaves
    Halloween

3. Let the class select the topic they would prefer to discuss further.

[9] The list of topics and words listed here were suggested by a fourth-grade class approximately one week before Halloween.

4. If, for example, the topic Halloween is chosen by the group, the teacher might ask the question, "What are some ideas that come to your mind when you think of Halloween?" Place a list of ideas on the chalkboard in columns:

candy	bats	skeletons
masquerades	witches	devils
parties	black cats	costumes
spooks	goblins	fairies
pumpkins	ghosts	graveyards

5. Suggest to the class that, with the preceding list of words in mind, they think of some complete ideas or sentences.
   a. Call on four or five students to recite their ideas.
   b. Let the class vote and select the idea they like best. Then write it on the chalkboard.
   c. Repeat the procedure until a short poem of four lines has been developed.

6. Develop a feeling for accent.
   a. Ask the class to read the poem aloud in unison.

Cincinnati Public Schools

Topics of current interest to children provide excellent motivation for the creating of songs.

      b. Read it again and accent the important words.

      c. Underline the important words on the chalkboard and place a vertical line before the accented words.

7. Determine the mood of the poem. Ask the question "Is the poem happy and carefree, or sombre and scary?" In a natural sequence of events, this step usually is determined rather quickly.

8. Determine the mode. The teacher should play major and minor chords and scales on the piano. Let the class vote and select the mode (either major or minor) which they feel best fits the mood of the poem.

9. Instruct the children to think of appropriate melodies to go with the first line of the poem.

      a. Request the entire class to sing together silently.

      b. Ask four or five students to sing their melodies for the class.

      c. The class should then vote and select the melody they like best.

      d. The teacher should notate the appropriate syllables on the chalkboard under the words.

      e. Repeat procedure for the other lines of the poem. (Later, when convenient, the teacher may notate the song on the chalkboard and/or on manuscript paper. If the students have a reasonable degree of understanding of notation, they may assist the teacher in this process.)

10. Duplicate copies of the song in order that the children may have a record of their cooperative group achievement.

11. Utilize the song as a part of the children's regular song repertoire.

The following two songs, "Lightning" and "Birthdays," were written by third-grade children and illustrate the use of their *own* topics, imagery, and vocabulary.

Lightning[10]

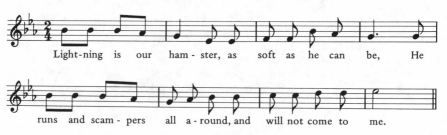

[10] This song was written by third-grade children at the Demonstration School, University of Wisconsin at Milwaukee; Dr. Nancy Nunnally, teacher.

Birthdays[11]

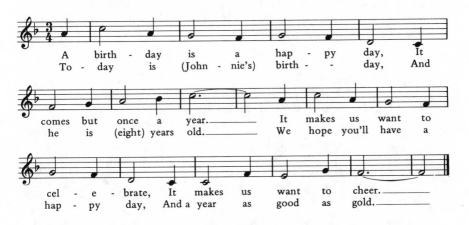

Seasons of the year or specific holidays may provide the motivation necessary for creative work. The song "Autumn Days," written by a fifth-grade class, grew out of a discussion of "events we enjoy in the autumn."

Autumn Days[12]

11 *Ibid.* Used by permission.

12 This song was written by fifth grade children at Glendale School, Cincinnati, Ohio; Grace Eilert, teacher.

Units of study organized around the social studies provide children with a necessary pool of thoughts and ideas which can be drawn upon for the creating of songs. The song "Annie Oakley" grew out of a fifth-grade unit on "Ohio—Our State."

Annie Oakley[13]

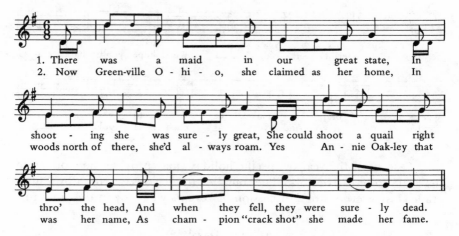

1. There was a maid in our great state, In shoot - ing she was sure - ly great, She could shoot a quail right thro' the head, And when they fell, they were sure - ly dead.

2. Now Green-ville O - hi - o, she claimed as her home, In woods north of there, she'd al - ways roam. Yes An - nie Oak-ley that was her name, As cham - pion "crack shot" she made her fame.

3. *In a contest with Butler she easily won, this made a match in more ways than one.*
   In the wild west show of Buffalo Bill, Annie Oakley continued to prove her skill.

4. *In remembering names of Ohio's great,*
   Please remember this champion of our state. (Repeat)

Topics for Discussion

1. Formulate a sequence of concepts about tempo, dynamics, and expression that moves from the general to the specific or from the specific to the complex.

2. Discuss how the artistic sensitivities developed through choral speaking can contribute to a more musical interpretation of songs.

3. How does the existence, or nonexistence, of creative expression in

---

[13] *Ibid.* Used by permission.

other fields, such as language arts, social studies, and art, affect the attitudes and accomplishments of children in the music class?

4. In what ways may self-expression through the creation of songs contribute to the musical, emotional, and social development of children?

5. What conditions are requisite to creative endeavor in the classroom and how can they be achieved by the teacher?

6. Why is motivation so important to the successful completion of a creative endeavor?

Suggestions for Further Study

MACHLIS, JOSEPH, *The Enjoyment of Music* (3rd ed.). New York: Norton, 1970, chapters 6 and 7.

TIPTON, GLADYS, and ELEANOR TIPTON, *Teacher's Guide: Adventures in Music.* Camden, N.J.: RCA Victor, 1961. (See guides for all albums, grades 1–6.)

WILT, MIRIAM E., *Creativity in the Elementary School.* New York: Appleton-Century-Crofts, 1959.

chapter 10

MUSICAL STYLE

Musical style may be defined simply as the distinctive manner or mode in which musical thought is expressed. It includes those character-istics that make a particular musical work uniquely different from others.[1] Style is a result of the manner or way in which a composer com-bines various musical elements, and thus a knowledge of these elements is a necessary prerequisite to an understanding of style. The word *style* may refer to the type of work—for example, symphonic, operatic, oper-etta, musical comedy; folk, popular, jazz, rock, country-western; homo-phonic, polyphonic, and monophonic—and also to the general historical period in which the music was written, and to the style of a particular composer.

Basic styles of music have changed throughout the course of history as a result of various social, political, and economic forces.[2] In spite of these gradual changes, enough common traits have existed in the arts to enable musicologists to delineate various historical periods, and each may be said to have its own unique *style* and characteristics. Although the style of each individual composer is unique and different from that of his contemporaries, common traits exist between the styles of composers living at a particular time. In studying the characteristics of music in a given period, it is desirable to know the social, political, and economic forces that influenced composers and thus shaped their crea-tive endeavors.

There are many music educators who feel that concepts about musical style and interpretation should be an integral part of the ex-periences of elementary school children. There are others, however, who

[1] Robert L. Garretson, *Conducting Choral Music,* 4th ed. (Boston: Allyn & Bacon, 1975), p. 112.
[2] *Ibid.,* p. 112.

feel that such concepts are much too advanced for children of this age level. In view of this divergence of opinion, this chapter is included, first of all, for the music teacher who needs this historical perspective of music; secondly, it is included so that teachers may judiciously use some of the content with highly motivated intermediate-grade students who, in their opinion, may benefit from it.

Musical style reflects the culture out of which it grew. The content of this chapter, therefore, can be most meaningful if it is related to and taught approximately at the time that similar historical periods are being covered in social-studies classes. For example, when the Revolutionary War period and the founding of our country are being studied, it might be appropriate for children to compare the American culture of the "George Washington era" with that of Europe. That composers of the Classic period worked for a patron and that their compositions were affected by the patron's position or status is relevant and needs to be understood. It follows, then, that after comprehending these basic facts, students may be receptive to learning some of the stylistic characteristics of the music of this period. The study of all historical periods should be approached from the same basis if it is to be at all valid as a learning experience. Particularly in IGE schools, where team teaching is employed, the social-studies teacher, in working with the music teacher, can assist children in developing insights about historical influences on musical style.

Stylistic considerations contribute to children's musical development when, through listening and discussion, they are able to hear and to verbalize the unique manner in which musical elements are employed in a composition. Furthermore, stylistic points of reference are helpful in classifying and comparing different compositions; through such classification and comparison, children are provided with greater insight and understanding into the art of music.

STYLE AND HISTORICAL PERIODS

While the characteristics of the music of any given period begin to develop in the previous period and carry over to the next, definite points of demarcation have been determined and the following are generally accepted: the Renaissance period (c. 1400–1600), the Baroque period (1600–1750), the Classic period (1750–1820), the Romantic period (1800–1900), and the Modern period (1890 to the present).

The characteristics of the music of each particular period are discussed in terms of five musical factors—meter and stress, tempo, dynamics, texture, and expression. Throughout the course of history these factors have undergone change, and they serve as identifiable points of reference to guide children's discussions about the uniqueness of particular compositions and comparisons of music of differing styles.

Renaissance Period

During the Renaissance period (c. 1400–1600), the religious orientation of the Middle Ages declined before rising secular interests. The Renaissance intellectual began to realize his destiny here on earth, rather than considering life only as a prelude to the hereafter. He developed a new confidence in his own ability to solve his problems and to determine his fate. Although Renaissance man did not deny the wisdom of the church, he began to accept other sources of truth. This shift of interest ultimately culminated in the development during the seventeenth century of the modern method of scientific inquiry. During the Renaissance there was an increased emphasis on the value of human personality and upon a person well-versed in all the arts and sciences. The development of this "ideal" existed in stark contrast to a society in which treachery, lust, and ignorance still remained somewhat commonplace. Nevertheless, the new intellectual emphasis in the Renaissance charted a course which has led over the years to a gradual improvement in the recognition of and provision for fundamental human rights.

During the Renaissance, music remained largely under the influence of the Church and the nobility. The composers' task was to write music for the church; thus, it was conceived primarily vocally, although it was performed interchangeably by voices or instruments. The following are some specific characteristics of Renaissance music:

Meter and stress. Much vocal music was devoid of regularly recurring accents, and stress occurred only through the emphasis of important syllables in the text. Bar lines were generally not used, but when they came into being in the latter part of the period, they indicated a measure of elapsed time and provided a means of keeping the singers together. Music of this period should be performed in a smooth, flowing manner, and phrases should be considered as long ascending and descending lines.

Tempo. The tempo of Renaissance music should remain relatively steady throughout the entire composition, or at least throughout a particular section. Any change in tempo should result only through a change in the mood of the text, and any changes within a given section of a piece should be very gradual and subtle. *Ritardando* did not exist, as we know it today, in the music of this period. Composers, however, were aware of the effect, and when it was desired they wrote it into the music itself.

Dynamics. Dynamic levels should be moderate and extremes should seldom occur. Any changes in dynamics should be made only with a change in the tempo and a contrasting mood between sections of a composition. As a result of the high degree of consonance and the lack of harmonic complexity in the music, climaxes seldom occurred and generally were not considered appropriate or necessary by the composers of this period.

Texture. Music was mostly contrapuntal in texture; i.e., the vocal lines were thought of as horizontal in nature. Music usually contained from three to six or more parts.

Expression. The masses and motets are impersonal in nature and are generally performed with an atmosphere of quiet reflection—as a "prayer unto God," rather than as a work for a concert audience. The tone quality of voices performing Renaissance music should be light and devoid of excessive vibrato, which is inappropriate to the character of the music.

Baroque Period

The Baroque period (1600–1750) had its beginnings in the latter part of the sixteenth century and ended in 1750, the year of the death of J.S. Bach. The spirit of the Baroque grew out of the Counter-Reformation, in which the papacy utilized all the resources possible in an attempt to regain the faith of its people previously lost to Protestantism. The art forms, therefore, were characterized by expansiveness, grandeur, and impressiveness. The architecture of the Baroque was expansive and monumental and the interior decoration of the churches was highly ornate. Paintings of Baroque artists were dramatic, filled with tension and alive with color. The canvases of El Greco (*c.* 1542–1614) reflect and are representative of the Baroque spirit.

Opera first developed in the early Baroque and the first complete production was of *Euridice* by Peri, presented in 1600. In contrast to the emphasis on polophony in the Renaissance, the Baroque period opened with a new style, known as *monody,* in which there was a single melody for one singer with instrumental accompaniment. The objective of this new style was to heighten the emotional impact of the text.

The organ, the harpsichord, and the clavichord were the three important keyboard instruments of the era, and composers devoted considerable compositional effort to these instruments. The Baroque also marked the first time in history that instrumental music assumed an equal status with vocal music, and much effort was devoted to the development of new musical instruments. The spirit of the Baroque necessitated a more brilliant tone than that in the past; the violin replaced the viol, and the guitar the lute. Composers also made more extensive use of brass and woodwind instruments, such as the trumpet, trombone, flute, oboe, and bassoon.[3]

The following are some specific characteristics of Baroque music:

Meter and stress.   The bar line and metered music came into being during the Baroque period, and accentuations at regular intervals can be noticed. Baroque music generally requires a crisp, clear manner of articulation and this is often accomplished by the performance practice of lengthening the dotted notes and shortening the complimentary notes. Thus, ¢ 𝅘𝅥𝅮· 𝅘𝅥𝅯𝅘𝅥𝅯· 𝅘𝅥𝅯𝅘𝅥 becomes ¢ 𝄾 𝄾 𝅘𝅥𝅯𝅘𝅥𝅯·· 𝅘𝅥𝅯 𝅘𝅥 . Children should be asked to listen for the type of articulation.

Tempo.   The tempo of Baroque music is moderate and deliberate, and extremes are generally avoided. An important characteristic of Baroque music is its steady, pulsating drive, which generally deviates only very slightly until it reaches a cadence, where a slight holding back of the tempo will be noticed. *Accelerando* and *ritardando* were not commonly practiced during this period of artistic expression.

Dynamics.   Because the instruments of the period generally lacked flexibility, the concepts of *crescendo* and *decrescendo* did not widely exist. Contrast in dynamics, therefore, was achieved primarily by so-called *terraced dynamics,* i.e., by adding or dropping out various voices or instruments.

Texture.   The period began with a change from a texture of independent but interrelated parts to a single melody or voice supported by a chordal accompaniment. This new style necessitated a change in the tonal system—from the medieval church modes to a major-minor tonal system. Initially the new style was homophonic in nature, but after a number of years polophony returned to vogue, doing so within the new major-minor system of tonality.

Expression.   The expressive possibilities of harmonic tension within the major-minor system of tonality were well understood by composers and were used as compositional devices. There was an increase

[3] Cf. Joseph Machlis, *The Enjoyment of Music,* 3rd ed. (New York: Norton, 1970), p. 358.

in intensity in contrast to the previous period, and dissonance was used considerably more for the purpose of achieving emotional intensity. Generally, Baroque composers were freer to express themselves, and thus gave greater vent to their emotions.

Classic Period

During the Classic period (1750–1820), the center of cultural life was the palace. The ruling aristocracy surrounded themselves with the arts, and composers were employed to contribute what they could to their patrons' cultural surroundings. The patron was generally more interested in the composer's creative output than in the composer as a person; therefore, a degree of reserve existed between employer and employee. Thus composers avoided becoming too personal in their art, as this could be offensive; as a result, objectivity and restraint became a predominate characteristic of their music.

The following are some specific characteristics of Classic music:

Meter and stress. The music of the period was characterized by elegance and delicate proportions. In contrast to the music of the Baroque period, the music of the Classic era was delicately marked.

Tempo. Tempo in the music of the Classic period was usually moderate, and extremes were avoided. *Tempo rubato* was used, but with discretion and restraint. The use of *ritardando* and *accelerando* became more frequent during the latter part of the period, but these devices were also employed with restraint.

Dynamics. Dynamic contrast was an important part of the music of the period; however, composers did not use or even desire the extremes that were employed during the later periods. *Crescendo* and *decrescendo* should be performed with restraint, and the dynamic level should generally change only one degree higher or lower.

Texture. Composers of the period sought lightness and simplicity in their music and thus they used a variety or combination of musical textures, including chordal patterns, running figures, unsupported melodies, and other devices. Contrapuntal devices were sometimes used, primarily in masses; polyphony, however, was generally employed to a comparatively limited extent by composers of the period.

Expression. Composers utilized phrases of a regular two- or four-bar length. The harmonic progressions of the period were comparatively less weighty in contrast to those of the Baroque period, although the harmonic vocabulary was similar. Ornamentation developed to its ultimate during this period, in which so much emphasis was placed on the importance of elegance and grace. Composers' endeavors were summarized by symmetry, balance, clarity, and restraint.

Romantic Period

The French Revolution, which began in 1789, led to a breakdown of the aristocratic way of life. Composers, no longer in debt to their patrons, were able to express themselves more freely, and thus they sought new means of musical expression. This resulted in a greater emphasis on emotion, which was previously inhibited or restrained. The following are some specific characteristics of music of the Romantic period:

Meter and stress. Composers often utilized meter changes without changing the meter signature, and accents, therefore, often occurred where they were not normally expected. Composers also were inclined toward the use of phrases of various lengths. Syncopation, intricate rhythmic patterns, and rhythmic surprise were also characteristic of the music of the period.

Tempo. As regards tempo, this was a period of extremes—fast tempi were often performed very fast and slow tempi very slow. Abrupt changes in tempo also often occurred. Both *accelerando* and *ritarando* and also *tempo rubato* were used to a greater extent than in the previous period.

Dynamics. Composers used extremes in dynamics ranging from *ppp* to *fff*. *Crescendo* and *decrescendo,* or the gradual increasing and decreasing of tone, were devices used extensively by composers of the period. The use of dynamic accents, such as *sforzando* (*sfz*), became much more frequent.

Texture. During this period there was an increased use of melodic and harmonic chromaticism. Deceptive resolutions and obscured cadences as a part of a "wandering" chromaticism were often contrasted by sudden shifts of the tonal center. Harmony was employed more extensively than counterpoint, but when the latter was used, it emphasized the opposition of masses of sound instead of vocal lines.

Expression. Individual expression was the goal of the composer, who thus drew upon all the musical devices and resources of the time. Unusual harmonic and rhythmic effects, wide contrasts in dynamics, changing moods and musical textures, and tone color were all effectively employed.

The Modern Period

The Modern period began with the Impressionists in about 1890. This movement began as a reaction against the excessive emotionalism of Romanticism. Claude Debussy and Maurice Ravel were the two leading exponents of musical Impressionism. Debussy was highly influenced by the Impressionist painters and the Symbolist poets, who sought to create an "impression" of things, rather than a clear-cut representation.

Expressionism appeared in about 1910 as a reaction to the "vagueness" of Impressionism and also received its impetus from painting and poetry. Artists were influenced by the ideas of Sigmund Freud and sought to capture on canvas thoughts from the unconscious mind. Distorted images, therefore, were often expressed through the visual arts. In music, expressionism is characterized by continuous intensity, dissonance, angular melodic fragments, complex rhythms, and fluctuating tempi.

Neo-Classicism appeared after World War I, and through this means of musical expression composers sought to recapture the ideals of eighteenth-century classicism. They particularly desired to achieve a balance between form and emotion, with form being considered of primary, and emotion of secondary, importance.

Neo-Romanticism grew out of World War II and allowed composers the opportunity for a more personal means of musical expression, with a greater emphasis on the poetic and emotional aspects of the music. Neo-Romantic composers used many of the same compositional devices as did the Neo-Classicists; however, they did so in such a way as to create warmth and feeling in the music. The following are some specific characteristics of modern music:

Meter and stress. Impressionistic music, in contrast to music of the Romantic period, contains much less tension and rhythmic drive. Accent and stress occur much less frequently.

The rhythm of Expressionistic music is incisive and clear-cut. Expressionists often distorted the normal syllabic emphasis of words, and thus often employed changing meters to reflect and support the rhythm.

Rhythm is a predominant characteristic of Neo-Classic music. Shifting accents within a measure (without changing the meter signature), additive rhythm, in which each measure contains one more or one less beat, and the use of traditional rhythmic patterns in nonsymmetrical forms are all characteristic of Neo-Classic music. An example of the latter would be a 4/4 measure of eighth notes emphasized or stressed as 3 / 3 / 2 or 3 / 2 / 3, rather than as 4 / 4.

Neo-Romantic composers use many of the same rhythmic devices as do Neo-Classic composers, but they use them in moderation.

Tempo.   Although the tempo of Impressionistic music is generally moderate, later music has shown a strong rhythmic drive. Expressionistic music possesses rhythm that is generally irregular and complex, with considerable fluctuation in tempo. The tempo of Neo-Classic music is moderate, and that of Neo-Romantic music often demands considerable flexibility.

Dynamics.   Impressionistic music generally has a relatively low dynamic level, but composers since the Impressionists have utilized a variety of dynamic effects, including extreme contrasts, rapid *crescendos* and *decrescendos,* and dynamic accents.

Texture.   The Impressionists, in seeking to avoid use of the major-minor tonal system, employed a variety of harmonic devices in their music, including the medieval modes, the whole-tone scale, the pentatonic scale, block-like chords in parallel motion (gliding from one to another), and escaped chords.

The twelve-tone method or serial technique is an integral part of Expressionistic music; however, it was not utilized by all composers of the period.

The Neo-Classic composer frequently employed polyphony (sometimes called "linear counterpoint") which was often noted for its dissonance, transparency of texture, and driving rhythm.

Neo-Romantic music generally is harmonically uncomplicated in contrast to previous styles, and it is noted for its lyricism and richness of harmony.

Expression.   Music of the Impressionistic period is generally performed in a restrained manner. Expressionistic music generally lacks any degree of consonance, and the continuing dissonance, along with angular melodic fragments, irregular rhythm, and abrupt changes in tempo, combine to create a high degree of tension in the music. Neo-Classic music is impersonal and objective and contains a minimum degree of emotional expression. Neo-Romantic music seeks a means of communication that is personal in nature, thus extremes are avoided and the musical devices used by the composer convey warmth and feeling.

Topics for Discussion

1. Discuss the word *style* as it relates to specific changes in music, art, literature, clothing, speech habits, and general customs.

2. Describe some specific social and economic forces that affected the compositional style of the composers of a particular period.

3. Discuss the similarities and differences in the style of two composers who were contemporary with each other.

Suggestions for Further Study

BUKOFZER, MANFRED F., *Music in the Baroque Era*. New York: Norton, 1947.

DART, THURSTON, *The Interpretation of Music* (rev. ed.). London: Hutchinson University Library, 1960.

DORIAN, FREDERICK, *The History of Music in Performance*. New York: Norton, 1942.

EINSTEIN, ALFRED, *Music in the Romantic Era*. New York: Norton, 1947.

GARRETSON, ROBERT L., *Conducting Choral Music* (4th ed.). Boston: Allyn & Bacon, 1975, chapter 3.

HOWERTON, GEORGE, *Technique and Style in Choral Singing*. New York: Carl Fischer, Inc., 1957.

MACHLIS, JOSEPH, *The Enjoyment of Music* (3rd ed.). New York: Norton, 1970.

REESE, GUSTAV, *Music in the Renaissance* (rev. ed.). New York: Norton, 1959.

SACHS, CURT, *Rhythm and Tempo: A Study in Music History*. New York: Norton, 1953.

ULRICH, HOMER, and PAUL A. PISK, *A History of Music and Musical Style*. New York: Harcourt, Brace & World, Inc., 1963.

Films and Filmstrips[4]

Composers: The American Tradition (Copland, Harris, Thomson, Piston, Sessions, Ives) (NET Film Service), 30 minutes, college.

Famous Composers and Their Music: Chopin, Schumann, Mendelssohn, Tchaikovsky, Grieg, Brahms (Jam Handy). Filmstrips with six $33\frac{1}{3}$ r.p.m. recordings.

Great Composers and Their Music: Bach, Handel, Haydn, Mozart, Beethoven, Schubert (Jam Handy). Filmstrips with six $33\frac{1}{3}$ r.p.m. recordings.

Jazz in the Concert Hall. Young People's Concert Series (McGraw-Hill Films). Part 1, 26 minutes, Part 2, 27 minutes.

What Does Classical Music Mean? Young People's Concert Series (McGraw-Hill Films). Part 1, 27 minutes, Part 2, 27 minutes, intermediate grades.

What Is American Music? Young People's Concert Series (McGraw-Hill Films). Part 1, 27 minutes, Part 2, 27 minutes, intermediate grades.

What Is Impressionism? Young People's Concert Series (McGraw-Hill Films). Part 1, 27 minutes, Part 2, 27 minutes, college.

[4] For addresses of producers and distributors of educational films and filmstrips, see the Appendix, pp. 287–288.

chapter 11

CONTEMPORARY INFLUENCES
ON MUSIC EDUCATION
IN AMERICA

Years ago the classroom teacher of music could feel somewhat content in passing along to children the "great wealth of our musical heritage." While imaginative teachers, always on the lookout for new ways to stimulate children's musical responsiveness, have always existed, others were simply content to "teach as they were taught." With the recent educational explosion, however, teachers are bombarded with new ideas, and music education has absorbed a wide range of new techniques, materials, and procedures for teaching music. Among these new influences are the Carl Orff approach to teaching music, the Kodály Method, the Manhattanville Music Curriculum Project (MMCP), the Contemporary Music Project (CMP), and the Popular Music Movement. Teachers should be completely familiar with all these approaches, so that if specific ideas are drawn upon from them, these ideas can be integrated in a more meaningful way into the teacher's total approach to teaching.

A number of the ideas presented in the following pages are incorporated into the content of the previous chapters on the teaching of musical concepts. They are included in this chapter so that the reader may develop and gain an understanding of their interrelatedness and a clearer perspective of the totality of the educational method or approach.

The Carl Orff Approach

Carl Orff is considered one of Germany's foremost composers, and such works as his *Carmina Burana, Catulli Carmina,* and *Antigonæ,* for example, are well-known to the musical world. He has become equally well-known for his work in music education. The first edition of his

Schulwerk appeared in 1930, but was written for an older age group. In 1948, Bavarian Radio, intrigued after hearing an out-of-print recording of his earlier work, asked Orff to write music "along these lines" that children would be able to play for a series of broadcasts. The present edition of *Schulwerk*, then, grew out of this effort and from the experience of working with children in preparing these and subsequent programs.[1]

The basic purpose underlying the Orff approach is "the development of a child's creative faculty which manifests itself in the ability to improvise."[2] Orff's beginning point is rhythm, taught initially through speech patterns which the child can readily comprehend. Through this approach a clearer understanding of tonal contrast, dynamics, phrasing, and note values is developed.[3] Clapping, knee-slapping (*patschen*), stamping, finger snapping, and percussion instruments are all used as a means of achieving a clearer perception of rhythm.

Orff has designed a complete set of instruments, which take into consideration the physical limitations of children (certain American manufacturers are currently producing similar instruments for use with Orff-Schulwerk activities). These are the Glockenspiel (soprano and alto), the Metallophone (soprano, alto, and bass), the Xylophone (soprano, alto, and bass), the Bordun (a two-stringed instrument), Timpani (small, medium, and large in size), a bass drum, small drums, woodblock, cymbals, triangle, and jingles or shells (small sleigh bells). Other instruments used are the recorder and tuned water glasses.

Melodic experiences begin with the falling minor third, because of children's familiarity with the interval. The range is gradually widened to include the pentatonic (five-tone) scale (C,D,E,G,A), which Orff feels is well-suited for children's early experiences with music.[4] (The first volume of *Music for Children* is pentatonic; however, the subsequent volumes deal with major and minor.)

Echo clapping, in which the teacher claps a one- or two-measure rhythmic pattern that is immediately imitated by the children, appropriately leads into echo playing on the Xylophone and Glockenspiel. For example, the pitches G and E may be used initially and the surrounding pitches (A, F, and D) removed, thus simplifying the echo

---

[1] Carl Orff, "The Schulwerk—Its Origin and Aims," trans. Arnold Walter, *Music Educators Journal*, vol. 49, no. 5 (April–May, 1963), pp. 69–74.

[2] Carl Orff and Gunild Keetman, *Music for Children, Book I, Pentatonic*, Mainz, Germany: B. Schott's Söhne, 1956, p. iv.

[3] Doreen Hall, *Teacher's Manual, Music for Children* (Mainz, Germany: B. Schott's Söhne, 1960), pp. 6, 13–19. For other examples of speech patterns, see *Book I, Pentatonic*, pp. 66–70.

[4] This is the most common form of the pentatonic scale; it follows the scheme of the black keys on the piano (beginning on F♯), i.e., whole step, whole step, minor third, and whole step.

response of the child. Later the A pitch is added. These three pitches comprise the familiar sound of the children's chant:

Eventually, after the children have had appropriate experiences, all five tones in the pentatonic scale are used.

Rhythmic canon, a form of simple polyphony in which one group imitates the patterns begun by another group (usually after one measure), is another device used to develop children's musicality. It grows out of experiences with echo clapping and speech canons. (For specific teaching suggestions, see pp. 22–23 in the *Teacher's Manual* by Doreen Hall.) Melodic canon grows out of experiences with echo playing. The following is an example of a simple melodic canon.[5]

Prior to playing canons on instruments, it is suggested that children have ample experience in singing vocal canons. (For other examples of rhythmic and melodic canons, see pp. 82–83 in *Book I, Pentatonic*.)

Rhythmic phrase building, in which rhythmic phrases are clapped by the teacher and then continued and concluded by the children in various ways, is considered as the first step toward improvisation. For example:[6]

Teacher claps   Possible children's responses

---

[5] Carl Orff and Gunild Keetman, *Music for Children, Book I, Pentatonic*, p. 83. Copyright 1958 by Schott & Co. Ltd. Used with permission of Belwin-Mills Publishing Corp. All rights reserved.

[6] *Ibid.*, p. 84. Used by permission.

Each child should have ample opportunity to complete the phrases begun by the teacher, and should be encouraged to create his or her own unique responses. This experience, of course, leads into melodic phrase building, in which the teacher plays a melodic pattern that is then continued and concluded by the child. For the initial experiences it is desirable to use only the tones E, G, and A, thus simplifying the response of the child. For example:[7]

As the child progresses in the ability to complete phrases, other tones may be added and the phrases may be lengthened to eight and even sixteen measures.

Ostinato (a figure repeated throughout a composition) is used as an accompaniment for improvisation. Rhythmic ostinati may involve combinations of clapping, *patschen,* finger snapping, and various percussion instruments. (For examples, see pp. 71–78, *Book I, Pentatonic.*) The Glockenspiel, Metallophone, Xylophone, Timpani, and Gamba are used in playing melodic ostinati. Melodic accompaniments begin with the bourdon, or open fifth. Moving bourdons may be created by changing either or both the notes (melodically—by steps or leaps, or rhythmically), thus developing the ostinato figure. Various ostinati are used, of which the following are only a few of the many possibilities.[8]

---

[7] *Ibid.,* p. 85. Used by permission.
[8] *Ibid.* Used by permission.

The rondo is considered to be the best form for improvisation. In the rhythmic rondo the teacher and the class clap and stamp the theme, with individual children improvising the contrasting sections.[9] This activity quite naturally leads into the use of the melodic rondo, in which the same general approach is used, but with instruments rather than clapping. Until the children comprehend the form and develop their ability to improvise, the melodic rondo may be taught as a piece with interludes played by individuals. (For examples of rhythmic and melodic rondos, see pp. 86–90 in *Book I, Pentatonic*.)

The above discussion highlights only some of the principal ideas in the Orff approach. For those persons interested in developing a broader understanding of these methods, the following publications are recommended.

ORFF, CARL, "The Schulwerk—Its Origin and Aims," trans. Arnold Walter, *Music Educators Journal*, vol. 49, no. 5 (April–May, 1963), pp. 69–74. (Also in *The Canadian Music Educator*, October–November, 1962.)

ORFF, CARL, and GUNILD KEETMAN, *Music for Children* (English adaptation by Doreen Hall and Arnold Walter). Mainz, Germany: B. Schott's Söhne (available from Belwin-Mills Publishing Corp.). Includes "Nursery Rhymes and Songs," "I, Pentatonic," "II, Major: Bordun," "III, Major: Triads," "IV, Minor: Bordun," "V, Minor: Triads."

HALL, DOREEN, *Teacher's Manual, Music for Children*. Mainz, Germany: B. Schott's Söhne, 1960. (Available from Belwin-Mills.)

LANDIS, BETH, and POLLY CARDER, *The Eclectic Curriculum in American Music Education: Contributions of Dalcroze, Kodály, and Orff*. Washington, D.C.: Music Educators National Conference, 1972.

NICHOLS, ELIZABETH, *Orff Instrument Source Book*, vols. 1 and 2. Morristown, N.J.: Silver Burdett Company, 1970.

WHEELER, LAWRENCE and LOIS RAEBECK, *Orff and Kodály Adapted for the Elementary School*. Dubuque, Iowa: Wm. C. Brown Publishers, 1972.

Film: *Music for Children*. (Available from Contemporary Films.)

Recording: *Music for Children*. Angel 3582.

For sources of the Orff-designed instruments, see the Appendix, pp. 288–290.

Increasing interest is being shown in the Orff approach by music educators throughout America. Workshops are held periodically, usually on college and university campuses, to clarify this approach. For the music educator who wishes to gain more knowledge of the Orff method, attendance at one of these workshops is highly recommended.

[9] For a discussion of the rondo form, see p. 215.

THE KODÁLY METHOD

Zoltan Kodály, eminent Hungarian composer, was dedicated to the improvement of school music in his native country and, through his articles, speeches, and books of music has inspired teachers and influenced music teaching throughout Hungary. His influence has gradually broadened and some of his methods have taken root in America as well.

Kodály felt that children's musical education should begin not later than kindergarten and that the ages between 3 and 7 were very formative years and the most important period in a child's development.[10] Kodály also felt that pentatonic tunes were particularly suitable for children's initial experiences, as the child need not be concerned about the half steps in the diatonic scale and could thus achieve "clear intonation."[11]

In consideration of the importance of rhythmic experiences in the early training of children, Kodály wrote the pieces in *Pentatonic Music* and the *333 Elementary Exercises* to be used as songs and tunes for walking and marching. One of a teacher's first tasks is to develop children's response to the regularity of the pulse in music, and Kodály suggests that tunes with notes of equal length be used initially, such as numbers 13 and 15 in the *50 Nursery Songs*. Later, songs combining quarter and eighth notes are to be introduced, and those in *50 Nursery Songs* are recommended because of their rhythmic as well as their tonal simplicity (a number of songs include only two or three different pitches).[12]

The strong-weak beat structure of music is to be emphasized by children's clapping or playing instruments such as the cymbal on strong beats. Rests are also to be introduced to young children, and this, it is suggested, can be done best through marching tunes, where the beat will coincide with children's steps. Initial songs should include the rest at the end of the phrase. Children may walk or clap on the notes and be asked to make a specific sound on the rests. (For example, in song number 3 in *50 Nursery Songs,* it is suggested that the children walk and clap on the notes of the song, which is about the wind, and to "hiss" on the rests, the sound of which is to represent the wind).[13]

Prior to singing a song, and while the class listens, the teacher may play the first four-measure phrase on a xylophone and then have the children walk or stamp the rhythm. This activity, by focusing on the rhythm, makes it easier for them to sing an imitation of the phrase.[14]

[10] Helga Szabó, *The Kodály Concept of Music Education* (London: Boosey & Hawkes Music Publishers Ltd., 1969), p. 4.
[11] *Ibid.,* p. 5.
[12] *Ibid.,* p. 6.
[13] *Ibid.,* p. 7.
[14] *Ibid.,* p. 7.

Kodály felt that it is generally best to "separate the rhythm and practice it before the pitch."[15] Although marching, clapping, and other types of bodily movement provide an initial approach to the study of rhythm, they later give way to a system of chanting rhythmic notation using the following syllables:

For example,

Kodály also felt that one should "devise some simple pictorial representation of the rhythm elements which correspond with the single down stroke of the crotchet (quarter note) and the two down strokes joined by a ligature for the pair of quavers (eighth notes)." An illustration which Kodály took from an early textbook is that of different size boots—large ones to represent the slower step of the father and the smaller ones to represent the shorter faster moving steps of a child.[16] To help reinforce the differences between the quarter and eighth notes, flash cards may be prepared. Initially, both the pictorial and musical elements are combined.

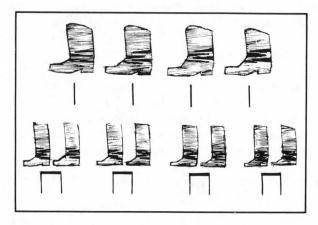

15 *Ibid.*, p. 8.
16 *Ibid,* p. 9. Used by permission.

An example which more closely resembles music notation is that of cherries, with single stems representing quarter notes and two cherries with connecting stems representing eighth notes.

After children are familiar with chanting notation with the syllables *ta* and *ti,* the word *rest* may be introduced. An example of an illustration which Kodály used is a succession of birdhouses with birds perched in each doorway to represent the beat notes (|) and an empty birdhouse to represent the rest (𝄽).

In adapting these aspects of the Kodály method, teachers may devise their own charts or use those in publications specifically designed for this purpose. It is particularly meaningful if the illustrations are pictorially related in some way to the text of a song. For example, for the song "See My Little Ducklings," the chart following will be found useful and helpful.[17]

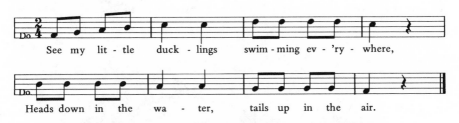

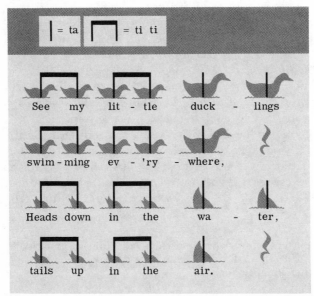

[17] From Aden G. Lewis, *Listen, Look and Sing,* vol. I (Morristown, N.J.: Silver Burdett Company, 1971). Used by permission. (Actual size of the published chart is 23″ × 17″.)

Whereas Carl Orff was concerned more about musical creativity and experimentation, Kodály felt strongly about the necessity for children to learn to read music. While the preceding procedures and activities provide important musical insights, Kodály stressed the desirability of the *sol-fa* system as a basis for developing a feeling for intervals. It is suggested that the initial experience of singing syllables be with songs including only two different pitches (preferably *sol* and *mi*).

Perhaps the aspect of the Kodály system that is best known among American music educators is the use of hand signals or positions, each designating a different scale step (for an illustration of hand signals see p. 69). These hand signals serve further to reinforce the tonal relationships of syllables and are later used as ear-training devices, with the children responding to and singing the syllables indicated by the teacher.

In focusing upon notation, paper discs representing *sol* and *mi* are initially placed on a card in an appropriate position and then a one line staff is introduced with *sol* above and *mi* below the line.

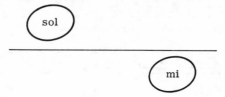

It is suggested that the third note to be introduced is *la,* and after appropriate experiences the fourth note to be presented is *do*. As new songs are learned which contain the added notes, the new hand signals representing these pitches also are introduced.[18]

Let Us Sing Correctly is a book of two-part exercises which Kodály wrote for the purpose of introducing two-part singing to children. The book is not for children to read from, but for the teacher's guidance in providing appropriate hand signals for two groups in a class.[19] In this sense, the book may be said to include a series of "ear-training devices."

The fifth pitch to be introduced to children is *re,* after which the full five-line staff may be presented. At this point, it is suggested that a number of exercises utilizing only *do* and *re* be used initially, and that these be selected from *333 Elementary Exercises*. Initial procedures are as follows:

1. Teacher taps or claps the rhythm with children imitating.
2. Teacher sings the rhythm on a neutral syllable, such as "la, la," and the children respond.

18 Szabó, *op. cit.,* p. 12.
19 *Ibid.,* p. 13.

3. Children sing the tune by following the *sol-fa* notations written underneath the rhythm symbols.
4. Teacher sings the tune on a neutral syllable while children say the *sol-fa* names.
5. Finally, the actual printed music is provided for the children and after the beginning syllables have been identified, they sing the song with *sol-fa* syllables.

Certainly as children gain some reading skill, then one or more of the steps above may be omitted, until finally the children are able to actually read music "at sight."[20]

It was mentioned earlier that the xylophone is the first instrument to be introduced to children. The second instrument may be the recorder, and it is at this time that the letter names of the lines and spaces are introduced and not before, primarily because they become more meaningful when connected with the study of an instrument.

The preceding discussion highlights some of the principal ideas in the Kodály Method. For further reading and study, the following publications are suggested:

Darazs, Arpad, "The Kodály Method for Choral Training," Bulletin No. 8, *Council for Research in Music Education* (Fall, 1966).

Darazs, Arpad, and Stephen Jay, *Sight and Sound.* Oceanside, N.Y.: Boosey & Hawkes, Inc., 1965.

Kodály, Zoltan, *Choral Method,* 15 vols., adapted by Percy M. Young. New York: Boosey & Hawkes Music Publishers Ltd., 1964.

Landis, Beth, and Polly Carder, *The Eclectic Curriculum in American Music Education: Contributions of Dalcroze, Kodály, and Orff.* Reston, Va.: Music Educators National Conference, 1972.

Lewis, Aden, *Listen, Look and Sing.* Morristown, N.J.: Silver Burdett Company, 1975.

Moll, Betsy McLaughlin, and Christine Kunko, eds., *Kodály Envoy.* Pittsburgh, Pa.: Organization of American Kodály Educators, Duquesne University School of Music.

Richards, Mary Helen, *Threshold to Music.* San Francisco: Fearon Publishers, 1964.

Szabó, Helga, *The Kodály Concept of Music Education.* London: Boosey & Hawkes Music Publishers, Ltd., 1969. (Textbook, English edition by Geoffry Russell-Smith; and three LP records, SBHED 0001–3.)

Szönyi, Elisabeth, "Zoltan Kodály's Pedagogic Activities," *International Music Educator* (March 1966), p. 418.

Wheeler, Lawrence, and Lois Raebeck, *Orff and Kodály Adapted for the Elementary School.* Dubuque, Iowa: Wm. C. Brown, 1972.

20 *Ibid.,* p. 14.

THE MANHATTANVILLE MUSIC CURRICULUM PROGRAM

The Manhattanville Music Curriculum Program was developed between 1965 through 1970, under the direction of Ronald B. Thomas, and was sponsored by the Arts and Humanities Program of the United States Office of Education. In the MMCP, the student functions as a musician in most of the activities and, by being involved in "doing" and using music, is motivated toward learning as a result of fulfilling personal needs and in meeting personal objectives of performance, composition, and interpretation.[21]

The *discovery approach* is one of the focuses of the MMCP, and the student is personally involved in creative activity—in composition or in combining or shaping musical sounds. Through personal involvement "the student can discover for himself those concepts of organization and interaction which are fundamental to musical understanding."[22]

The MMCP also focuses on musical concepts, or points of musical understanding, and upon musical skills, or the means of implementing the concepts. In the MMCP, "the core of the program is a spiral of musical concepts which begins with the broadest possible view and progresses to levels of higher specificity and complexity."[23]

Another aspect of the MMCP is its emphasis on relevance. In other words, stress is on the music of today that is most meaningful to the student. The music of yesteryear is brought into the study in various ways, but it is done so within a frame of reference that is meaningful today.[24]

Still another point of emphasis is the focus on the totality of the musical experience. Musical elements do not stand alone, in other words, but are related to one another, e.g., pitch to timbre, rhythm to dynamics, and so forth. While in specific educational strategies the emphasis or focus may be on one concept, it is necessary that such focus take place within a total musical framework. Furthermore, if students are to develop sensitivity to music they must have a breadth or variety of experience that will allow for the development of a proper perspective.[25]

The MMCP includes seven major areas of activities: (1) MMCP strategies involving composing, performing, evaluating, conducting, and listening, (2) student recitals, (3) listening to recordings, (4) research and

[21] Ronald B. Thomas, *MMCP Synthesis: A Structure for Music Education* (Bardonia, N.Y.: Media, Inc., 1970), p. 5.

[22] *Ibid.*, p. 16.

[23] *Ibid.*, pp. 16–17.

[24] *Ibid.*, p. 19.

[25] *Ibid.*, p. 20.

oral reports, (5) guest recitals, (6) singing (for joy and pleasure), and (7) skill development.[26]

As previously mentioned, the primary thrust of MMCP is upon the understanding of concepts. This is accomplished through the MMCP Spiral Curriculum—"an open-ended and flexible organization of concepts that focuses on the interaction and relationship of concepts, factors and elements."[27] To allow for the greatest possible flexibility, the curriculum is not organized by grade levels, but by *cycles*—16 in all. MMCP sample teaching strategies representing cycles 1,[28] 8,[29] and 15[30] are included on the following pages to illustrate the teaching approach unique to MMCP and the scope of musical concepts and activities from simple to complex.

Readers interested in further information regarding the MMCP Concept Spiral are referred directly to pages 39–119 in the *MMCP Synthesis: A Structure for Music Education* by Ronald B. Thomas, available through Media Materials, Inc., P.O. Box 533, Bardonia, N.Y. 10954.

SAMPLE STRATEGY

Cycle 1. The plan, the shape, the order of a piece of music is determined by the composer.

Each student may perform his three sounds at his own desk.
Focus on "listening" to distinctive qualities of sounds performed.

Encourage students to focus attention on other exploratory possibilities by investigating the sound producing materials with greater depth. Can you produce a sound on your object that is bright, dull, shrill, intense, etc.? How is this done?

Discuss any points of interest relative to the activity.
Extend the discussion by focusing on the following questions:
Why is silence in the room necessary for performance to be effective?
How did sounds vary or seem similar?
Which objects produced the brightest, dullest, most shrill, most intense sounds?
What makes a sound dull, bright, intense, etc.

Divide the class into groups of 5 or 6 students. A conductor-composer should be selected by each group. He will determine the order of

26 *Ibid.*, pp. 24–25.
27 *Ibid.*, p. 37.
28 *Ibid.*, p. 43. Used by permission.
29 *Ibid.*, pp. 82–83. Used by permission.
30 *Ibid.*, p. 114. Used by permission.

sounds and the overall plan of the improvisation. Conducting signals should be devised and practiced in each group so that directions will be clear.

Allow approximately 10 minutes for planning and rehearsal.
At the end of the designated time each group will perform.

Tape all improvisations for playback and evaluation. Discussion should focus around the following questions:
Did the improvisation have a good plan? Did the music hold together?
What was the most satisfying factor in this piece?
How would you change the improvisation?
What are some of the conductor's concerns?

In listening to the recorded examples focus attention to the overall shape or plan of the music. In listening to a single example two or three times students may map out a shape or a plan which represents the composition. These plans can be compared and used for repeated listenings.

Suggested Listening Examples:
Construction in Metal—Cage, John; K08P-1498
Poème Electronique—Varèse, Edgar; Col. ML5478; MS6146

SAMPLE STRATEGY

Cycle 8. In a composition built on a prescribed series of pitches, the manipulation of other elements brings variety, contrast, and meaning.

The teacher should write a 7-tone row on the board. When the students have copied the row, 3 or 4 students should improvise on the row attempting to achieve variety through the creative use of rhythm, dynamics, octave transposition, and rests.

After the improvisational demonstrations, a recording of a serial composition for a small chamber ensemble should be played as a reference for the class. Each student should identify two characteristics of serial music which he wishes to use in his own composing.

The class should be divided into groups of five students to form ensembles of three pitched instruments and two non-pitched percussion. Using the row prepared by the teacher and the characteristics the students have previously identified, each group should construct a composition of 1- to 2-minute duration. All musical factors should be first improvisationally explored and then accurately notated.

Since the process of composing, notating and rehearsing is rather complicated, adequate time must be allowed for the students to feel that they are satisfied with their creative work. Because the time required by each group will vary considerably, each group may record its own work when completed and pass judgment on its own achievement. If they wish to revise the composition, time should be allowed for this. After all groups have completed their assignment, a performance for the class is in order.

In the discussion of compositions, the focus should be on the variety, unity and identified characteristics. Was the total aural nature of the piece appropriate in terms of the reference recordings? Did the composition have a sense of unity? How was this achieved? How was variety handled?

Possible Extensions:

Play the tape of these compositions for the art teacher and the English teacher. What suggestions do they have?

Include some of these row compositions along with others on a student composition recital for the parents. Suggest recordings that the parents may purchase.

Suggested Listening Examples:

Music for Brass Quintet—Schuller, Gunther; CRI 144

Trio—Ives, Charles; Decca DL710126

Marteau sans Maître—Boulez, Pierre; Turnabout 4081

SAMPLE STRATEGY

Cycle 15.

Select a scale involving any seven successive white keys on the piano. Pick any one of them to function as the sound of resolution.

Experiment, melodically, to discover ways to allow musical phrases to come to a logical ending on the pitch selected to be the sound of resolution. Choose still another pitch to function as an alternate sound of resolution. Again, experiment to discover ways in which this note will become the final note of a phrase.

Write a melody which is five or six phrases in length. Some phrases should end on one of the sounds of resolution, others on the alternate. With the melody complete, consider which instrument or voice relates best to the character of the piece. Score the melody for the instrument or voice selected.

After several of the melodies have been heard, consider the musical implications of the notes of resolution which were not commonplace as contrasted with those that were.

Questions can be focused on interesting meter or phrasing concepts, the use of other instruments (percussion, for example) with the melody, or other melodies in combination.

CONTEMPORARY MUSIC PROJECT (CMP)

The Contemporary Music Project had its beginnings in 1959, when its initial program, known as the Young Composers Project (YCP), was established. The YCP involved the placing of thirty-one young composers over a three-year period in public secondary schools throughout the United States. This program was supported by the Ford Foundation and was administered by the National Music Council of the Ford Foundation through a "committee of selection" under the chairmanship of Norman Dello Joio. The placement of these composers in schools, where they could compose for particular performing groups, contributed to their own development and provided students with an opportunity to gain new insights into the creative process.

In 1965, the Young Composers Project became known as the Composers in Public Schools (CPS) program, and the music of the involved composers changed from a basically traditional tonal framework, where the innovations focused upon rhythm and meter, to music in almost all current styles and practices, including aleatoric and electronic techniques.[31] The Composers in Public Schools program resulted in a repertoire of unique contemporary compositions which was available from the CMP Library through University Microfilms.[32] In 1968, the idea of Composers in Public Schools was extended to include Professionals-in-Residence in Communities. In addition to working in the public schools, composers were to develop associations with artistic and educational groups in the community as a demonstration that education is not confined to the classroom, but embraces a range of experiences within the community.

Growing out of the YCP was an increased awareness that public-school music teachers lacked understanding of contemporary compositional techniques and that the use of contemporary music in schools needed to be much more extensive if a creative approach to music education were to be achieved.[33]

In 1962, the MENC submitted a proposal to the Ford Foundation to expand the YCP by organizing contemporary music seminars and workshops in the schools, and by establishing pilot projects through which composers could identify and help develop creative talent among students in elementary and secondary schools. This proposal was approved and MENC received a grant of $1,380,000 to establish and operate this expanded program from 1963 to 1969, which was known as the Contemporary Music Project for Creativity in Music Education (CMP).[34] Out of the pilot projects grew an increased awareness of the need to

---

[31] Comprehensive Musicianship: An Anthology of Evolving Thought (Washington, D.C., Contemporary Music Project, MENC, 1971), pp. 23–24.

[32] Music from the CMP Library has not been available for purchase since March, 1971.

[33] Comprehensive Musicianship: An Anthology of Evolving Thought, op. cit., p. 29.

[34] Ibid., p. 31.

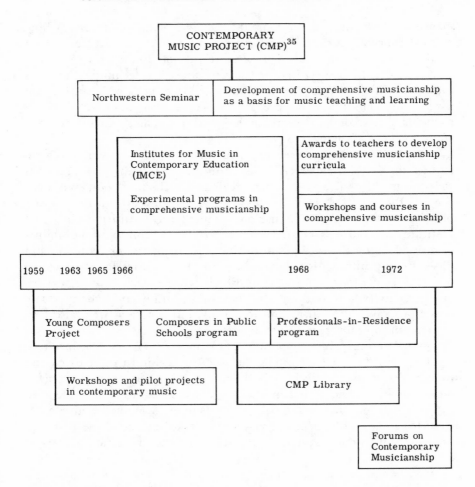

reconsider the education of school music teachers, and in April, 1965, the Northwestern University Seminar on Comprehensive Musicianship was held "to examine and revise existing structures of theoretical studies to develop better-trained public school music teachers."[36]

Implications of this seminar for college and secondary school music curricula focus upon the reorganization of courses in basic musicianship and a "move toward the teaching of concepts that are applicable in greater or lesser degree to all music, not just to the style of a particular composer or a single period of Western tradition."[37] And while the emphasis in secondary schools is appropriately centered upon perfor-

[35] Contemporary Music Project. Music Educators National Conference. Used by permission.

[36] *Comprehensive Musicianship, op. cit.,* p. 34.

[37] *Ibid.,* p. 40.

mance organizations, teachers should not ignore the values of teaching musical concepts, such as melody, harmony, form, and texture, as part of the ensemble rehearsal. Furthermore, although the college theory class provides the best setting for teaching analytical techniques, analysis should not be limited to this class, but should be included as an integral part of any class that "purports to further musical understanding—the elementary or secondary classroom, the studio, the music literature class, and the rehearsal room."[38]

In 1966, CMP organized experimental programs known as the Institutes for Music in Contemporary Education (IMCE). The programs were grouped into five geographical regions paralleling the different divisions of the MENC.[39] IMCE was set up to put into action the working premises set forth by the Seminar on Comprehensive Musicianship. "The Institutes were to be considered as centers for continuing self-examination of educational practices in music, as focal points for receiving and disseminating information, and as working laboratories for the creative minds in contemporary music education."[40] The primary area of experimental activity was training in basic musicianship in undergraduate music programs. Pre-college and upper-division programs were also considered appropriate areas of investigation.

One of the principal points that came out of the Northwestern Seminar was the need to restore the study of music to the curriculum, that is, the study of music in its highest form. Another, perhaps even more important, move that gradually gained recognition was the idea "why should teaching at the college level differ in method and content from teaching in the elementary school?" In other words, the basic approach to instruction should be the same for the first grade as it is at college.[41]

Although IMCE was concluded in 1968, a number of schools continued experimental programs supported by CMP into 1969. In 1970, summer workshops were held at several universities to familiarize music teachers with the principles of comprehensive musicianship and with ways to apply them in the classroom. Summer courses for college teachers were also held at other universities to acquaint college teachers with the principles of comprehensive musicianship and ways to apply them to undergraduate courses in basic musicianship.

In speaking about the Contemporary Music Project, Samuel Adler stated, "CMP has been a 'nagging conscience' to many of us and has

---

38 *Ibid.,* p. 48.

39 A sixth regional institute was established later in 1966.

40 *Comprehensive Musicianship: An Anthology of Evolving Thought, op. cit.,* p. 55.

41 *Ibid.,* p. 58.

given us the impetus to try to correct some of the encrusted, outmoded doctrines embedded in our 'good old classical curriculum.' CMP has forced many of our schools to take a new look at the present-day 'job specifications' with which our 1968–1980 students are confronted. With the guidance of CMP, we have been able to change our attitude from a spoon-feeding type of education to a more creative, student-centered approach."[42] Robert J. Werner, Director of CMP, stated in 1970: "We have helped to create a dialogue among all the branches of our profession, a need that was the motivating force for the very inception of the ISME. [International Society for Music Education.]"[43]

For more detailed information on the Contemporary Music Project, see the following:

Comprehensive Musicianship: An Anthology of Evolving Thought. Reston, Va.: Contemporary Music Project, MENC, 1971, pp. ix–119.

"Contemporary Music Project," *Music Educators Journal* (May, 1973) ("CMP in Perspective," "Comprehensive Musicianship," "Putting Ideas Into Practice," "Relationship of CMP to MENC Programs," "The Continuation of An Idea").

What Is Music? Reston, Va.: Contemporary Music Project, MENC, 1973 (a 20-minute film on the elements of music).

THE POPULAR MUSIC MOVEMENT

Some teachers feel that the almost exclusive use of popular music will provide a means for maximum motivation for learning; therefore, their music programs are centered on the use of current popular tunes —tunes with which many children are generally familiar. The basic justification set forth for this approach is that children have heard the music and are highly responsive to it. Thus, activities designed to increase musical enjoyment will facilitate the development of musical growth.

Supporting this movement are various prominent music educators throughout the United States who present workshops on procedures for using popular music to develop musical understanding, and who write and publish articles on this subject. The National Association of Jazz Educators also supports this movement, and articles on the teaching of jazz and popular music appear frequently in *The Educator,* the official magazine of the NAJE.

The use of popular music as a core of musical studies has definite

42 *Ibid.,* p. 87.
43 *Ibid.,* pp. 99–100.

limitations when only current popular favorites are utilized. Greater musical understanding can be achieved if children are taught about the historical development of jazz and the specific stylistic differences between Dixieland, "swing music" from the so-called big band era, rock and roll, soul music, acid rock, rhythm and blues, jazz-rock, and the current use of synthesizers. The development of children's ability to differentiate between the previously mentioned types of music will help establish a foundation for the analysis and subsequent understanding of other types and styles of music.

Topics for Discussion

1. What ideas in the Carl Orff approach to teaching music seem to have made the greatest inroads into music education in the United States?

2. Discuss the idea of implementing so-called "pure" Orff in the American elementary schools.

3. What aspect of the Kodály system of music instruction is best known among American music educators?

4. What similarities exist between the Orff and Kodály methods? How do these methods compliment each other?

5. What is the central philosophy of the Manhattanville Music Curriculum Project (MMCP)?

6. Describe the Spiral Curriculum of the Manhattanville Music Curriculum Project (MMCP).

7. Discuss the contributions of the Contemporary Music Project (CMP) to music education.

8. What is the position of the Contemporary Music Project as regards the teaching of music concepts?

9. Discuss the role of popular music in elementary-school music programs. What are some contrasting attitudes and what might be considered a reasonable approach?

Suggestions for Further Study

The Carl Orff approach; see p. 262.
The Kodály Method; see p. 267.
The Manhattanville Music Curriculum Program; see p. 269.
The Contemporary Music Project; see p. 275.
The popular music movement; see *The Educator,* the official magazine of the NAJE.

chapter 12

MUSIC AND
OTHER CURRICULAR AREAS

Some years ago the inclusion of music in the curriculum was justified not only because of the aesthetic satisfactions it brought to persons, but also on the basis of how it could be integrated with other subjects as a means of making all learning more meaningful. As mentioned earlier, music as a school subject did not at one time have an organized body of content enabling it to assume an equal position with other school subjects; music has always had a basic content, but this content needed to be developed and clarified. "Sputnik" and the need to improve American education changed all this. Conceptual learning came into vogue and was soon reflected in articles in professional journals, at national, regional, and state meetings of music educators, and in the basic music series textbooks. The pendulum has thus swung toward emphasizing music for its own sake, with a concrete, recognized body of knowledge that is considered as basic and important to the general education of children as any other school subject.

The music specialist today is generally concerned with the development of children's musicality, and the task is great indeed! Music, however, is not a subject that remains in isolation from the other school subjects, and there are aspects of the course content of other curricular areas that either relate to or substantially support children's comprehension of and attitudes toward music. The classroom teacher is a strong ally of the cause of music and, by relating aspects of the content of other curricular areas to music, contributes substantially to the children's overall musical education. The music specialist should be especially cognizant of these contributions and, if employed as a music consultant in a school system, should in turn endeavor to assist classroom teachers whenever possible to utilize music to support and strengthen other curricular areas.

SOCIAL STUDIES AND MUSIC

As stated earlier, the objective of world peace is dependent to a great extent upon an understanding of other cultures in addition to our own. Because music is an integral part of all cultures, complete understanding of other peoples cannot be achieved unless all aspects of their cultures, including music, are included in the units of study. This indeed places a major responsibility upon the social-studies teachers; the music specialist in each school should, therefore, assist by providing source information and teaching materials whenever possible. The following are some ways in which music can be used to meet the specific objectives of the social studies class.[1]

1. Various customs, ideals, and attitudes of the people of a particular culture are often revealed in its music. The following songs are given as examples of the wide range of information and ideas contained in the music of various peoples.
   a. After-dinner madrigal singing, popular during the Elizabethan era, "Now in the Month of Maying" by Thomas Morley (*This Is Music*, Book 5)
   b. A Nova Scotia courting song, "Madam, Madam, You Came Courting," folksong from Nova Scotia (*This Is Music*, Book 5)
   c. A Pennsylvania Dutch mother-daughter conversation about work and spinning, "Spin, Spin, My Darling"—Pennsylvania Dutch song (*This Is Music*, Book 5)
   d. Humor in song, "The Young Man Who Wouldn't Hoe Corn"—traditional American song, arr. Burl Ives (*This Is Music*, Book 5)
   e. Attitudes about home on the Western frontier, "The Little Old Sod Shanty"—American pioneer song (*Exploring Music*, Book 5)
   f. A northern lumberman's attitude toward work, "The Shanty Man's Life"—American folksong (*Exploring Music*, Book 5)
   g. Attitudes toward love in old England, "When Love Is Kind"—old English melody (*The Magic of Music*, Book 4)
   h. Attitudes toward life, "Our Life Is Like a River"—Felix Mendelssohn (*This Is Music*, Book 5).

2. Music often describes various important historical events of a country and some music was written for commemorative purposes.
   a. Prince Charles of England, triumphal entry into Scotland,

---

[1] On another day, classroom teachers may wish to use the same materials to help children achieve a comprehension of specific music concepts. Familiarity with the songs should facilitate the learning process and the achievement of teaching objectives.

"Charlie Is My Darling"—Scottish folksong (*Making Music Your Own,* Book 4)

b. A British song making fun of the early Yankees (who later adopted the song as their own), "Yankee Doodle"—traditional (*Making Music Your Own,* Book 4)

c. American colonists celebrating a victory over the British Redcoats, "Riflemen of Bennington"—song of the American Revolution (*Making Music Your Own,* Book 5)

d. The Battle of Quebec in 1759 between the French and the English, "The Maple Leaf Forever" by Alexander Muir (*This Is Music,* Book 5)

e. An old colonial song commemorating Independence Day, "The Glorious Fourth"—old colonial song (*This Is Music,* Book 5).

3. During times of national crisis, such as war, the people of a country unite and this *esprit-de-corps* is reflected in their music. Many songs have grown out of such events and are always well remembered. Several American examples are as follows:

a. Revolutionary War—"Chester," by William Billings (*The Magic of Music,* Book 5)

b. Civil War—"When Johnny Comes Marching Home," by Louis Lambert (*Exploring Music,* Book 5)

c. World War I—"Yankee Doodle Boy," by George M. Cohan (*Exploring Music,* Book 5).

4. In the expansion of our country, and the westward movement in particular, songs describing various types of transportation were popular. Several examples are as follows:

a. "Erie Canal," American work song (*Exploring Music,* Book 5)

b. "Down the Ohio," river shanty (*Making Music Your Own,* Book 5)

c. "The Railroad Cars Are Coming," American folksong (*Exploring Music,* Book 5)

d. "Roll On, Wagons" by Shirley Granger (*This Is Music,* Book 5)

e. "Sailing for San Francisco," Forty-Niner's song (*This Is Music,* Book 5).

SCIENCE AND MUSIC

Many aspects of music involve science, the study of which may broaden children's knowledge and make them generally more appreciative of the art of music. Although music teachers sometimes endeavor to teach the scientific aspects of music, they usually would be well advised to leave this topic to the science teacher and devote their energies to the development of musical comprehensions. The following topics, though only suggestive, are appropriate for units of study in science classes.

1. Acoustics, the science of sound.[2]
   a. What is sound?
   b. Why are some sounds pleasant and others unpleasant?
   c. Listen to everyday sounds in the environment. How can you tell one sound from another?
   d. Difference between noise and a musical tone.
   e. Loudness or intensity, frequency, pitch, fundamentals and overtones, vibrato and tremolo.

2. The recording and reproduction of sound.
   a. Tape recorders—how they function.
   b. Sound reproduction on reel to reel tapes, discs, cassettes.

3. Uses of music in radio, television, and motion pictures.

4. Electronic music—synthesizers and how they function.

5. The physiology and anatomy of the human vocal mechanism.
   a. The component parts and their location.
   b. The functioning of the vocal mechanism resulting in phonation.
   c. Correct posture and breathing techniques.

LANGUAGE ARTS AND MUSIC

As one of the creative arts, the language arts program in the schools has had a long and close relationship to music, with various aspects of each somewhat overlapping, but contributing to and strengthening the other. The following are some specific activities in the language arts program that particularly relate to music.

1. The rhythm of poetry is similar to that of music in that it has meter, accent, and various phrase lengths. Help children to compare these elements in both poetry and music.

2. The interpretation of poetry through individual analysis and reading.

3. Group interpretation of poetry through choral speaking (see pp. 238–242 for further information on choral speaking and its relationship to the objectives of the music program).

4. Selection of appropriate background music for poetry reading or dramatizations.

5. Setting poetry to music (see pp. 242–246 for suggested procedures).

6. Reading books about music and musicians.[3]

[2] For a demonstration album, with accompanying booklet, see *The Science of Sound* (Folkways Records, 117 West 46th Street, New York, N.Y.)

[3] For an annotated listing of appropriate materials, see Peggy Flanagan Baird, *Music Books for the Elementary School Library* (Reston, Va.: Music Educators National Conference, 1972).

7. Creative dramatizations:
   a. Favorite-song charades are perhaps the simplest form of dramatization. All the children in a class write the name of a favorite song on a piece of paper and drop it into a box. Children then take turns and the one chosen to reach into the box selects a song title. A child who needs assistance chooses a partner, and the two confer briefly before presenting their charade.
   b. Pretend to be a particular animal, or a workman, such as a fireman or a policeman, or a character on television, such as Dr. Marcus Welby. Select music to accompany the actions.
   c. Dramatize heavy things, such as iron, stones; light things, such as feathers, air; fast things, such as an airplane, a train; slow things, such as a turtle, a worm; quiet things, such as a statue, a library; noisy things, such as a chain saw, a motorboat.[4] Children should select and choose appropriate music for the dramatization.
   d. Dramatization of favorite songs—usually those with multiple verses, for example, "Sweet Betsy from Pike," "Old MacDonald"; or recorded instrumental music with a programmatic idea behind it, such as "Of a Tailor and a Bear" by MacDowell.
   e. Dramatization of a favorite story.[5]

PHYSICAL EDUCATION AND MUSIC

Singing games and folk dances are considered by music and physical education specialists to be important instructional activities in both their areas. These activities can contribute substantially not only to the objectives of social-studies units of study, but also to the music program, for students' accurate response to rhythmic notation is dependent to a large extent upon their internalization of rhythm, which is developed through various types of bodily movement (see chapter 4, pp. 128–130).

ART AND MUSIC

Art and music have similar components, such as rhythm, form, intensity, and contrast, and for this reason some basic music texts include examples of art to help clarify and strengthen children's understanding of various music concepts.[6] Conversely, the art teacher can appropriately use music examples to clarify various art concepts. *Variety* is an important characteristic of design. The artist creates variety by

[4] Cf. Dorothy Hickok and James A. Smith, *Creative Teaching of Music in the Elementary School* (Boston: Allyn & Bacon, 1974).

[5] For appropriate and suitable materials, see Burdette Fitzgerald, *World Tales for Creative Dramatics and Storytelling* (Englewood Cliffs, N.J.: Prentice-Hall, 1962).

[6] See, for example, the basic music series *The Spectrum of Music* (New York: Macmillan, 1974).

the use of contrasting shapes, colors, or other visual elements, whereas the composer creates variety through changes in melody, rhythm, and harmony. Both the art and music teachers may use each other's medium to clarify concepts in their own subject areas.

Suggestions for Further Study

Social Studies

CHASE, LINWOOD, and MARTHA TYLER JOHN, *A Guide for the Elementary Social Studies Teacher* (2nd ed.). Boston: Allyn & Bacon, 1972.

GILLESPIE, MARGARET C., and A. GRAY THOMPSON, *Social Studies for Living in a Multi-Ethnic Society: A Unit Approach.* Columbus, Ohio: Charles E. Merrill, 1972.

MICHAELIS, JOHN, *Social Studies for Children in a Democracy* (4th ed.). Englewood Cliffs, N.J.: Prentice-Hall, 1968.

SMITH, JAMES A., *Creative Teaching of the Social Studies in the Elementary School.* Boston: Allyn & Bacon, 1968.

Science

FRIEDL, ALFRED E., *Teaching Science to Children.* New York: Random House, 1972.

LEWIS, JUNE E., and IRENE C. POTTER, *The Teaching of Science in the Elementary School* (2nd ed.). Englewood Cliffs, N.J.: Prentice-Hall, 1970.

NELSON, LESLIE, and GEORGE LORBEER, *Science Activities for Elementary Children* (5th ed.). Dubuque, Iowa: Wm. C. Brown, 1972.

PILTZ, ALBERT, and ROBERT SUND, *Creative Teaching of Science in the Elementary School.* Boston: Allyn & Bacon, 1974.

VICTOR, EDWARD, *Science in the Elementary School.* New York: Macmillan, 1970.

Language Arts

ARNSTEIN, FLORA J., *Children Write Poetry: A Creative Approach.* New York: Dover Publications, 1967.

BAMMAN, HENRY J., MILDRED A. DAWSON, and ROBERT J. WHITEHEAD, *Oral Interpretation of Children's Literature.* Dubuque, Iowa: Wm. C. Brown, 1964.

BURNS, PAUL C., and ALBERTA L. LOWE, *The Language Arts in Childhood Education.* Chicago: Rand McNally, 1966.

CHAMBERS, DEWEY W., *Children's Literature in the Curriculum.* Chicago: Rand McNally, 1971.

FITZGERALD, BURDETTE, *World Tales for Creative Dramatics and Storytelling.* Englewood Cliffs, N.J.: Prentice-Hall, 1962.

GREENE, HARRY A., and WALTER T. PETTY, *Developing Language Skills in the Elementary Schools* (4th ed.). Boston: Allyn & Bacon, 1971.

SMITH, JAMES A., *Creative Teaching of the Language Arts in the Elementary School* (2nd ed.). Boston: Allyn & Bacon, 1973.

Physical Education

(See pp. 130–132 for a listing of books on bodily movement).

Art

HURWITZ, AL, ed., *Programs of Promise: Art in the Schools.* New York: Harcourt Brace Jovanovich, 1972.

JEFFERSON, BLANCHE, *Teaching Art to Children.* Boston: Allyn & Bacon, 1959.

LOWENFELD, VIKTOR, and LAMBERT W. BRITTAIN, *Creative and Mental Growth.* London: Collier-MacMillan, 1970.

APPENDIX

BIBLIOGRAPHY ON FUNDAMENTALS OF MUSIC

BENWARD, BRUCE, *Sightsinging Complete* (2nd ed.). Dubuque, Iowa: Wm. C. Brown Company Publishers, 1973.

BERKOWITZ, SOL, GABRIEL FONTRIER, and LEO KRAFT, *A New Approach to Sight Singing*. New York: W. W. Norton & Company, Inc., 1960.

CASS, JEANNETTE, *Rudiments of Music*. Englewood Cliffs, N.J.: Prentice-Hall, Inc., 1956.

CASTELLINI, JOHN, *Rudiments of Music*. New York: W. W. Norton & Company, Inc., 1962.

CLOUGH, JOHN, *Scales, Intervals, Keys, and Triads: A Self-Instruction Program*. New York: W. W. Norton & Company, Inc., 1964.

ELLIOTT, RAYMOND, *Fundamentals of Music* (3rd ed.). Englewood Cliffs, N.J.: Prentice-Hall, Inc., 1971.

FRACKENPOHL, ARTHUR, *Harmonization at the Piano* (2nd ed.). Dubuque, Iowa: Wm. C. Brown Company Publishers, 1970.

KIELY, DENNIS, *Essentials of Music for New Musicians*. Englewood Cliffs, N.J.: Prentice-Hall, Inc., 1975.

KNUTH, ALICE SNYDER, and WILLIAM E. KNUTH, *Basic Resources for Learning Music* (2nd ed.). Belmont, Calif.: Wadsworth Publishing Company, 1973.

NYE, ROBERT E., and BJORNAR BERGETHON, *Basic Music: Functional Musicianship for the Non-Music Major* (4th ed.). Englewood Cliffs, N.J.: Prentice-Hall, Inc., 1973.

OTTMAN, ROBERT, and FRANK MAINOUS, *Rudiments of Music*. Englewood Cliffs, N.J.: Prentice-Hall, Inc., 1970.

PACE, ROBERT, *Piano for Classroom Music* (2nd ed.). Englewood Cliffs, N.J.: Prentice-Hall, Inc., 1971.

SEXTON, JEANETTE, *Musical Awareness Through Songs*. Englewood Cliffs, N.J.: Prentice-Hall, Inc., 1971.

WARDIAN, JEANNE FOSTER, *The Language of Music: A Programmed Course*. Englewood Cliffs, N.J.: Prentice-Hall, Inc., 1967.

WINOLD, ALLEN, and JOHN REHM, *Introduction to Music Theory*. Englewood Cliffs, N.J.: Prentice-Hall, Inc., 1971.

WINSLOW, ROBERT W., and LEON DALLIN, *Music Skills for Classroom Teachers* (3rd ed.). Dubuque, Iowa: Wm. C. Brown Company Publishers, 1970.

WISLER, GENE C., *Music Fundamentals for the Classroom Teacher* (3rd ed.). Boston: Allyn & Bacon, Inc., 1971.

PUBLISHERS OF BASIC MUSIC TEXTBOOKS

ALLYN AND BACON, INC., 150 Tremont Street, Boston, Massachusetts 02111.
This Is Music for Today.

AMERICAN BOOK COMPANY, 300 Pike Street, Cincinnati, Ohio 45202.
New Dimensions in Music.

FOLLETT PUBLISHING COMPANY, 1010 West Washington Blvd., Chicago, Illinois 60607.
Discovering Music Together.

GINN AND COMPANY, 191 Spring Street, Lexington, Mass. 02173.
The Magic of Music.

HOLT, RINEHART AND WINSTON, INC., 383 Madison Ave., New York, New York 10017.
Exploring Music.

MACMILLAN PUBLISHING COMPANY, INC., 100F Brown Street, Riverside, New Jersey 08075.
The Spectrum of Music.

PRENTICE-HALL, INC., Englewood Cliffs, New Jersey 07632.
Growing With Music.

SILVER BURDETT COMPANY, Park Avenue and Columbia Road, Morristown, New Jersey 07960.
Silver Burdett Music.

SUMMY-BIRCHARD PUBLISHING COMPANY, 1834 Ridge Avenue, Evanston, Illinois 60204.
Birchard Music Series.

BASIC RECORD SERIES

Adventures in Music (A New Record Library for Elementary Schools). RCA Victor, LES 1000–1009.
Complete series, ten volumes—one volume each for grades 1 and 2, two volumes for grades 3–6.
Available in 33⅓ r.p.m., stereo, and 45 r.p.m.
Teacher's Guide, prepared by Gladys Tipton and Eleanor Tipton, is included with each album. Order from the nearest Ginn and Company Sales Office.

Bowmar Orchestral Library, Bowmar Educational Records. 18 albums, each of which includes suggestions to the teacher and wall charts of musical themes.

Series 1: Bol #51 Animals and Circus, Bol #52 Nature and Make-Believe, Bol #53 Pictures and Patterns, Bol #54 Marches, Bol #55 Dances, Part I Bol #56 Dances, Part II, Bol #57 Fairy Tales in Music, Bol #58 Stories in Ballet and Opera, Bol #59 Legends in Music, Bol #60 Under Many Flags, Bol #61 American Scenes.

Series 2: Bol #62 Masters in Music, Bol #63 Concert Matinee, Bol #64 Miniatures in Music, Bol #65 Music, USA, Bol #66 Oriental Scenes, Bol #67 Fantasy in Music, Bol #68 Classroom Concert.

PUBLISHERS OF GUITAR INSTRUCTION BOOKS

ALFRED MUSIC CO., 145 West 45th Street, New York, New York 11050

C.G. CONN, LTD., Oakbrook, Illinois 60521

CHARLES HANSEN EDUCATIONAL MUSIC AND BOOKS, 1860 Broadway, New York, New York 10023

HAL LEONARD PUBLISHING CORPORATION, 960 East Mark, Winona, Minnesota 55987

MEL BAY PUBLICATIONS, 107 West Jefferson, Kirkwood, Missouri 63122

YAMAHA INTERNATIONAL, Buena Park, California 90620

PRODUCERS AND DISTRIBUTORS OF EDUCATIONAL FILMS[1]

AMERICAN MUSIC CONFERENCE, 332 South Michigan Ave., Chicago, Ill. 60604

BAILEY FILMS, 6509 De Longpre Ave., Hollywood, Calif. 90028

BOWMAR RECORDS, 622 Rodier Dr., Glendale, Calif. 91201

CARL F. MAHNKE PRODUCTIONS, 215 East 3rd St., Des Moines, Iowa 50300

CLASSROOM MATERIALS CO., 93 Myrtle Dr., Great Neck, N.Y. 11020

CONTEMPORARY FILMS, 267 West 25th St., New York, N.Y. 10001

CORONET INSTRUCTIONAL FILMS, 65 East South Water St., Chicago, Ill. 60601

EMC CORPORATION, 180 East 6th St., St. Paul, Minn. 55101

ENCYCLOPAEDIA BRITANNICA FILMS, 1150 Wilmette Ave., Wilmette, Ill. 60091

INTERNATIONAL FILM BUREAU, 322 South Michigan Ave., Chicago, Illinois 60604

JAM HANDY, 2821 East Grand Blvd., Detroit, Mich. 48211

JOHNSON HUNT PRODUCTIONS, 6509 De Longpre Ave., Hollywood, Calif. 90028

McGRAW-HILL FILMS, 1221 Avenue of the Americas, New York, N.Y. 10020

MODERN TALKING PICTURE SERVICE, 1212 Avenue of the Americas, New York, N.Y. 10036

NET FILM SERVICE, Indiana University, Audio-Visual Center, Bloomington, Ind. 47401

[1] This list is limited only to the producers and distributors of films included in this publication. For addresses of firms not included in this Appendix, see the *Index to Producers and Distributors,* 2nd ed. (Los Angeles: National Information Center for Educational Media [NICEM]), 1973.

SOCIETY FOR VISUAL EDUCATION, 1345 West Diversey, Chicago, Ill. 60614

UNITED WORLD FILMS, INC., 221 Park Avenue South, New York, N.Y. 10003

UNIVERSITY OF CALIFORNIA, University Extension, Education Film Sales Department, Los Angeles, Calif. 90024

WALT DISNEY PRODUCTIONS, Educational Film Division, 500 S. Buena Vista Ave., Burbank, Calif. 91503

XEROX FILMS, 245 Long Hill Road, Middletown, Conn. 06457

SOURCES OF CATALOGS OF
EDUCATIONAL RECORDINGS

BOWMAR EDUCATIONAL RECORDS, INC., 622 Rodier Dr., Glendale, Calif. 91201

CHILDREN'S MUSIC CENTER, 5373 West Pico Blvd., Los Angeles, Calif. 90019

COLUMBIA RECORDS, INC., Educational Dept., 799 Seventh Ave., New York, N.Y. 10019

EDUCATIONAL RECORD SALES, 157 Chambers Street, New York, N.Y. 10007. Branch offices: 500 South Douglas St., El Segundo, Calif., and 3300 North Harlem Ave., Chicago, Illinois

FOLKWAYS RECORDS, 701 Seventh Street, New York, N.Y. 10036

JOHN W. GUNTER, INC., Curriculum Materials, P. O. Box G, San Mateo, Calif. 94402

KEYBOARD JR. PUBLICATIONS, INC., 1346 Chapel St., New Haven, Conn. 06511

MCA RECORDS, 445 Park Avenue, New York, N.Y. 10019

MERCURY RECORD CORP., 35 East Wacker Dr., Chicago, Ill. 60601

PHOEBE JAMES RECORDS, P. O. Box 475, Oak View, Calif. 93022

RADIO CORPORATION OF AMERICA, 1133 Avenue of the Americas, New York, N.Y. 10036

RHYTHM-TIME RECORDS, P. O. Box 1106, Santa Barbara, Calif. 93100

RHYTHMS PRODUCTIONS, Whitney Bldg., Box 34485, Los Angeles, Calif. 90034

RUTH EVANS, Childhood Rhythm Records, P. O. Box 132, Forest Park Branch, Springfield, Mass. 01100

SOUND BOOK PRESS SOCIETY, INC., 117 West 46th St., New York, N.Y. 10036

VOX PRODUCTIONS, INC., 211 East 43rd St., New York, N.Y. 10017

YOUNG PEOPLE'S RECORDS, 225 Park Avenue South, New York, N.Y. 10003

SOURCES OF CLASSROOM INSTRUMENTS
AND EQUIPMENT

CHILDREN'S MUSIC CENTER, 5373 West Pico Blvd., Los Angeles, Calif. 90019
Rhythm instruments, resonator bells, song bells, Autoharp, Latin-American instruments, Flutophones, Tonettes, Song flutes, recorders, instruments for Orff-Schulwerk.

CONN CORPORATION, 616 Enterprise Dr., Oak Brook, Ill. 60521

EDUCATIONAL MUSIC BUREAU, 1834 Ridge Ave., Evanston, Ill. 60204
Rhythm instruments, Latin-American instruments, melody bells, resonator bells, instruments for Orff-Schulwerk, Autoharps, recorders, Flutophones, Tonettes, Song Flutes, visual teaching aids.

FRED GRETSCH MANUFACTURING CO., 630 Eden Park Entrance, Cincinnati, Ohio 45202
Latin-American instruments.

GAMBLE HINGED MUSIC CO., 312 South Wabash Ave., Chicago, Ill. 60604
Rhythm instruments, Tonettes, Song Flutes, Flutophones, recorders, tone bells, song bells, Autoharps, pitch pipes.

G. C. JENKINS COMPANY, P. O. Box 1707, Decatur, Ill. 62526
Orchestra bells.

GEORGE KELISCHEK, 386 Allendale Dr. S.E., Atlanta, Ga. 30317
Recorders, instruments for Orff-Schulwerk, instructional materials.

HARGAIL MUSIC PRESS, 28 West 38th St., New York, N.Y. 10018
Imported recorders and recorder music.

HARMOLIN, INC., P. O. Box 244, La Jolla, Calif. 92037
Harmolins, resonator bells, psalteries.

JOHN W. GUNTER, INC., Curriculum Materials, P. O. Box G, San Mateo, Calif. 94402
Rhythm instruments, Latin-American instruments, Autoharps, resonator bells.

KITCHING EDUCATIONAL DIVISION OF LUDWIG INDUSTRIES, 1728 North Damen Dr., Chicago, Ill., 60647
Melody bells, orchestra bells, resonator bells, rhythm instruments, tuning forks, tuning bars.

LYONS BAND DIVISION OF THE MAGNAVOX CO., 430 Wrightwood Ave., Elmhurst, Ill. 60126
Tonettes, Flutophones, Autoharps, ukuleles, resonator bells, Song Bells, Chord Lyre (bells), orchestra bells, Latin-American instruments.

MAGNAMUSIC-BATON, 10370 Page Industrial Blvd., St. Louis Mo. 63132
Studio 49 instruments for Orff-Schulwerk.

MELODY FLUTE COMPANY, P. O. Box 276, Laurel, Md. 20810
Melody Flutes and recorders.

M. HOHNER, INC., Andrews Rd., Hicksville, Long Island, N.Y. 11802
Resonator bells, glockenspiels, xylophones, Metallophones, rhythm instruments, Latin-American instruments, melodicas, harmonicas, recorders, Sonor Instrumentarium for Orff-Schulwerk.

OHIO FLOCK-COTE CO., 5713 Euclid Ave., Cleveland, Ohio 44103
Music-graph flannel boards.

OSCAR SCHMIDT-INTERNATIONAL, INC., Garden State Rd., Union, N.J. 07083
Autoharps and Guitaros.

PERIPOLE PRODUCTS, INC., P. O. Box 146, Lewistown Rd., Brownsmills, N.J. 08015
Rhythm instruments, Latin-American instruments, song bells, resonator bells, Autoharps, Flutophones, Song Flutes, Tonettes, recorders, Sonor Instrumentarium for Orff-Schulwerk.

RHYTHM BAND, INC., P. O. Box 126, Fort Worth, Tex. 76101
   Rhythm instruments, Latin-American instruments, Autoharps, Flutophones,
   Tonettes, Song Flutes, melody bells, resonator bells, recorders, fifes, har-
   monicas, ukuleles, Premier instruments for Orff-Schulwerk.

TROPHY MUSIC COMPANY, 1278 West 9th St., Cleveland, Ohio 44113
   Flutophones, recorders.

VIKING COMPANY, 113 South Edgemont St., Los Angeles, Calif. 90004
   Resonator bells, music charts.

WALBERG AND AUGE, Route 20 and Millbury St., Auburn, Mass. 01501
   Song bells, marimba bells, resonator bells, Autoharps, rhythm instruments,
   Latin-American instruments, Song Flutes, Tonettes, Flutophones, recorders.

WM. KRATT CO., 988 Johnson Place, Union, N.J. 07083
   Harmonicas and pitch pipes.

WILLIS MUSIC COMPANY, 7380 Industrial Road, Florence, Ky. 41042
   Rhythm instruments, melody bells, resonator bells, Flutophones, Song
   Flutes, Tonettes, recorders, Autoharps, pitch pipes, staff liners.

ZIM-GAR MUSICAL INSTRUMENT CORP., 762 Park Place, Brooklyn, N.Y., 11216
   Rhythm instruments, Latin-American instruments, Autoharps, zithers, psalteries, Flutophones, Tonettes, Song Flutes, resonator bells, melody bells,
   orchestra bells, xylophones, stepbells, recorders, pitch pipes.

INDEX

Popular youth music, 34
Pounds, Ralph L., 44 n
Presto and *largo*, 235
"Program music," 223
Prokofiev, Sergei, 215
Psychological blocks, 44
Pulse, 99–100
  and accent, 114
  physical response to, 175

Q

Quality and range, 200

R

Raebeck, Lois, 34 n.7, 138 n
Rapport, maintaining, 53
Ravel, Maurice, 235, 255
Recordings:
  catalogue sources, 288
  using, 51
Record series, 287
Renaissance period, 249, 250–51
Repeat signs, 212
Reser, Harry, 156 n
Resonator bells, 6, 136, 139, 160, 161, 163, 188
Respighi, Ottorino, 223
Rhythm:
  and bodily movement, 101–4
  concepts of, 93–128
  even or uneven, 100
  meter, and bodily movement, 92–132
"Rhythm conversation," 110–11
Rhythmic:
  canon, 260
  patterns, 117
  phrase building, 260
  rondo, 262
Rhythm instruments, 180–82
Rhythm patterns, devising, 111–12
Ritard, 238
Romantic period, 249, 254
Rondo form, 215
Rossini, Gioacchino, 221
"Rote-note" process, 63
Rounds, 136, 141
Rounds and canons, 133
  singing, 149–52

S

Saint-Saëns, Camille, 190
Scale, defined, 66
Scales:
  "blues," 88–89
  chromatic, 81
  diatonic, 75
  major, 84–85
  middle-eastern, 89–90
  minor, 85
  modal, 89
  pentatonic, 79, 86, 259 n.4, 260
  whole-tone, 87
Schubert, Franz, 223
Sections, contrasting, 220, 222
Self-expression:
  need for, 2–3
  through singing, 237–38
Sequence, 73–74
Simple wind instruments:
  introducing, 203
  playing, 201–5
Singing, two-part, 172
Singing games and folk dances, 128–30
Slurs and ties, 235
Smith, James A., 282
Socratic method, 8
Sonata-allegro form, 222–23
Song and record collections, 33
Songflute, 201
Songs:
  children's composed, 33
  creating, 242–46
  singing combined, 153
  two-part, 165
Song-teaching procedures, 48–55
  alternative procedures, 55–56 n
Song text, interpretation of, 226
Sounds:
  exploring different, 186, 187
  exploring "everyday," 183
Spiral curriculum, 269
Starr, Robert J., 31 n
Strauss, Richard, 223, 233
String instruments, producing sound on, 189–90
Syllables, 160, 202
Symphonic poem, 223
Syncopation, 123, 125
Szabó, Helga, 263 n